ECONOMIC ISSUES, PROBLEMS AND PERSPECTIVES

UNEMPLOYMENT

ECONOMIC, POLITICAL AND SOCIAL ASPECTS

ECONOMIC ISSUES, PROBLEMS AND PERSPECTIVES

Additional books in this series can be found on Nova's website under the Series tab.

Additional e-books in this series can be found on Nova's website under the eBooks tab.

ECONOMIC ISSUES, PROBLEMS AND PERSPECTIVES

UNEMPLOYMENT

ECONOMIC, POLITICAL AND SOCIAL ASPECTS

TABITHA FLETCHER
EDITOR

nova publishers
New York

Additional color graphics may be available in the e-book version of this book.

Library of Congress Cataloging-in-Publication Data

Names: Fletcher, Tabitha, editor.
Title: Unemployment : economic, political and social aspects / editor, Tabitha Fletcher.
Description: Hauppauge, New York : Nova Science Publishers, Inc., [2016] | Series: Economic issues, problems and perspectives | Includes index.
Identifiers: LCCN 2016017066 (print) | LCCN 2016022542 (ebook) | ISBN 9781634851817 (hardcover) | ISBN 9781634852180 ()
Subjects: LCSH: Unemployment.
Classification: LCC HD5707.5 .U5535 2016 (print) | LCC HD5707.5 (ebook) | DDC 331.13/7--dc23
LC record available at https://lccn.loc.gov/2016017066

Published by Nova Science Publishers, Inc. † New York

CONTENTS

PREFACE

This book discusses unemployment and its relations to economic, political and social aspects. The first chapter studies the relationship of unemployment to the level of confidence that characterizes some macroeconomic relevant agents, such as consumers or investors. Chapter Two investigates the effects of productivity growth shocks on unemployment, both in the short run and in the medium - long run. Chapter Three reviews finite sample inference for unemployment-inflation tradeoff. Chapter Four focuses on understanding how the Great Recession of 2007-2009 and/or long-term labor market changes may have separately or jointly affected health among employed workers in 2010. Chapter Five evaluates the persistence of the unemployment rate in the following emerging European countries: Slovenia, Slovakia, the Czech Republic, Poland, Hungary, Cyprus, Malta, Estonia, Latvia and Lithuania. Chapter Six discusses the case of election results on the political aspects of unemployment. Chapter Seven studies the relationship between unemployment and the (individual) perceived levels of well-being, such as life satisfaction or happiness. Chapter Eight assesses the association between homelessness and survival in a population of unemployed individuals in one region of northern Poland. Chapter Nine studies the impact that educational level and vocational training programmes had on the labour market of semi-peripheral EU countries, using Greece as a case study. Chapter Ten estimates the effects of area unemployment rate on smoking and drinking in China.

In: Unemployment
Editor: Tabitha Fletcher

ISBN: 978-1-63485-181-7

Chapter 1

ON THE ECONOMIC ASPECTS OF UNEMPLOYMENT: THE CASE OF CONSUMER CONFIDENCE

António Bento Caleiro*
Department of Economics, University of Évora, Portugal

ABSTRACT

Unemployment is related to economic, political and social aspects. One of the least analysed economic aspects is the relationship of unemployment to the level of confidence that characterizes some macroeconomic relevant agents, such as consumers or investors. Expanding previous work on this matter, this chapter considers a fuzzy logic methodology in order to uncover the relationship that exists between the unemployment rate and the consumer confidence level for a large group of European Union countries, in the period 1995-2015. It is concluded that this relationship is stronger than apparently it looks, especially in certain countries. This result should therefore be used as an extra argument in making economic decisions leading to the diminishment of unemployment, which will boost economic confidence.

Keywords: confidence, European Union, fuzzy logic, unemployment

1. INTRODUCTION

Some variables, inherently subjective, such as (consumer) confidence are known to be important in the evolution of the economic situation, which is measured by a multitude of other, (much) more objective, variables, such as the level of output, the unemployment and/or inflation rates. In fact, there is empirical evidence that supports the existence of an influence of confidence on the business cycle (Constantinescu, 2012; Matsusaka & Sbordone, 1995; Mourougane & Roma, 2003; Santero & Westerlund, 1996, and Utaka, 2003). Reflecting this importance, consumer sentiment surveys have become quite common (Curtis, 2007).

*Corresponding author: caleiro@uevora.pt.

Particularly for Europe, the European Commission (EC) itself unmistakeably acknowledges the importance of the economic climate on the understanding of the European business cycle (European Commission, 2000). Associated with this recognition is the fact that business surveys, carried on by the Directorate General for Economic and Financial Affairs of the EC, in order to obtain information about the economic sentiment or the consumer confidence, allow, in the EC's own words "comparisons among different countries' business cycles and *have become an indispensable tool for monitoring the evolution of the EU and the euro area economies*, as well as monitoring developments in the applicant countries."[1] [italics added]. In accordance with this institutional position, Møller et al. (2014) find that, for many European countries, consumer confidence and the output gap are highly positively correlated.

Given the undeniable importance of confidence, one should determine what factors turn out to be relevant or causal to this (subjective) variable (Ramalho et al., 2011). Our hypothesis is that unemployment, as an objective variable, cannot be discarded from the key elements explaining confidence (Caleiro, 2006; 2007).[2] In order to be able to test this hypothesis, an appropriate methodology has to be considered, given the characteristics of confidence.

As a matter of fact, due to incomplete information, economic agents may be characterised by a certain level of confidence given a vague perception of the economic situation. As clearly pointed out in Santero & Westerlund (1996), confidence is a concept which cannot be defined precisely. This means that, when looking at the economic situation, even if all the information provided by those objective variables, such as unemployment, could be fully exploited, economic agents may still base their judgements on subjective criteria such as '*high*' or '*large*', '*normal*' or '*mean*' and '*low*' or '*small*' values for those objective variables. If this is the case, a fuzzy logic approach rather than a crisp one is (much) more appropriate.

As is well-known, since the seminal paper of Zadeh (1965), fuzzy logic has undergone a tremendous growth, both in theoretical and applied fields. Far from being a surprise, despite the delay, a considerable number of applications of fuzzy logic in diverse fields of Economics have been made; see, for instance, Bagnoli & Smith (1998) on real estate valuation, and/or Draeseke & Giles (1999), and/or Yu et al. (2006) on underground economy, and/or Landajo (2000) on forecasting, and/or West & Linster (2003) on game theory. The diversity of the nature of these applications is indeed a characteristic that indicates the richness of fuzzy logic; see Díaz & Morillas (2012) for a literature review of several other applications of this nature.[3]

To sum up, given that one of the main concerns of fuzzy logic is to capture approximate rather than exact forms of reasoning, and this also characterises many economic situations, such as in fact forming intrinsically subjective measures of confidence, this logic can and should indeed be used to understand how confidence is related to unemployment. This task is

[1] See http://ec.europa.eu/economy_finance/db_indicators/surveys/index_en.htm (accessed on January 26, 2016). See also European Commission (2014).

[2] If this hypothesis is confirmed to be accurate, then clearly, the unemployment rate should have been chosen in many countries as a target variable, long before it actually happened (in the EU, eventually as soon as the inflation rate), particularly as the EC itself recognizes the importance of confidence level. Of importance to this remark, in Caleiro (2007) is concluded, using the same methodology of this chapter, that, in the European Union, inflation could not be related to confidence as much unemployment was.

[3] Despite the large number of applications of fuzzy logic in numerous fields of Economics, it is surprising that, to the best of our knowledge, so very few applications have been made in modelling approximations of subjective economic variables, such as confidence (or life satisfaction), by objective ones, such as unemployment, output or inflation. In fact, to the best of our knowledge, the only references in this field are Caleiro (2003; 2006; 2007).

accomplished in the chapter by the use of data for a large group of European Union countries, in the period 1995-2015. It is concluded that this relationship is stronger than apparently it looks, especially in certain countries. This result should therefore be used as an extra argument in making economic decisions leading to the diminishment of unemployment, which will boost economic confidence.

That being said, the rest of the chapter is structured as follows: Section 2 presents and analyses, in a succinct manner, the data; the fuzzy logic methodology is presented in Section 3, being applied in Section 4, in which the results are presented and discussed; Section 5 concludes in the usual manner.

2. THE DATA

As for the data, we opted for a monthly frequency as this is the more suitable for our purposes, since only in the survey for this frequency there is a question about the forecasts regarding unemployment. In addition, we also wanted to have a sufficiently long time horizon in order to be demanding about the robustness of the methodology, which led us to consider the period 1995-2015. In this chapter, the area of interest is the European Union (EU), for that being evident the resource to the data provided by the Eurostat. From the current EU-28 member states, given the chosen frequency and time period, data exist only for 14 of them, namely: Belgium; Denmark; Germany; Ireland; Spain; France; Italy; Hungary; Netherlands; Austria; Portugal; Finland; Sweden; and the United Kingdom. Figures 1 and 2 display the data.

With regard to the unemployment rate, it should be noted some perception of a cyclical behavior, being evident the effects of the 2008/09 economic crisis particularly in certain countries. Furthermore, it seems possible to identify two groups of countries with fairly high correlation coefficients between their unemployment rates,[4] namely the group constituted by Ireland, United Kingdom, Hungary, Spain, Denmark and Portugal, and another composed group by Belgium, France, Sweden and Netherlands. It is also pertinent to acknowledge the existence of many (significant) negative correlations, being relevant the case of Germany vis-a-vis Spain, Portugal, Ireland and even the United Kingdom.

With regard to consumer confidence it is relevant to point out the inexistence of negative correlations in the values recorded for that variable in the European countries under analysis.[5] Again, it seems possible to identify two groups of countries with fairly high correlation coefficients between their levels of consumer confidence, namely the group constituted by Belgium, France and Austria, and another group constituted by Ireland, Spain, Portugal, Italy, Netherlands and the United Kingdom. A general decline in confidence registered after the 2008/09 crisis is also apparent.

That being said, it appears that it does not exist an evident relationship between the unemployment rate and the level of consumer confidence, which seems to be confirmed by Table 1.

[4] See the complete table of the correlation coefficients in the Annex.

[5] See the complete table of the correlation coefficients in the Annex.

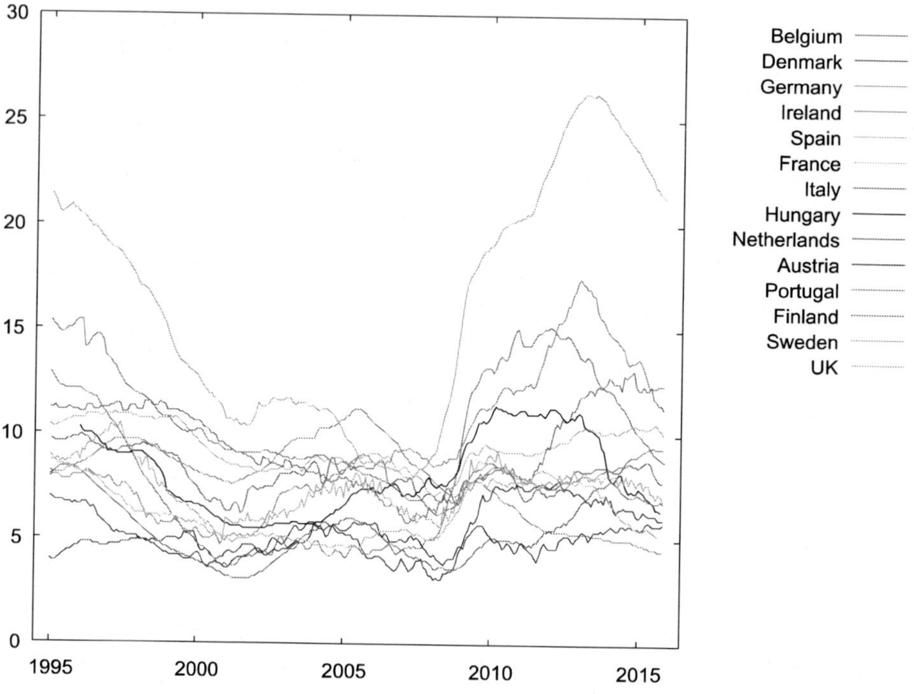

Figure 1. The unemployment rate.

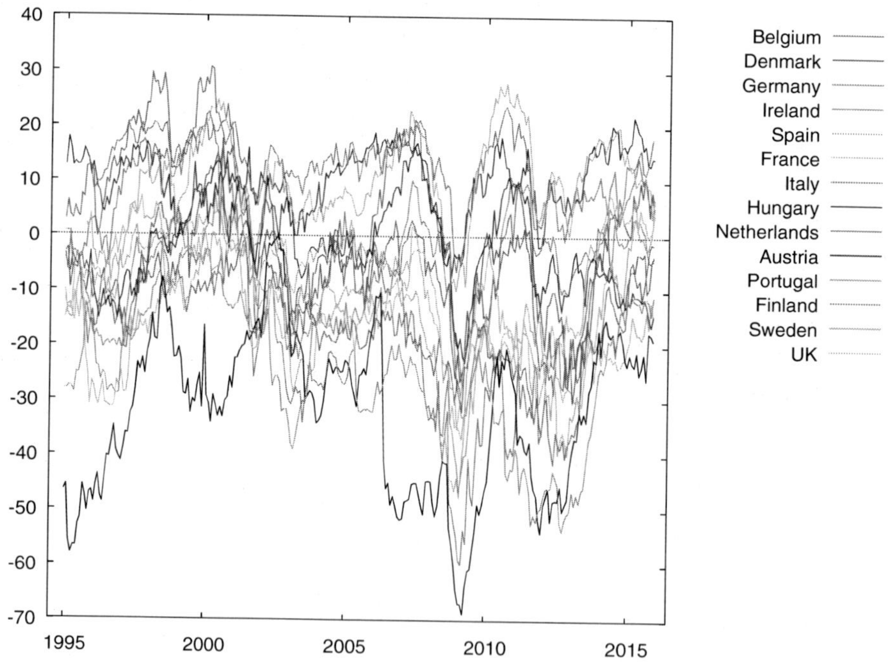

Figure 2. The consumer confidence.

Table 1. Correlation coefficients between the unemployment rates and consumer confidence[6]

Portugal = -0.6437****; t(249) = -13.273	Hungary = -0.5042****; t(236) = -8.970
UK = -0.4823****; t(247) = -8.652	Germany = -0.4652****; t(249) = -8.294
Austria = -0.3945****; t(240) = -6.651	Belgium: -0.2880****; t(249) = -4.746
Ireland = -0.2715****; t(249) = -4.451	Spain = -0.2368***; t(249) = -3.846
Sweden = -0.2153***; t(240) = -3.4159	France = -0.1759**; t(249) = -2.819
Netherlands = -0.1076; t(249) = -1.707	Denmark = 0.0677ns; t(249) = 1.071
Italy = 0.2346***; t(249) = 3.808	Finland = 0.2534***, t(239) = 4.049

From Table 1 it appears that the correlation coefficient between the two variables is generally negative but not too negative -- except, possibly, in Portugal -- and may even be positive, but in this case, even less positive. These results confirm that there is no evident relationship between the unemployment rate and the levels of consumer confidence, therefore making it challenging to obtain values based on the unemployment rate that approximate those registered by the consumer confidence indicator. That may be the case from a crisp point of view but not the case with fuzzy logic.

3. The Fuzzy Logic Process

Following Caleiro (2006,2007) we continue with a brief presentation of the fuzzy logic approach that will be used throughout the chapter. Following the logic of crisp sets, the degree to which an element belongs to a set *A* is either 0 or 1. The generalisation to a fuzzy set is made by relaxing the strict separation between elements belonging or not to *A*, allowing the degree of belonging/membership to take more than those two values, typically by allowing any value in the closed interval [0,1]. See, for instance, Zimmermann (1991) or Chen (1996).

The values then assigned by the membership function of a fuzzy set to the elements in the universal set indicate the membership grade or degree of adherence of each element in the set. Larger/smaller values naturally indicate higher/lower membership grades, degrees, or consistency between an element of the set and the full characteristics that the set describes.[7] Hence, using fuzzy logic, one can deal with reasoning like: 'the observed value for the unemployment rate, say 8%, can be considered high, normal or low with some degrees of membership'.

In terms of fuzzy logic, 'high', 'normal' or 'low' values (for the variable under question) can be considered to be subjective categories, as economic agents often evaluate those concepts differently. In what follows, it will be assumed that consumers use these kinds of subjective categories to 'construct' an approximate indicator of their confidence, therefore assuming an approximate or qualitative reasoning. In general, this corresponds to the assumption of an inference mechanism based on *if-then* decision rules described as follows.

[6] The t statistic (and the p-value) are computed under the (two-tailed test of the) null hypothesis of no correlation.

[7] Although many authors defend that membership defines the degree of adherence rather than the probability of an event, some others consider that the membership function may be considered akin to a subjective probability distribution (Chang & Stekler, 1977).

The linguistic variables 'high unemployment', 'normal unemployment' and 'low unemployment' constitute the so-called antecedent vector, say *X*, in the universe of discourse of unemployment, say *U*. A fuzzy algorithm relating those linguistic variables with consumer confidence, as a fuzzy variable, is then constructed on the basis of statements or *if-then* decision rules such as: 'if the observed value for the unemployment rate is considered low with a higher degree of membership then consumer confidence also rises'.

To sum up, the structure of the fuzzy system that will be used can be presented as follows:

1. Fuzzification: Transformation of quantitative data on the unemployment rate (crisp inputs) into qualitative categories, that is linguistic terms such as 'high', 'normal' or 'low' (fuzzified inputs);
2. Inference: Construction of fuzzy rules from the membership functions of inputs-antecedents and outputs-consequences, followed by the determination of fuzzy output linguistic terms;
3. Defuzzification: Transformation of the previous qualitative/linguistic terms back into real numbers, i.e., the translation of fuzzy to crisp output(s), in the case the 'low' unemployment category, which will constitute an approximation to the values of the consumer confidence indicator.

In what concerns the fuzzification stage, let us assume that consumer confidence is related with unemployment and that the unemployment rate can be characterised by three qualitative categories (subjective terms) according to: 'unemployment rate' $\in$ {low, normal, high}. The translation of the unemployment rates, measured on the real axis, into those categories will be achieved through the use of membership functions associated with the fuzzy sets of 'low', 'normal' and 'high' values. In our case, these functions were derived from the empirical distributions of the unemployment rates for the selected EU member states for the period Jan/1995-Dec/2015.

Concerning the choice of the shape for the membership function, the gaussian curve type will be used because it is consistent with the data and it does not exclude data from coming from all – 'low', 'normal', 'high' – possible distributions, as might happen, in an 'ad-hoc' way, with trapezoidal/triangular membership functions.

As pointed out in Evans & Honkapohja (1999), following Sargent's (1993) suggestion, one possibility of substituting fully rational agents by agents possessing bounded rationality is by considering that agents' memory is also bounded. In a sense, this suggestion was followed in the determination of the membership values given that they were obtained using a rolling window with a fixed length. As such, we consider that consumers, when forming their confidence at a moment t, go through a fuzzification process applied to the unemployment rates observed during the last w months (including the present one), i.e., from $t - w + 1$ until t, for $t \geq w$ covering all the period under analysis.

To put it more formally, we start by computing a moving average:

$$\bar{u}_t = \frac{\sum_{j=t-w+1}^{t} u_j}{w}, \text{ for } t \geq w \tag{1}$$

and a moving standard deviation

$$\sigma_t = \sqrt{\frac{\sum_{j=t-w+1}^{t} (u_j - \bar{u}_t)^2}{w-1}} \tag{2}$$

where w is the length of the rolling window.[8]

Given our choice for the type of membership function, i.e., a normal density function:

$$f(x,\mu,\sigma) = \frac{1}{\sqrt{2\pi}\sigma} \exp\left(-\frac{(x-\mu)^2}{2\sigma^2} \right), \tag{3}$$

the non-normalised membership values for the unemployment rate associated with the categories 'low', 'normal' and 'high' were determined as

$$f(u_t, \bar{u}_t - k\sigma_t, \sigma_t) \rightarrow low \tag{4}$$

$$f(u_t, \bar{u}_t, \sigma_t) \rightarrow normal \tag{5}$$

$$f(u_t, \bar{u}_t + k\sigma_t, \sigma_t) \rightarrow high \tag{6}$$

where f is defined as in (3). Plainly, the separation between the average position for the three categories of unemployment, given by (4), (5) and (6), is made proportional, through the parameter k, to the dispersion of the data.

In what concerns the inference stage, it will be assumed that the behaviour of consumers can be approximated by simple '*if-then*' decision rules as follows: if $u \in U$ then $z \in Z$, where U and Z are fuzzy sets and u and z are real numbers. As we are using only one objective measure, this stage assumes a particularly simple form. Given that consumer confidence is plausibly related, in an inverse way, with the unemployment rate, we simply consider that the only category to be considered is the 'low' one.[9] In other words, in this stage consumers transform the qualitative factors of unemployment rates into their confidence.

Finally, in what concerns the defuzzification stage, the use of fuzzy rules during the inference stage produced fuzzy outputs, which have to be translated back into crisp outputs. In our case, this means that the inference output must be defuzzified into real numbers which will constitute the proxy values of the confidence indicator. As the most plausible

---

[8] This means that, for each new observation on the unemployment rate, consumer forget the oldest in their minds. The length of the window can thus be associated with the number of observations that consumers keep in their memory. Consequently, throughout the period under analysis, the mean and the standard deviation, in which are based the membership values, will vary. This also mean that the context is relevant in the sense of providing a baseline that may evolve through time. In a sense, this is in agreement with Casey & Owen (2013) that, when testing test for asymmetric reactions of consumer confidence to changes in economic fundamentals, concluded that reference points are important in determining consumer reactions.

[9] Given that symmetry was considered in determining the membership values, the 'high' category is a just a mirror image of the 'low' one.

approximation, we simply consider the values assumed by the normalised degrees of membershipness of the ‘low’ category for unemployment.[10]

4. The Results

We then consider that consumers, when forming their confidence at a *moment t*, go through a fuzzification process applied to the unemployment rates observed during the last w months (including the present one), i.e., from $t - w + 1$ until t, for $t \geq w$ covering all the period under analysis. The normalised membership values for the ‘low’, ‘normal’ and ‘high’ values of the unemployment rates were then obtained considering, for a grid of values of w, the value of k leading to the maximum correlation between the consumer confidence values and the normalised membership values for the ‘low’ unemployment category.

We also admit that consumers, when forming their confidence level, possess decaying memory, in the sense of giving less importance to observations far away in time. A straightforward way to accommodate the effects of decaying memory is to consider that the membership values are filtered by exponentially decaying factors:

$$p_j = \exp(\mu(j-t)) \tag{7}$$

for $t - w + 1 \leq j \leq t$, where μ relates to the degree of memory loss.

Table 2. A summary of the results

	Belgium	Denmark	Germany	Ireland	Spain	France	Italy
k	0,1694	1,0926	2,2334	0,0028	0,0034	0,2377	0,0125
μ	-0,7599	-0,4990	-0,3938	-0,0632	-0,0164	-1,4548	-1,1231
r	0,4389	0,4156	0,8175	0,9072	0,8130	0,6889	0,5569
	Hungary	**Netherlands**	**Austria**	**Portugal**	**Finland**	**Sweden**	**UK**
k	0,9652	0,4188	1,4941	0,7286	0,0062	0,0021	0,1366
μ	-0,0034	-0,8642	-0,6741	-0,0259	-2,7280	-1,3210	-0,9956
r	0,3406	0,8043	0,5260	0,7901	0,5485	0,5975	0,5677

Following the procedure described above the obtained results are displayed in Figures 3-16 (see the annex), which plot the original series of the consumer confidence indicator and the normalised membership values associated with the ‘low’ category for unemployment for that parameterisation. In general, one may state that the fit, in a visual way, is quite reasonable in the case of Spain, Ireland, Italy, Netherlands, Portugal and the United Kingdom, being a fair one in the rest of the countries, at least in the sense that, in the most part of the period, the trends presented by both variables are not in clear disagreement.

Table 2 summarises the results in terms of the separation parameter, k, the degree of memory loss, μ, and the correlation coefficient, r, between the low category of unemployment and the level of consumer confidence.

[10] The normalised membership values were obtained from (4), (5) and (6) in order that they add up to 1.

From a more formal perspective, Table 2 confirms a good fit between the unemployment rate and the consumer confidence indicator in the case of Germany, Ireland, Spain, France, Netherlands and Portugal, leading us to admit that, in fact, the level of confidence is much more related to unemployment than is apparent. In the case of no (or even weak) relationship between unemployment and confidence, we can certainly admit that the optimization routine could indeed lead to a fair approximation during part(s) of the period under analysis but would visibly fail during the rest of the period.

CONCLUSION

The objective of the chapter was to show how an objective measure, such as the unemployment rate, can be used, in a retrospective way, to understand the trajectory registered by a subjective measure, such as the consumer confidence indicator, which is intrinsically prospective.[11] To put it clearer we hypothesise that, from a fuzzy logic perspective, the unemployment rate is a proxy variable, in the econometrics sense, of confidence. To achieve this objective, 14 EU member-states were considered, during the period 1995-2015. The achievement of these objectives should indicate that ignoring the unemployment trajectory, when attaining high(er) levels of confidence is a policy objective, as it indeed sometimes happens, is likely to lead to failure.

The chapter shows that, for many European countries, it is, indeed, possible to approximate the trajectory of consumer confidence by the unemployment rate. In this sense, the chapter reveals the apparent importance that unemployment has upon confidence. Moreover, it illustrates that retrospectiveness may be used in order to understand prospectiveness (Delorme et al., 2001; Koshal et al., 2015).

In particular, given that, at least at an aggregate level, confidence is much more related to unemployment than is apparent, this should be taken into account in the design of the EU economic policies. Paying more attention to unemployment at a European level may indeed impose that each of the member states performs this task. As a matter of fact, given the results obtained here, one may conclude that ignoring the unemployment trajectory, when attaining high(er) levels of confidence is a policy objective, as it indeed sometimes happens, is likely to lead to failure.

If indeed confidence is not inseparable from unemployment, an understanding of this link between these two economic measures may be of crucial importance, for instance, to economic policies designed to increase perceived well-being or life satisfaction by the inevitable use of objective aggregates. In particular, these issues seem to be of crucial importance for an incumbent which, due to re-election goals, wants the electorate to feel particular confident at the day of the elections.[12] In fact, a casual observation on the reality may point out that re-elections tend to be associated with peaks on consumer confidence (Ramalho et al., 2011; Adam, 2014) but it also indicates that, in what gives respect to confidence, probably more important than the *level* is the *direction* assumed by the

[11] As considered by the European Commission (2003), "the consumer confidence indicator is the arithmetic average of the balances (in percentage points) of the answers to the questions on the financial situation of households, the general economic situation, unemployment expectations (with inverted signs) and savings, *all over the next 12 months*." [italics added].

[12] As is well-known, ever since the seminal paper of Nordhaus (1975) many political business cycle models consider the unemployment rate as crucial for the electorate.

unemployment rate, just as fuzzy logic would prescribe. We also would like to consider these matters in future research.

ANNEX

Austria_unemployment rate

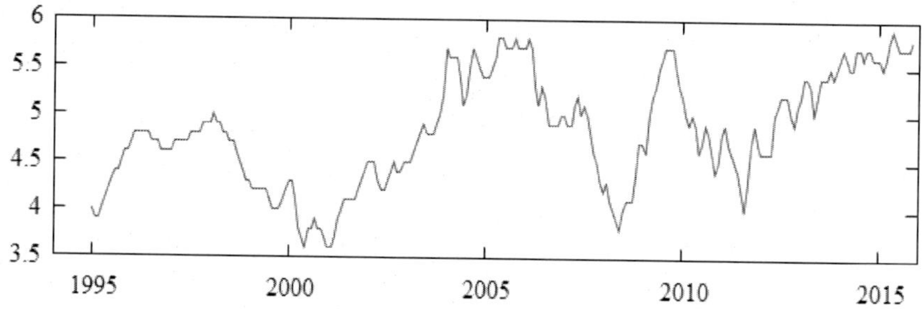

Austria_consumer confidence

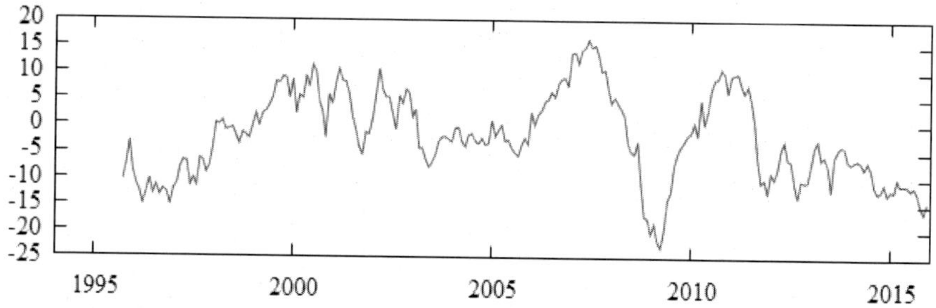

Belgium_unemployment rate

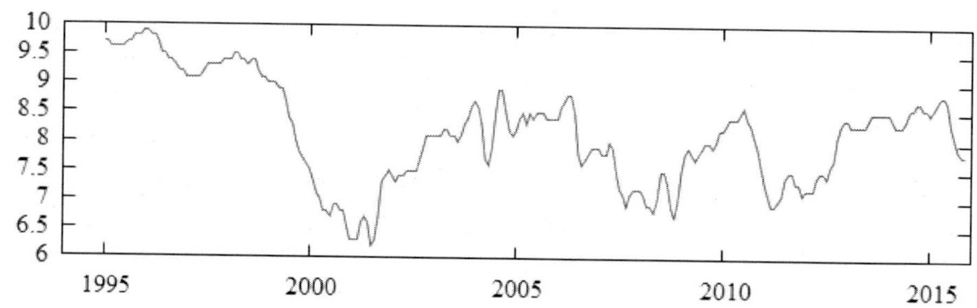

Belgium_consumer confidence

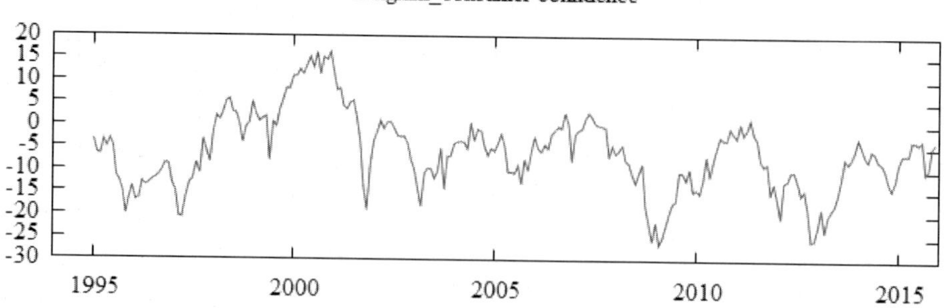

Denmark_unemployment rate

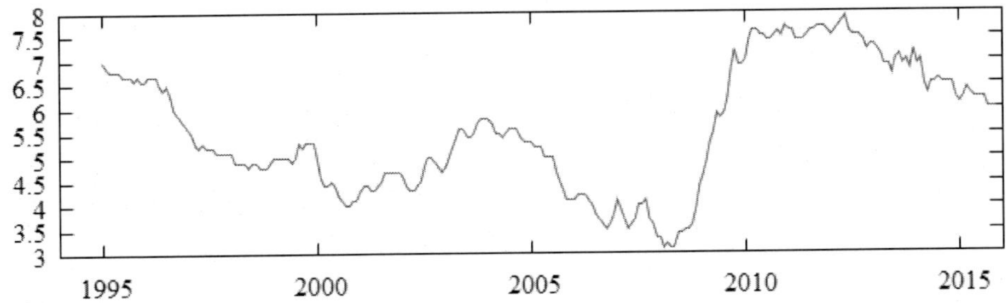

Denmark_consumer confidence

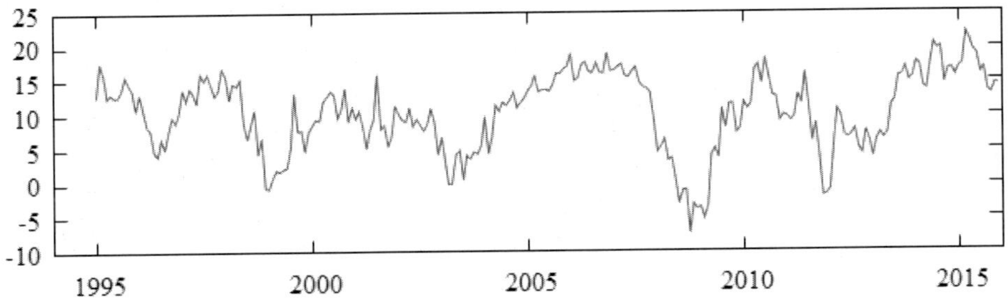

Finland_unemployment rate

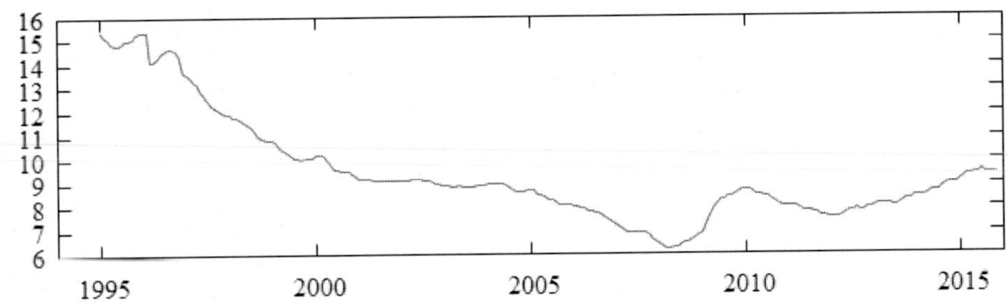

Finland_consumer confidence

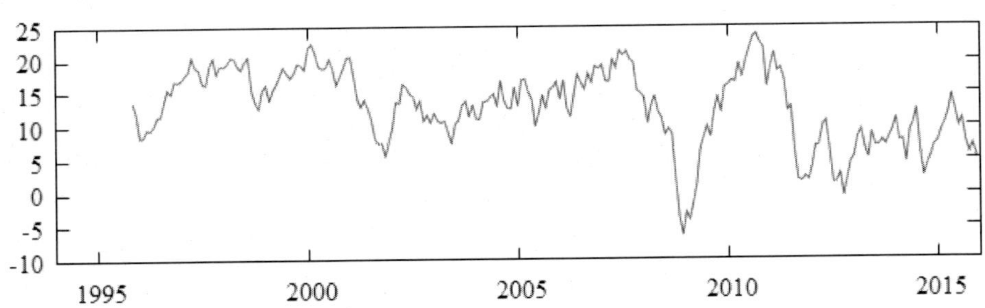

France_unemployment rate
11
10.5
10
9.5
9
8.5
8
7.5
7
1995
2000
2005
2010
2015

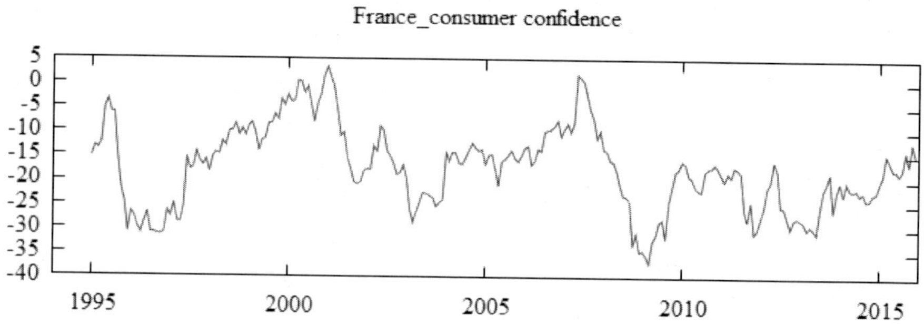
France_consumer confidence
5
0
-5
-10
-15
-20
-25
-30
-35
-40
1995
2000
2005
2010
2015

Germany_unemployment rate
12
11
10
9
8
7
6
5
4
1995
2000
2005
2010
2015

Germany_consumer confidence
15
10
5
0
-5
-10
-15
-20
-25
-30
-35
1995
2000
2005
2010
2015

Hungary_unemployment rate

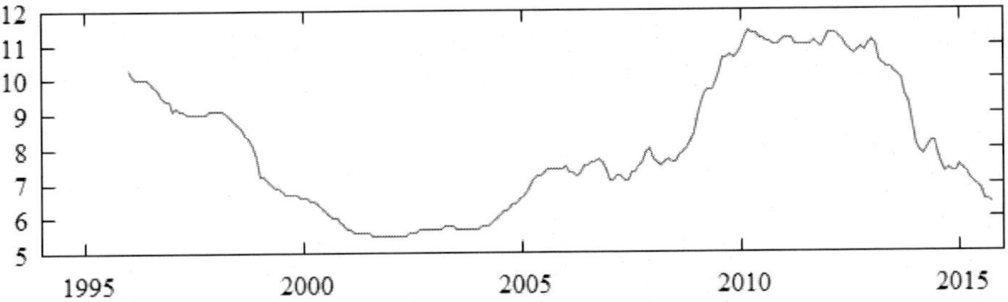

Hungary_consumer confidence

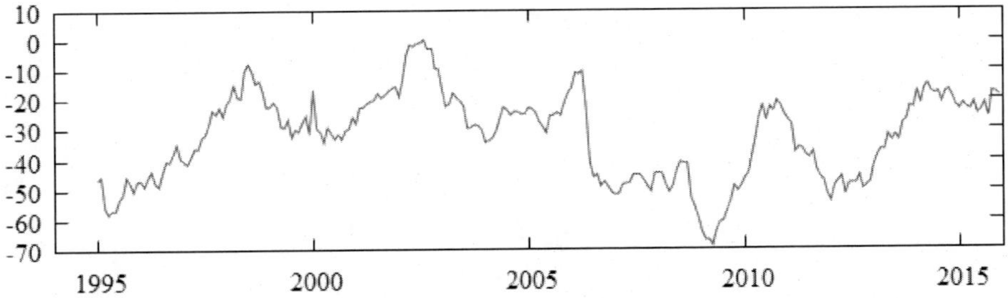

Ireland_unemployment rate

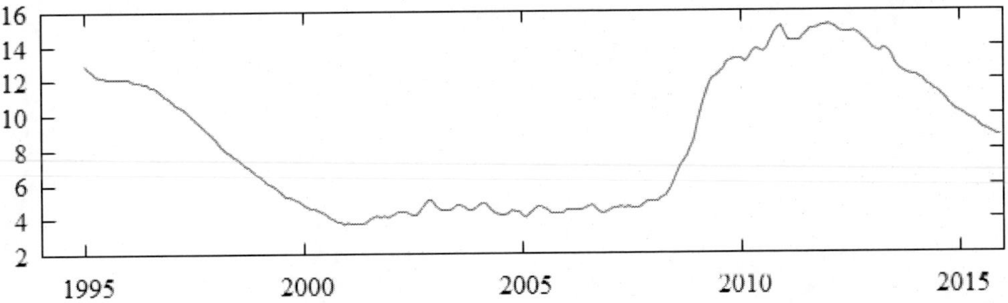

Ireland_consumer confidence

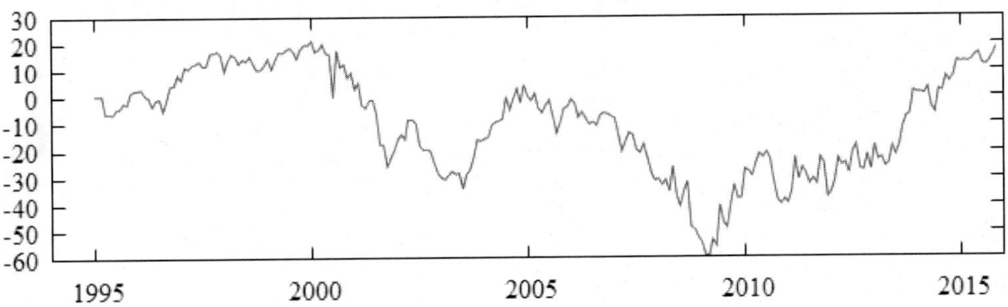

Italy_unemployment rate
14
13
12
11
10
9
8
7
6
5
1995
2000
2005
2010
2015

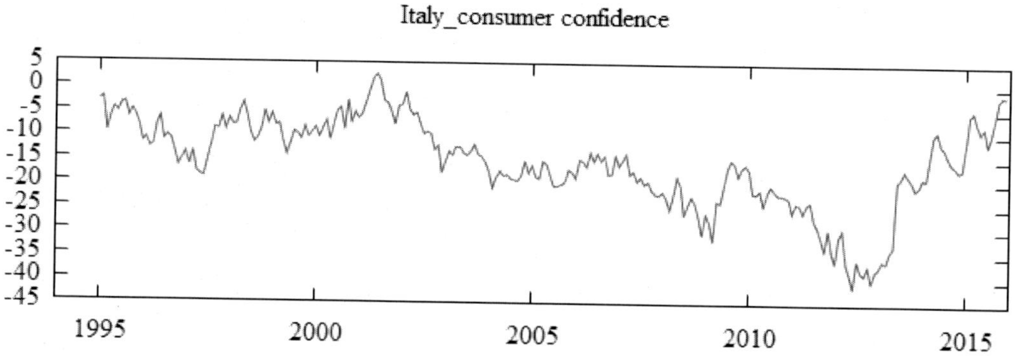
Italy_consumer confidence
5
0
-5
-10
-15
-20
-25
-30
-35
-40
-45
1995
2000
2005
2010
2015

Netherlands_unemployment rate
9
8
7
6
5
4
3
1995
2000
2005
2010
2015

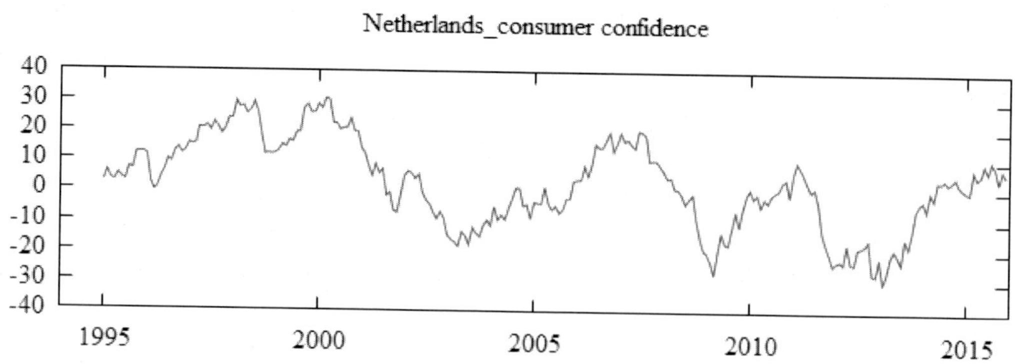
Netherlands_consumer confidence
40
30
20
10
0
-10
-20
-30
-40
1995
2000
2005
2010
2015

Portugal_unemployment rate
18
16
14
12
10
8
6
4
1995
2000
2005
2010
2015

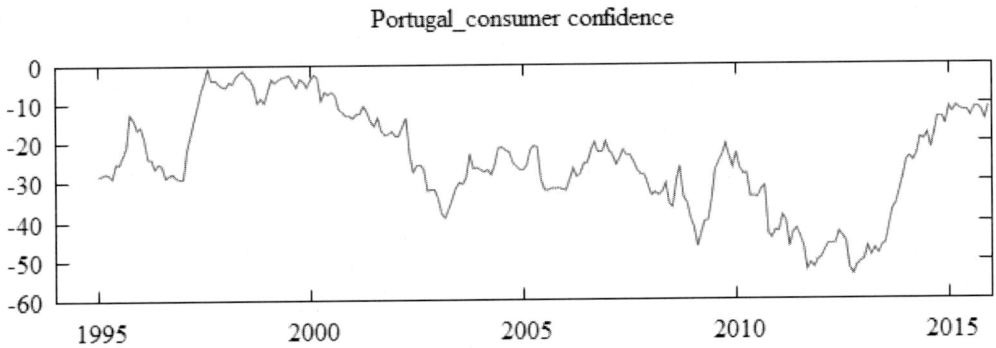
Portugal_consumer confidence
0
-10
-20
-30
-40
-50
-60
1995
2000
2005
2010
2015

Spain_unemployment rate
28
26
24
22
20
18
16
14
12
10
8
6
1995
2000
2005
2010
2015

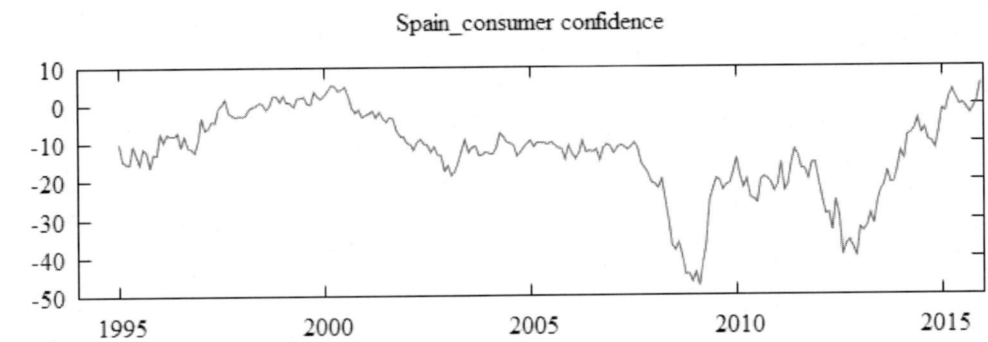
Spain_consumer confidence
10
0
-10
-20
-30
-40
-50
1995
2000
2005
2010
2015

Sweden_unemployment rate

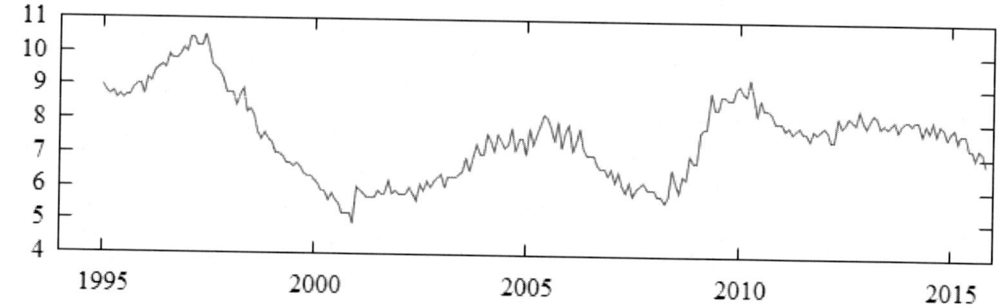

Sweden_consumer confiden

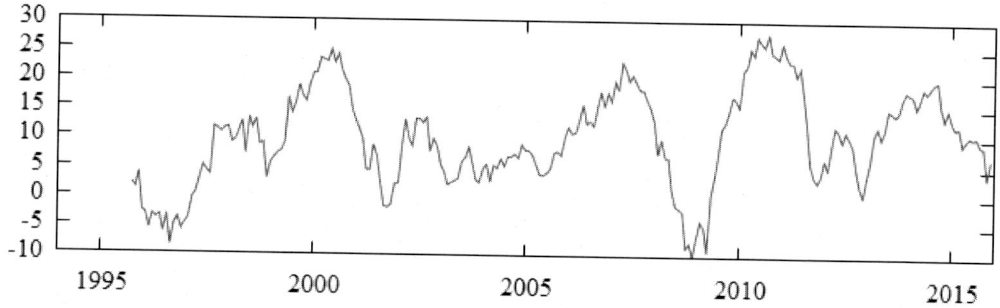

UK_unemployment rate

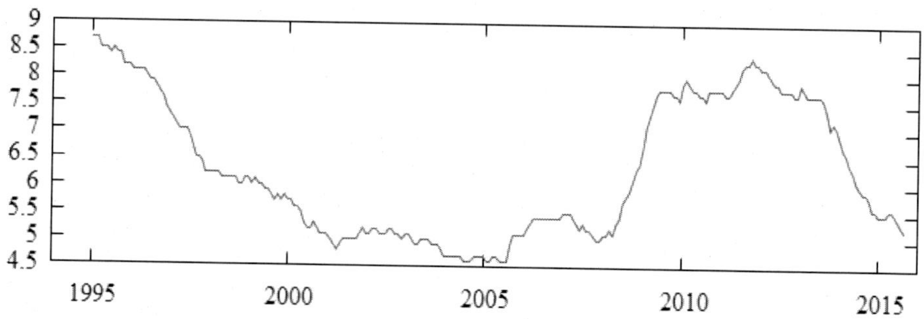

UK_consumer confidence

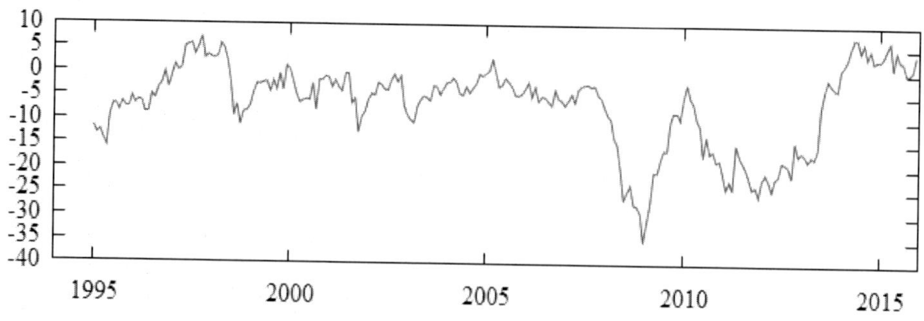

Unemployment rates correlation coefficients, using the observations 1996:01 - 2015:09
5% critical value (two-tailed) = 0.1275 for n = 237

Belgium	Denmark	Germany	Ireland	Spain	France	Italy	
1.0000	0.2298	0.2582	0.2093	0.2983	0.7184	0.4707	Belgium
	1.0000	-0.5826	0.8653	0.8469	0.4935	0.4559	Denmark
		1.0000	-0.6702	-0.7653	-0.1968	-0.4428	Germany
			1.0000	0.9081	0.4912	0.4056	Ireland
				1.0000	0.6614	0.7128	Spain
					1.0000	0.8515	France
						1.0000	Italy
Hungary	**Netherlands**	**Austria**	**Portugal**	**Finland**	**Sweden**	**UK**	
0.2236	0.6970	0.4585	0.0524	0.6425	0.7084	0.2103	Belgium
0.6991	0.5633	0.3443	0.7140	0.0917	0.5793	0.7542	Denmark
-0.4390	-0.2334	-0.0487	-0.7306	0.2858	-0.0391	-0.5122	Germany
0.9134	0.5289	0.2459	0.7799	0.0662	0.6763	0.9355	Ireland
0.7142	0.6654	0.2926	0.7708	0.1750	0.6113	0.7860	Spain
0.3993	0.6975	0.2454	0.2196	0.7012	0.7032	0.4862	France
0.1840	0.6116	0.1018	0.2537	0.5639	0.4139	0.3289	Italy
1.0000	0.4061	0.1783	0.6658	0.0416	0.6905	0.9349	Hungary
	1.0000	0.6550	0.5682	0.3978	0.7307	0.4006	Netherlands
		1.0000	0.5398	-0.1197	0.4508	0.0499	Austria
			1.0000	-0.3811	0.3845	0.5959	Portugal
				1.0000	0.5223	0.1922	Finland
					1.0000	0.6652	Sweden
						1.0000	UK

Consumer confidence correlation coefficients, using the observations 1995:11 - 2015:11
5% critical value (two-tailed) = 0.1264 for n = 241

Belgium	Denmark	Germany	Ireland	Spain	France	Italy	
1.0000	0.2823	0.5577	0.4923	0.6408	0.8534	0.5419	Belgium
	1.0000	0.2872	0.4423	0.4072	0.3346	0.2572	Denmark
		1.0000	0.2105	0.2329	0.5384	0.0441	Germany
			1.0000	0.8244	0.4704	0.6126	Ireland
				1.0000	0.5866	0.7899	Spain
					1.0000	0.4507	France
						1.0000	Italy
Hungary	**Netherlands**	**Austria**	**Portugal**	**Finland**	**Sweden**	**UK**	
0.4336	0.6690	0.6825	0.5628	0.6499	0.5519	0.4036	Belgium
0.2828	0.3822	0.2063	0.2839	0.4036	0.5070	0.6145	Denmark
0.1995	0.3271	0.5482	0.1006	0.2820	0.6895	0.0423	Germany
0.4797	0.7037	0.0533	0.7866	0.4431	0.1251	0.7563	Ireland
0.5441	0.7228	0.2451	0.8220	0.5563	0.2119	0.7682	Spain
0.3326	0.6453	0.7336	0.5662	0.6630	0.5545	0.4303	France
0.5478	0.6251	0.1865	0.8159	0.4072	0.0347	0.6740	Italy
1.0000	0.2417	0.2129	0.4195	0.2774	0.2190	0.5603	Hungary
	1.0000	0.4322	0.7954	0.7332	0.3238	0.5475	Netherlands
		1.0000	0.1829	0.6676	0.6393	0.1109	Austria
			1.0000	0.5134	0.1273	0.7074	Portugal
				1.0000	0.5024	0.4407	Finland
					1.0000	0.1802	Sweden
						1.0000	UK

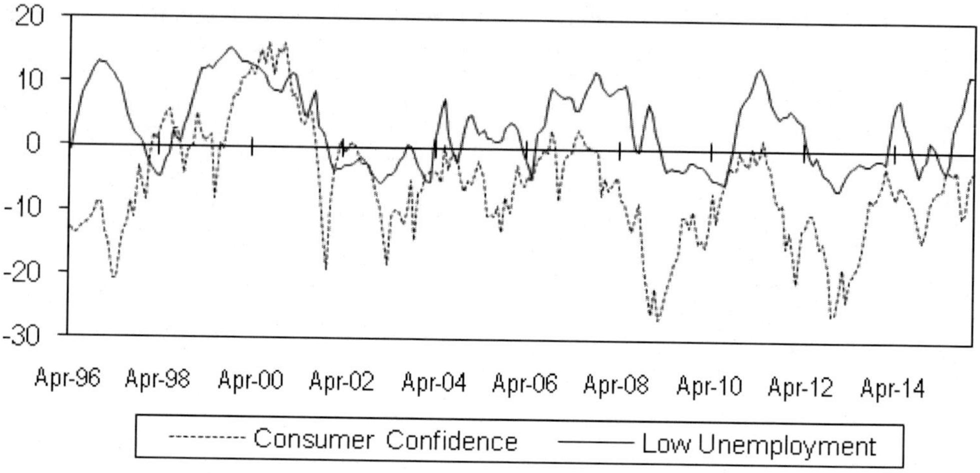

Figure 3. Belgium.

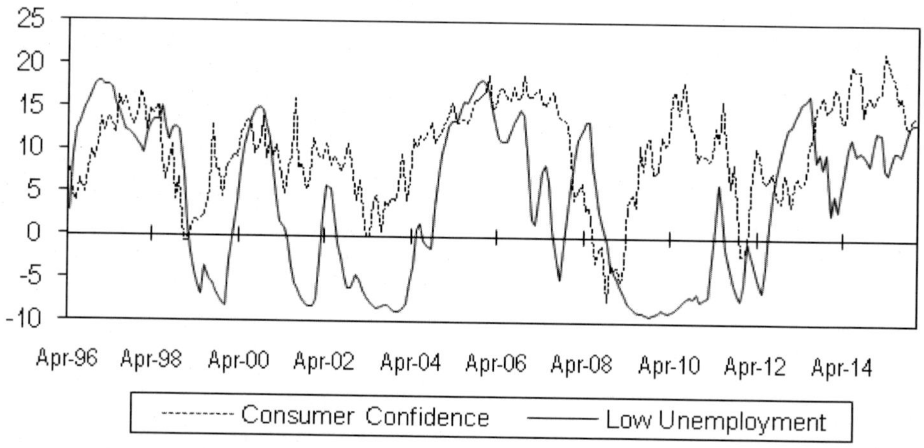

Figure 4. Denmark.

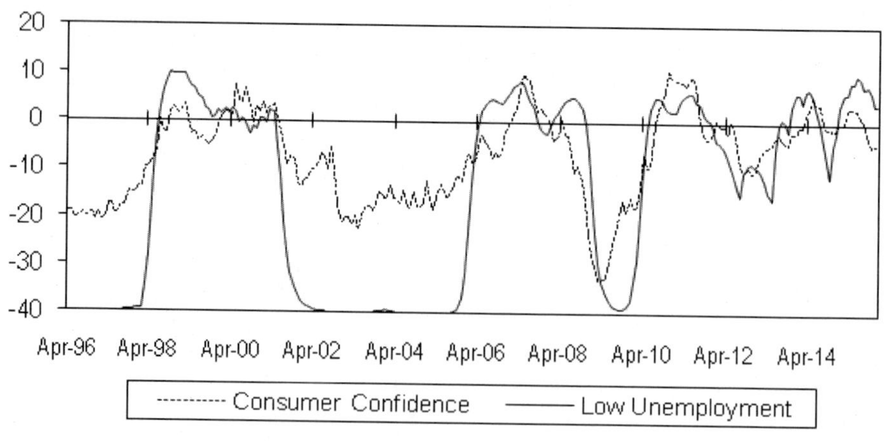

Figure 5. Germany.

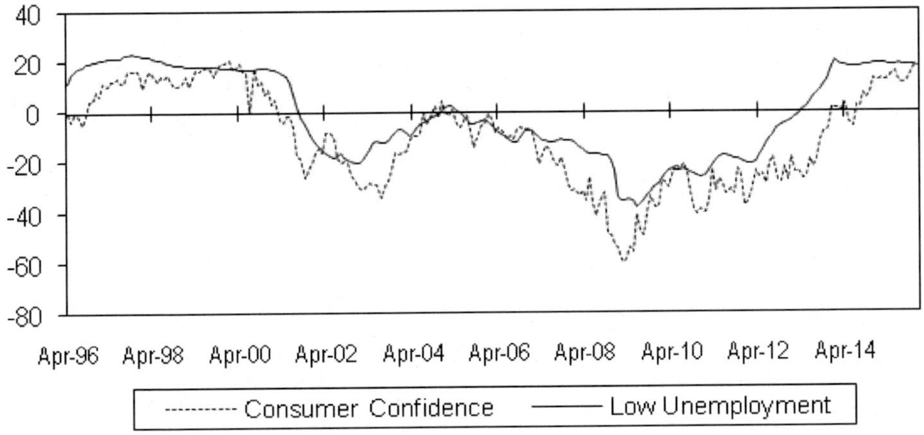

Figure 6. Ireland.

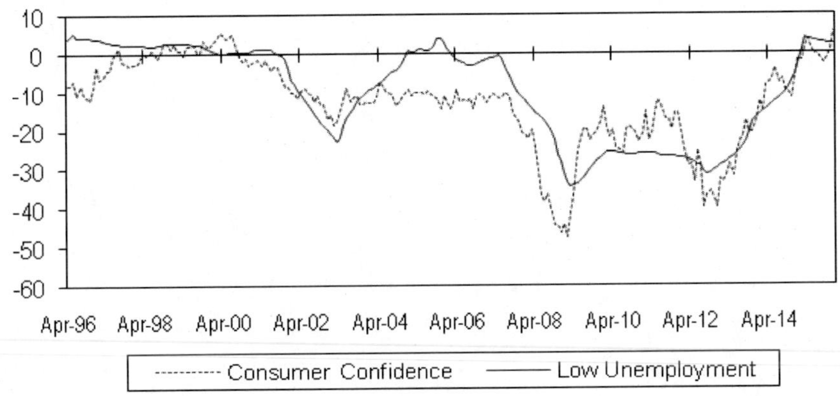

Figure 7. Spain.

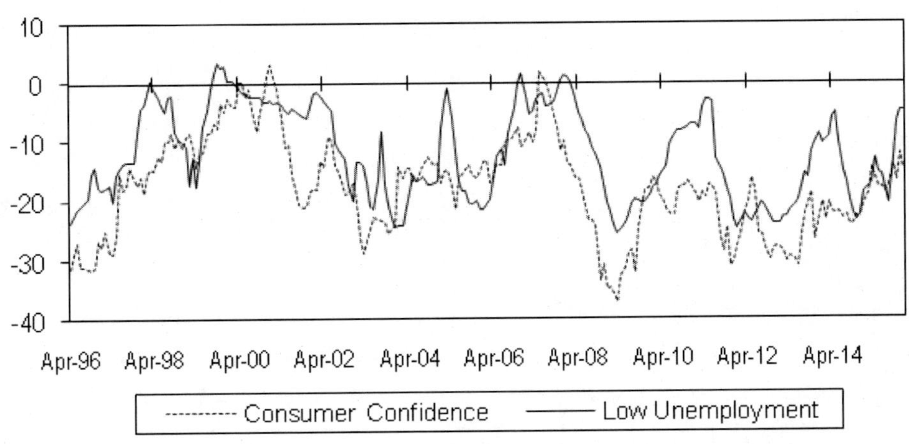

Figure 8. France.

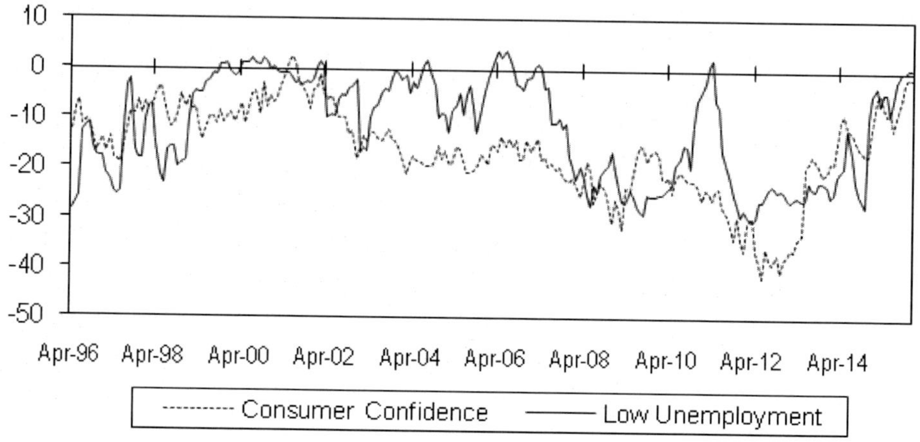

Figure 9. Italy.

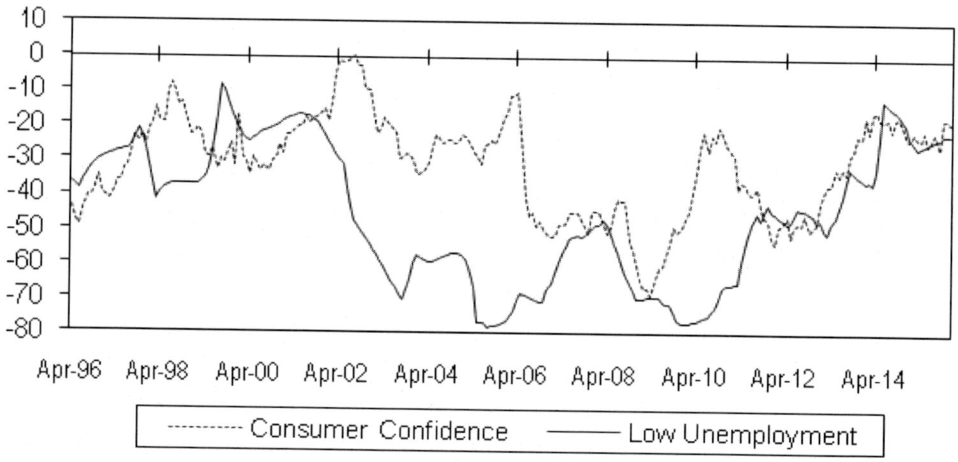

Figure 10. Hungary.

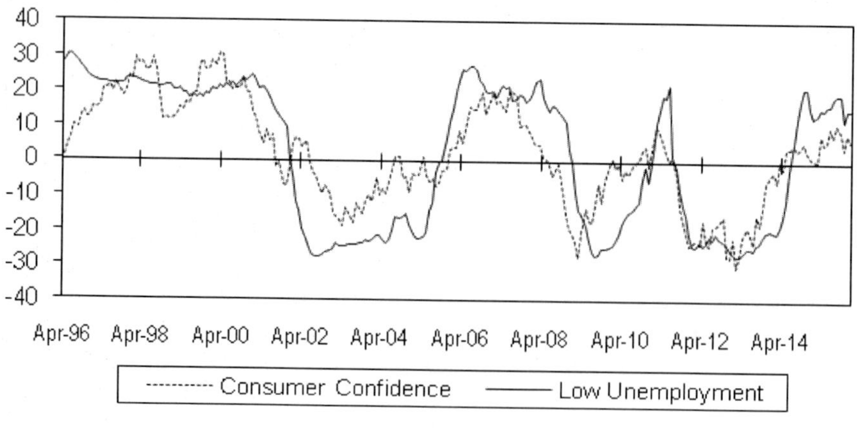

Figure 11. Netherlands.

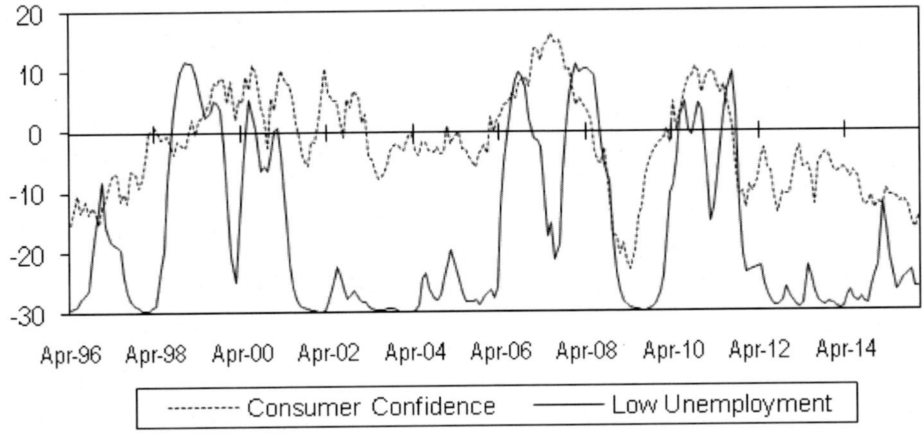

Figure 12. Austria.

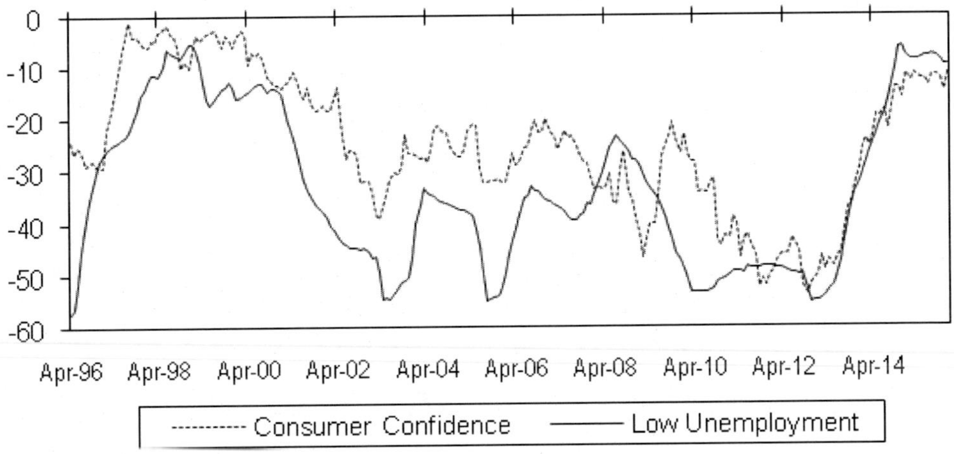

Figure 13. Portugal.

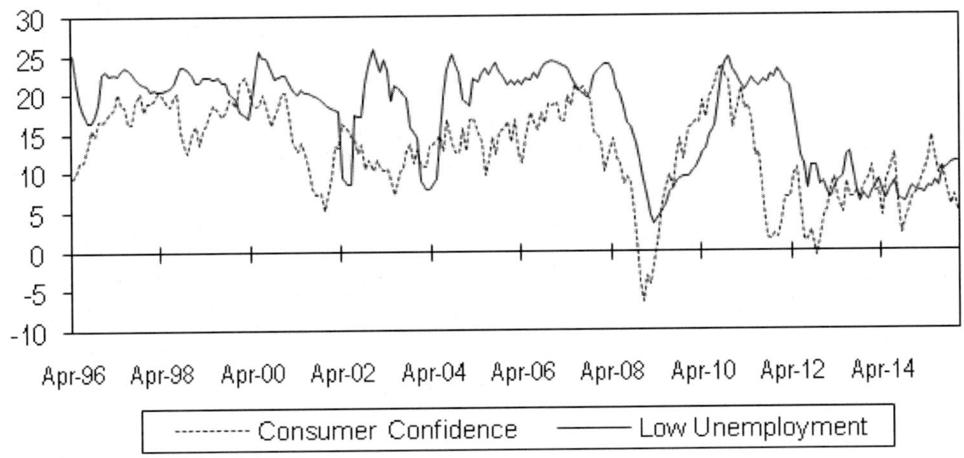

Figure 14. Finland.

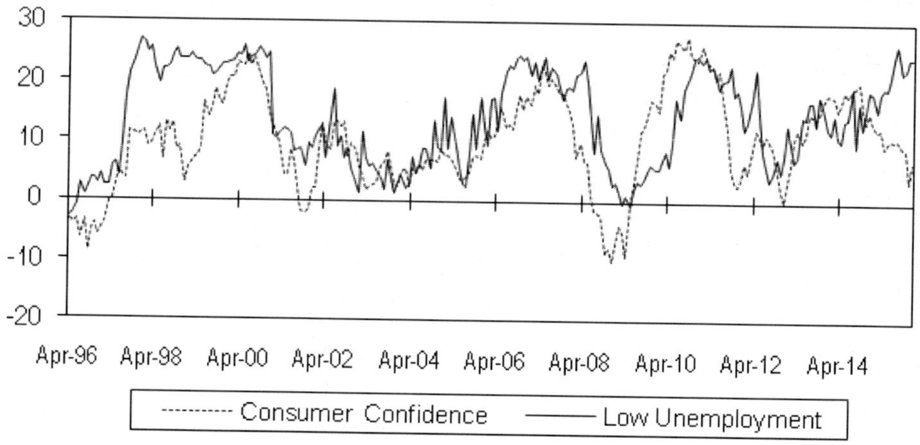

Figure 15. Sweden.

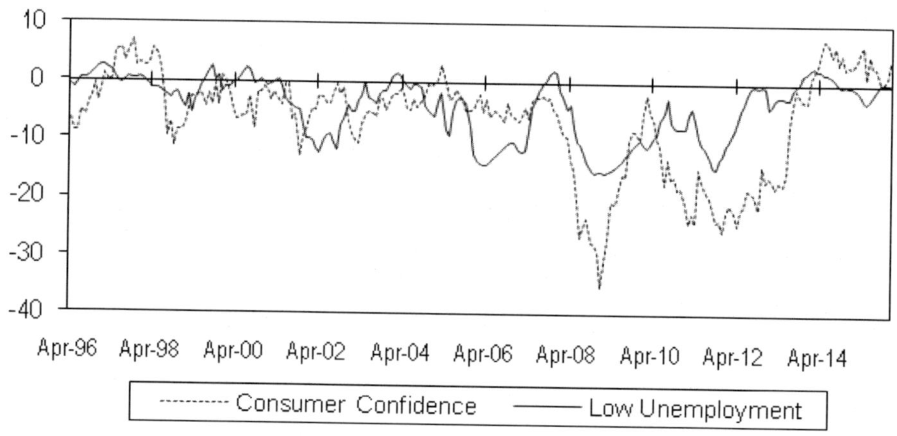

Figure 16. United Kingdom.

References

Adam, A. (2014). Do elections bring optimism? *Electoral Studies*, *33*, 137-143.

Bagnoli, C. & Smith, H. C. (1998). The theory of fuzzy logic and its application to real estate valuation. *The Journal of Real Estate Research*, *16*(2), 169-199.

Caleiro, A. (2003). "Subjective versus Objective Economic Measures: A fuzzy logic exercise". *Departamento de Economia Working Paper*, 2003/11, Universidade de Évora.

Caleiro, A. (2006). How is Confidence related to Unemployment in Portugal. *Applied Economics Letters*, *13*(13), 887-890.

Caleiro, A. (2007). Confidence and Unemployment in the European Union: A lesson from the 2004 enlargement. *Notas Económicas*, *26*, December, 15-26.

Casey, G. P. & Owen, A. L. (2013). Good news, bad news, and consumer confidence. *Social Science Quarterly*, *94*(1), 292-315.

Chang, S. S. L. & Stekler, H. O. (1977). Fuziness in Economic Systems, Its Modeling and Control. *Annals of Economic and Social Measurement*, *6*(2), Spring, 165-174.

Chen, C. H. ed. (1996). *Fuzzy Logic and Neural Network Handbook*. New York: McGraw-Hill.

Constantinescu, A. (2012). The business cycles and the influence of economic confidence indicators in the European region. *Romanian Economic Journal, 15*(44), 201-224.

Curtis, R. (2007). Consumer Sentiment Surveys: Worldwide Review and Assessment. *Journal of Business Cycle Measurement and Analysis, 1*, 7-42.

Díaz, B. & Morillas, A. (2012). Some Experiences Applying Fuzzy Logic to Economics. *In Soft Computing in Humanities and Social Sciences*, (pp. 347-379), Berlin, Heidelberg: Springer.

Delorme, C., Kamerschen, D. & Voeks, L. (2001). Consumer confidence and rational expectations in the United States compared with the United Kingdom. *Applied Economics, 33*, 863-869.

Draeseke, R. & Giles, D. E. (1999, July). A Fuzzy Logic Approach to Modelling the Underground Economy. In *Proceedings of the International Conference on Modelling and Simulation (MODISM 99),* (Vol. 2, pp. 453-458).

European Commission. (2000). "Business Climate Indicator for the Euro Area (Presentation Paper)". *Directorate General for Economic and Financial Affairs.*

European Commission. (2003). "The Joint Harmonised EU Programme of Business and Consumer Surveys: User Guide". *Directorate General for Economic and Financial Affairs, Economic Studies and Research, Business Surveys.*

European Commission. (2014). "A User Manual to the Joint Harmonised EU Programme of Business and Consumers Surveys". *Directorate-General for Economic and Financial Affairs, Unit Economic situation, forecasts, business and consumer surveys.*

Evans, G. W. & Honkapohja, S. (1999). Learning Dynamics. *in Handbook of Macroeconomics*, (pp. 449-542), Amsterdam: Elsevier Science.

Koshal, R. K., Koshel, M. & Lindley, J. D. (2015). Forecasting the Index of Consumer Sentiment. *In Proceedings of the 1985 Academy of Marketing Science (AMS) Annual Conference*, (pp. 450-451). Springer International Publishing.

Landajo, M. (2000). Neural and Fuzzy Models for Economic Forecasting: An econometric view and some practical experience. *Fuzzy Economic Review, 5*(1), May, 3-28.

Matsusaka, J. J. & Sbordone, A. M. (1995). Consumer Confidence and Economic Fluctuations. *Economic Inquiry, 33*(2), April, 296-318.

Møller, S. V., Nørholm, H. & Rangvid, J. (2014). Consumer confidence or the business cycle: What matters more for European expected returns? *Journal of Empirical Finance, 28*, 230-248.

Mourougane, A. & Roma, M. (2003). Can confidence indicators be useful to predict short term real GDP growth? *Applied Economics Letters, 10*, 519-522.

Nordhaus, W. D. (1975). The Political Business Cycle. *The Review of Economic Studies, 42*(2), 130, April, 169-190.

Ramalho, E. A., Caleiro, A. & Dionísio, A. (2011). Explaining Consumer Confidence in Portugal. *Journal of Economic Psychology, 32*(1), February, 25-32.

Santero, T. & Westerlund, N. (1996). "Confidence Indicators and their Relationship to Changes in Economic Activity", Economics Department Working Paper No. 170, OECD.

Sargent, T. J. (1993). *Bounded Rationality in Macroeconomics*. Oxford: Clarendon Press.

Utaka, A. (2003). Confidence and the real economy – the Japanese case. *Applied Economics, 35*, 337-342.

West, J. E. & Linster, B. (2003). The Evolution of Fuzzy Rules as Strategies in Two-Player Games. *Southern Economic Journal*, *69*(3), 705-717.

Yu, T. H. K., Wang, D. H. M. & Chen, S. J. (2006). A fuzzy logic approach to modeling the underground economy in Taiwan. *Physica A: Statistical Mechanics and its Applications*, *362*(2), 471-479.

Zadeh, L. A. (1965). Fuzzy Sets. *Information and Control*, *8*, 338-353.

Zimmermann, H. J. (1991). *Fuzzy Set Theory - and Its Applications*. 2nd edition, Boston: Kluwer Academic Publishers.

BIOGRAPHICAL SKETCH

Name: António Bento Caleiro

Affiliation: Departamento de Economia, Universidade de Évora, Portugal.

Education: BA in Economics (Universidade de Évora, Portugal); MSc in Mathematics applied to Economics (Instituto Superior de Economia e Gestão, Lisbon, Portugal); PhD in Economics (European University Institute, Florence, Italy).

Address: Largo dos Colegiais, 2, 7002-883 Évora, Portugal.

Research and Professional Experience: My research areas include demographic economics, electoral cycles, fuzzy logic applications to economics, spatial econometrics. My teaching courses include Economic Decision Analysis, Economic Policy, Public Economics, and Research Methodology.

Professional Appointments: Assistant professor at the Departamento de Economia, Universidade de Évora, Portugal, since 2001.

Publications Last 3 Years:

Articles:

Rego, Conceição; Baltazar, Maria da Saudade; Caleiro, António (2012), "Higher Education and Social Cohesion", Higher Education of Social Science, 2: 2, March, 17-24.

Caleiro, António (2012), "Output Persistence in Portugal"', International Journal of Latest Trends in Finance and Economic Sciences, 2: 3, September, 206-210.

Rego, Maria da Conceição; Caleiro, António (2012), "Em Torno do Contributo das Instituições de Ensino Superior para a Dinâmica Regional de Crescimento Económico", Desenvolvimento Regional em debate, 2: 2, Dezembro, 124-138.

Guerreiro, Gertrudes Saúde; Caleiro, António (2012), "Regional Income Differences in Borderlands: A Convergence Analysis", International Journal of Latest Trends in Finance and Economic Sciences, 2: 4, December, 305-307.

Caleiro, António (2013a), "A Self-Organizing Map of the Elections in Portugal", The IIOAB Journal, Special Issue (Neuroscience in Economic Decision Making), 4: 3, April-June, 9-14.

Baltazar, Maria da Saudade; Rego, Conceição; Caleiro, António (2013), "Ensino Superior e Crise Económica -- Contributos para o Estudo do Caso Português"', Revista Portuguesa de Estudos Regionais, 33: 2.º quadrimestre, 65-78.

Belbute, José Manuel; Caleiro, António Bento (2013), "Cross Country Evidence on Consumption Persistence", International Journal of Latest Trends in Finance and Economic Sciences, 3: 2, June, 440-455.

Caleiro, António (2013b), "How to Classify a Government: Can a perceptron do it?", International Journal of Latest Trends in Finance and Economic Sciences, 3: 3, September, 523-529.

Caleiro, António Bento (2014), "What if Output Persistence is Disregarded by an Opportunistic Incumbent?", International Journal of Latest Trends in Finance and Economic Sciences, 4: 4, December, 803-806.

Neto, José Chavaglia; Filipe, José António; Ferreira, Manuel Alberto M.; Caleiro, António (2015), "Neuroeconomics: Decisions in Extreme Situations", EC Business Management, 1: 1, January, 14-21.

Book Chapters:

Caleiro, António (2012a), "Why and How Must Portugal be Synchronized with the European Union", IN Bento-Gonçalves, A.; Vieira, A. (eds.), Portugal: Economic, Political and Social Issues, pp. 1-15, Nova Science Publishers, New York, (ISBN: 978-1-62257-474-2).

Caleiro, António (2012b), "Unemployment versus Happiness in Portugal", IN Bento-Gonçalves, A.; Vieira, A. (eds.), Portugal: Economic, Political and Social Issues, pp. 113-123, Nova Science Publishers, New York, (ISBN: 978-1-62257-474-2).

Rego, Conceição; Caleiro, António (2012a), "Acerca dos impactes da Universidade de Évora no seu meio envolvente. Síntese de alguns resultados obtidos", IN Pereira, S.M.; Vaz, F.L. (coords.), Universidade de Évora (1559-2009). 450 anos de modernidade educativa, pp. 751-762, Chiado Editora, Lisboa, Outubro (ISBN: 978-989-697-651-4).

Rego, Conceição; Caleiro, António (2012b), "Para uma análise custo-benefício da importância presente da Universidade de Évora. Que lições para o futuro?", IN Pereira, S.M.; Vaz, F.L. (coords.), Universidade de Évora (1559-2009). 450 anos de modernidade educativa, pp. 777-786, Chiado Editora, Lisboa, Outubro (ISBN: 978-989-697-651-4).

Galego, Aurora; Caleiro, António (2012), "Uma Análise do Tempo de Procura de Emprego dos Recém-Licenciados pela Universidade de Évora", IN Pereira, S.M.; Vaz, F.L. (coords.), Universidade de Évora (1559-2009). 450 anos de modernidade educativa, pp. 787-798, Chiado Editora, Lisboa, Outubro (ISBN: 978-989-697-651-4).

Mendes, Maria Filomena; Caleiro, António; Lagarto, Sandra; Ribeiro, Filipe (2013), "An Application of Statistical Methods of Indirect Estimation and Projection of Internal Migration Flows Within the Portuguese Mainland", IN Lita da Silva, João; Caeiro, Frederico; Natário, Isabel; Braumann, Carlos A. (eds.), Advances in Regression, Survival Analysis, Extreme Values, Markov Processes and Other Statistical Applications, pp. 401-408, Studies in Theoretical and Applied Statistics, Springer, June (ISBN: 978-3-642-34903-4).

Caleiro, António Bento (2013), "Acerca da Actualização das Matrizes Input-Output", IN Lopes, João Carlos; Santos, Jorge; St. Aubyn, Miguel; Santos, Susana (coords.), Estudos de Homenagem a João Ferreira do Amaral, pp. 225-239, Edições Almedina, Coimbra, (ISBN: 978-972-40-5198-7).

Rego, Conceição; Caleiro, António (2013), "O 'Mercado' do Ensino Superior em Portugal: uma caracterização da situação actual", IN Rego, Conceição; Caleiro, António; Vieira,

Carlos; Vieira, Isabel; Baltazar, Maria da Saudade (eds.), Redes de Ensino Superior: Contributos Perante os Desafios do Desenvolvimento, pp. 155-178, Évora: CEFAGE-UE, (ISBN: 978-989-20-4215-2).

Rego, Conceição; Caleiro, António; Vieira, Carlos; Vieira, Isabel; Baltazar, Maria da Saudade (2013), "Ensino Superior em Portugal e acesso ao mercado de trabalho: que relação?", IN Rego, Conceição; Caleiro, António; Vieira, Carlos; Vieira, Isabel; Baltazar, Maria da Saudade (eds.), Redes de Ensino Superior: Contributos Perante os Desafios do Desenvolvimento, pp. 239-261, Évora: CEFAGE-UE, (ISBN: 978-989-20-4215-2).

Baltazar, Maria da Saudade; Rego, Conceição; Caleiro, António (2013), "O contributo das instituições de ensino superior para a `construção' das cidades médias: o caso da Universidade de Évora", IN Rego, Conceição; Caleiro, António; Vieira, Carlos; Vieira, Isabel; Baltazar, Maria da Saudade (eds.), Redes de Ensino Superior: Contributos Perante os Desafios do Desenvolvimento, pp. 263-284, Évora: CEFAGE-UE, (ISBN: 978-989-20-4215-2).

Rego, Conceição; Caleiro, António; Vieira, Carlos; Vieira, Isabel; Baltazar, Maria da Saudade (2014), "Algumas notas sobre o contributo do ensino superior para a qualificação da população no Alentejo", IN Nico, B. (coord.) & Nico, L.P.; Ferreira, F.; Tobias, A. (orgs.), Educações no Alentejo, pp. 157-166, Colecção: Educação, Território e Desenvolvimento Local, Edições Pedago, Mangualde, Maio, (Depósito Legal: 375479/14).

In: Unemployment
Editor: Tabitha Fletcher

ISBN: 978-1-63485-181-7

Chapter 2

PRODUCTIVITY GROWTH SHOCKS AND UNEMPLOYMENT IN THE POSTWAR US ECONOMY

Antonio Ribba*
University of Modena and Reggio Emilia, Italy

Abstract

In recent years growing attention has been paid to the dynamic interaction between productivity growth and unemployment in the US economy. In this chapter we aim to investigate the effects of productivity growth shocks on unemployment, both in the short run and in the medium - long run. We adopt a structural VAR approach and find that, in the last decades, productivity shocks have exerted persistent effects on unemployment. Moreover, these shocks have played an important role in explaining the fluctuations in the unemployment rate at different frequencies. This conclusion seems to be robust to alternative identification strategies of the structural shocks.

Keywords: productivity growth shocks, unemployment, structural VARs

JEL Classification: C32, E24

1. Introduction

In this chapter we want to investigate the dynamic relation at different horizons between productivity growth and unemployment in the postwar US economy.

It is well known that in the 1970s adverse supply shocks were associated with a persistent increase in unemployment. Symmetrically, in the second half of the 1990s, the speed-up in productivity growth accompanied the decrease in the unemployment rate.

Grubb *et al.* (1982) were among the first to offer an explanation of the observed correlation in almost all the industrialized countries among the productivity growth deceleration of the 1970s and the joint increase of inflation and unemployment.

---

*E-mail address: antonio.ribba@unimore.it.

However Blanchard (1989), by using a structural VAR model identified in coherence with a Keynesian view of economic fluctuations, reached a different conclusion. Considering the period $1965 - 1986$, he found that in the US economy, following a productivity shock there was an increase in unemployment for some quarters.

As far as more recent decades are concerned, Ball and Moffitt (2002) presented evidence in favour of a significant role played by the acceleration in productivity growth of the $1990s$ in shaping the joint evolution of inflation and unemployment towards a decrease in that decade. Instead, in Ribba (2003) an empirical investigation was undertaken in order to separate transitory, aggregate demand shocks, moving inflation and unemployment in opposite directions in the short run, and permanent supply shocks, causing movement in the same direction for inflation and unemployment in the long run[1].

Ball and Mankiw (2002) and Ribba (2006) present empirical evidence on the low-frequency co-movements between inflation and unemployment, by structurally interpreting these co-movements in terms of a causal relation running from productivity growth to unemployment.

In a very recent paper, Benigno *et al.* (2015) have suggested the existence of a long-run relation between the volatility in productivity growth and long-run unemployment.

An alternative, theoretical interpretation of the dominant factors driving unemployment (and inflation) in the long run has recently been offered by Berentsen *et al.* (2011). The authors argue that a positive long-run relation between inflation and unemployment may be explained by monetary factors combined with a search-and-bargaining approach. Notice that the pre-eminent role attributed to monetary factors is in line with the Friedmanian interpretation of the stagflation which characterized the $1970s$. (cf. Friedman 1977).

Building on Berentsen *et al.*, Gomis-Porqueras, Julien and Wang (2013) develop a search-theoretic models of money and unemployment in order to derive optimal fiscal and monetary policies. In particular, they show that in a framework with search-and-bargaining frictions some market inefficiencies can be overcome with proper fiscal policies.

A monetary explanation of the long-run evolution of the rate of unemployment has also been offered by Ireland (1999). In Ireland's interpretation, the joint positive long-run relation between unemployment and inflation is explained by the inability of the central bank to pursue a credible low-inflation target.

Although Beyer and Farmer (2007) have criticized Ireland's explanation of the low-frequency movements of unemployment, even their interpretation rests on a dominant role played by shocks on the side of the aggregate demand. More precisely, they identify the roots of the simultaneous increase of inflation and unemployment in 1970s in a downward drift which affected the real interest rate.

On the empirical side, Haug and King (2014) have claimed in a recent investigation that their results concerning the US economy seem to be consistent with a monetary interpretation of the long-run behaviour of unemployment.

Thus, in the present chapter, we aim to investigate the response of unemployment to productivity growth shocks. Moreover, we want to measure the contribution of productivity growth shocks in composing the variability of unemployment at various horizons. We ac-

[1]However a different long-run story might have characterized the European economy in the 1980s and in the first part of the 1990s. For example in Ribba (2007) evidence is provided for Italy of a long-run increase in the unemployment rate driven, among other factors, even by contractionary monetary policy shocks.

complish this task by estimating and identifying a bivariate structural VAR model, using a sample data covering the period $1960 : 1 - 2014 : 4$. Indeed, as stressed by Hutton (2007), empirical research investigating the long-run effects of productivity growth on macroeconomic variables should, ideally, utilize samples covering longer periods than just a few decades.

Our main findings can be summarized as follows: (1) productivity growth and unemployment rate exhibit a negative correlation, both at business cycle frequencies and in the medium run; (2) a positive productivity growth shock moves the unemployment rate towards a significant reduction which lasts for many quarters; (3) the productivity growth shocks explain an important part of the variability of unemployment at various horizons; (4) A relevant role in driving unemployment fluctuations is also played by aggregate demand shocks, nevertheless structural disturbances on the demand side cause short-run movements of productivity growth and unemployment rate in the same direction.

Indeed these results seem to be robust to alternative identification strategies of the structural shocks. For, we first identify the productivity growth shock by imposing a recursive structure to the bivariate VAR model including productivity and unemployment, and after, in order to check for the robustness of the conclusion reached, we adopt a more agnostic approach in the spirit of Uhlig (cf. Uhlig 2005) and identify the productivity shock by imposing sign restrictions on the responses of unemployment.

It is worth stressing that although by adopting a sign restrictions approach we detect an increase in the persistence of the effects of productivity growth shocks on unemployment, as a whole the two identification strategies lead to quite similar results.

Let us also note that in the presence of a pre-eminent or, in the limit, exclusive role of monetary factors, one should not expect to detect in the data any significant role played by productivity growth shocks on unemployment fluctuations, at least at lower frequencies. Thus, given the empirical results obtained in the present research, our conclusion appears to be in contrast with researches pointing to a pure monetary explanation of the medium to long-run co-movement of inflation and unemployment.

Further, we want to point out that our empirical results might also be interpreted as a call for theoretical modelling to incorporate the influence of productivity growth on unemployment at different frequencies.

The rest of the chapter is organized as follows. In section 2 we present some facts concerning the correlations at different leads and lags between productivity growth and unemployment.

Section 3 presents the strategy of identification of the structural VAR model together with the dynamic responses of the two variables to the identified shocks. In this context, we complement the impulse-response function analysis with the decomposition of variance at different horizons, in order to measure the relative importance of the structural shocks.

In section 4 we undertake a sensitivity analysis in order to check the robustness of the results obtained in section 3 and thus we identify the productivity growth shock by imposing sign restrictions on the response of unemployment.

Section 5 concludes and some implications of the results obtained are also drawn.

2. Some Simple Facts on the Joint Evolution of Productivity Growth and Unemployment in the Postwar US Economy

In figure 1 productivity growth and unemployment rate in the US economy, for the sample period $1960:1-2014:4$, are reported.

We consider the annual rate of growth of labor productivity and the civilian unemployment rate. Both the series are taken from FRED at the St. Louis FED Web site.

Obviously, it is not possible to infer any causal relationship characterizing the variables by simply inspecting their joint evolution. An attempt to identify the causal relations between the two variables will be undertaken in the subsequent sections, by utilizing the structural VAR methodology. Nevertheless, some simple facts clearly emerge from the descriptive analysis conducted in the present section.

The first stylized fact concerns the strong, negative relation between the two variables in the first part of the 1970s, when a sudden and deep decline in productivity growth is associated with an increase in the unemployment rate. The same negative relation is also apparent in the second half of the 1990s, when an acceleration in the rate of growth of productivity is associated to a tendency of strong decrease in the unemployment rate.

However, an important difference characterizing the 1990s with respect to the 1970s consists in the smoother process which exhibits both the increase in productivity growth and the decrease of the unemployment rate in the more recent decade.

Another interesting fact which emerges from this simple graphical inspection concerns the positive relation between the two variables characterizing other historical periods. In particular, this positive co-movement is apparent in the first part of the eighties and in the more recent period, $2008-2014$, in which the US economy was affected by the so-called Great Recession. This evidence seems to suggest that in the presence of shocks arising on the side of aggregate demand, productivity growth and unemployment move in the same direction.

Once again, we stress that it is difficult to draw sound conclusion on the causality directions in the observed movements of the variables without the identification of a structural model. As a consequence, we will try to check this conjecture on the dynamic effects exerted by aggregate demand shocks on productivity growth and unemployment in the next section, by utilizing a more structural approach.

In Table 1 we present the cross correlations of productivity growth and unemployment at various leads and lags. The results show clear evidence of a negative relation between the two variables, both in the short and in the medium rum.

Table 1. Measuring the co-movements of productivity growth and unemployment in the US economy

		Lag						**Lead**			
0	4	8	12	24	36	0	4	8	12	24	36
-.071	-.02	-.32	-.26	-.092	.003	-.071	-.29	-.32	-.31	-.14	.10

Note: Cross correlations of productivity growth and unemployment rate at various leads and lags are reported for the sample period $1960:1-2014:4$.

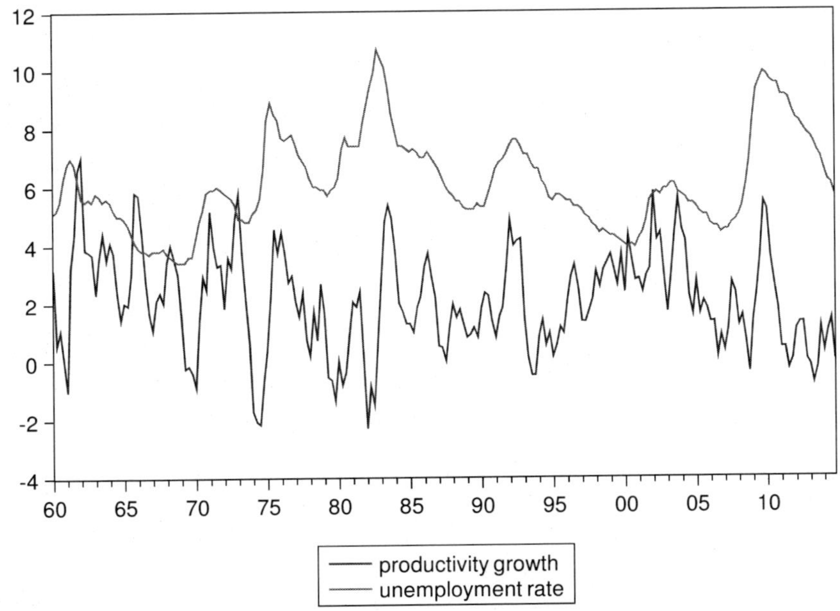

Figure 1. Productivity growth and unemployment rate in the US economy 1960:1 - 2014:4.

As shown in Table 1, there is evidence of positive cross correlations only at lead and lag of 36. Instead, all the other correlations, from lead and lag 0 to 24, have negative signs. The maximum values are obtained at lag 12 ($-.26$) and at lead 8 ($-.32$).

3. The Estimated Structural VAR Model

A bivariate VAR model for the US economy is estimated, covering the sample period $1960:1-2014:4$. It includes the labor productivity growth and the rate of unemployment.

We start with the estimation of the reduced form VAR model:

$$X_t = \mu + A(L)X_{t-1} + e_t \tag{1}$$

where for a VAR of order p, $A(L) = \sum_{i=1}^{p} A_i L^{i-1}$. We take, in accord with the Schwartz criterion, $p = 5$. L is the lag operator, such that: $L^i X_t = X_{t-i}$. μ is a vector of constant terms and e_t is the 2×1 vector of error terms, such that $E(e_t) = 0$ and $E(e_t e_t') = \Sigma_e$.

In order to fix notation, the 2×1 vector X_t is given by:

$$X_t' = (\; g_t \quad u_t \;)$$

where g_t is the annual rate of growth of labor productivity and u_t is the civilian unemployment rate.

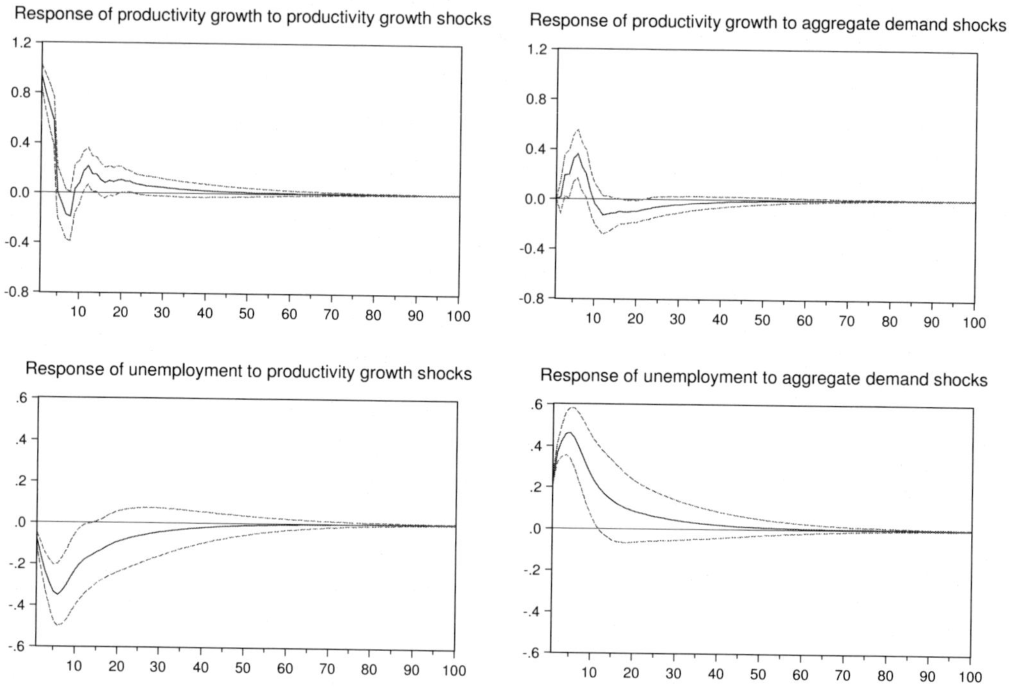

Figure 2. Responses of variables to the identified shocks.

Given an assumption of stationary variables included in X_t, we can write the following reduced-form moving average representation of the VAR model:

$$X_t = \gamma + C(L)e_t \tag{2}$$

where $C(0) = I$.

We recover the structural shocks by imposing a (contemporaneous) recursive structure to the estimated VAR model. The structural moving-average representation is given by:

$$X_t = \gamma + B(L)\eta_t \tag{3}$$

where $B(L) = C(L)B$ and $\eta_t = B^{-1}e_t$. B is the Cholesky factor of Σ_e, *i.e.* is the unique lower triangular matrix such that $BB' = \Sigma_e$. η_t is the 2×1 vector of orthonormal shocks.

Thus we are imposing the following restriction: an unexpected increase in the unemployment rate does not influence the productivity growth within the period (one quarter in our sample data). Moreover, by interpreting the structural shock obtained by the VAR unemployment equation as an aggregate demand shock, it follows that the zero, contemporaneous restriction implies imposing that an aggregate demand shock does not cause modification in the rate of growth of labor productivity in the current quarter.

In Figure 2 the impulse-response functions are reported.

As shown in Figure 2, there is a significant, negative effect on unemployment of a positive productivity growth shock. No less importantly, this negative effect is also quite persistent, since it requires around forty quarters to vanish. To be more precise, the median response of unemployment to the productivity shock exhibits this persistent effect. However, taking into account the confidence bands, the response becomes statistically non-significant after around fifteen quarters.

A different conclusion was instead reached by Blanchard (1989) in an investigation concerning the US economy for the period $1965:1-1986:4$. The author found, by identifying a structural VAR model in the spirit of the Keynesian view of economic fluctuations, that a positive productivity shock causes a temporary increase in unemployment.

As far as the aggregate demand shock is concerned, an unexpected reduction in aggregate demand, *i.e.* an unexpected increase in unemployment, causes a temporary increase, which lasts for around ten quarters, in productivity growth. Hence, we detect a good deal of persistence even in the shocks on the aggregate demand side.

It is important to point out that this structural analysis seems to reinforce the conclusion reached in the previous section, based on a descriptive analysis, of a positive relation induced by aggregate demand movements between productivity and unemployment.

Thus, on the basis of this analysis, the conclusion is that fluctuations in the rate of unemployment are significantly driven by movements in the productivity growth, both in the short and in the medium run. Another important conclusion is that also shock on the demand side play a relevant role in explaining the fluctuations in the rate of unemployment. Of course, the relevance of aggregate demand shocks is far from surprising and a subsequent step will be to measure the relative importance of these two structural shocks at different horizons.

Once analyzed the impulse-response functions, a potentially interesting and complementary analysis concerns the decomposition of the forecast error variance.

The structural representation [3] allows the error in forecasting X_t for each horizon s to be built:

$$X_{t+s} - E_t X_{t+s} = B_0 \eta_{t+s} + B_1 \eta_{t+s-1} + B_2 \eta_{t+s-2} + ... + B_{s-1} \eta_{t+1} \qquad (4)$$

From [4] and given the orthonormality of the structural disturbances, the variance of the forecasting error is:

$$Var(X_{t+s} - E_t X_{t+s}) = B_0 B_0' + B_1 B_1' + B_2 B_2' + ... + B_{s-1} B_{s-1}' \qquad (5)$$

By using equation [5] it is thus possible to decompose the total variance of the forecast error, for each variable, due to the variance of each structural shock. Clearly we would like to use [5] in order to measure the relative important importance of productivity growth shocks in composing the variability of unemployment at various horizons.
The main results are reported in Table 2.

At horizons comprised from one quarter to one year the productivity growth shock explains around one fifth of the total variability of unemployment. However, there is an increase in the subsequent periods and at horizons from 24 to 60 quarters the variance explained is around 37 percent. Hence a relevant, though not dominant, role is played by productivity growth shocks in explaining the variability of unemployment at different frequencies.

Table 2. Fraction of the forecast error variance of the rate of unemployment attributable to productivity growth shocks at different horizons

Horizon						
1	4	8	12	24	36	60
11.0	22.8	32.7	35.0	36.9	37.2	37.3

Note: The total variance of the forecast error for unemployment is computed and then decomposed in the part attributable to each structural shock (cf. formula [5]). The table presents the fraction of variability at various horizons which is due to the productivity growth shock.

It is worth stressing that in the context of the structural bivariate model utilized in this section, the forecast error variance analysis shows that the pre-eminent role is played by aggregate demand shocks in explaining the fluctuations in the rate of unemployment.

4. A More Agnostic Approach to Identification of Productivity Growth Shocks

In this section we provide an alternative strategy of identification of the productivity growth shock, based on sign restrictions.

Let us start with the estimation of the reduced form:

$$X_t = \mu + A(L)X_{t-1} + e_t \tag{6}$$

where, as stated in section 3, for a VAR of order p, $A(L) = \sum_{i=1}^{p} A_i L^{i-1}$, with $p = 5$ in this context. e_t is the 2×1 vector of error terms, such that $E(e_t) = 0$ and $E(e_t e_t') = \Sigma_e$.

We obtain the identification of the productivity growth shock in the following way: given the relation between the error terms, e_t, and the exogenous macroeconomic shocks, ϵ_t, $e_t = F\epsilon_t$, the covariance matrix of the vector of residuals matrix, Σ_e, is randomly drawn from the posterior distribution of the matrix of the VAR coefficients; since $E(\epsilon_t \epsilon_t') = I$, *i.e.* the vector contains orthonormal variables, and given $FF' = \Sigma_e$, we identify a set of impulse vectors, $f^1..f^n$, such that $f^i = F_i\alpha^i$, where $\|\alpha^i\| = 1$, which is consistent with some plausible macroeconomic hypothesis.

Thus, each impulse vector, f^i, is a column of F and, moreover, n, the number of identified shocks, is smaller than m, the number of total shocks driving the dynamic system. More precisely, in this empirical study, given $m = 2$, we identify $n = 1$ one single economic shock.

In particular, we impose the following sign restriction: the response of unemployment to a positive productivity growth shock is negative for 4 quarters.

It is important to note that this identification strategy allows a set of impulse vectors consistent with the imposed sign restrictions to be selected. Hence, in order to select a unique set of impulse vectors we apply a penalty function (cf. Mountford and Uhlig 2009).

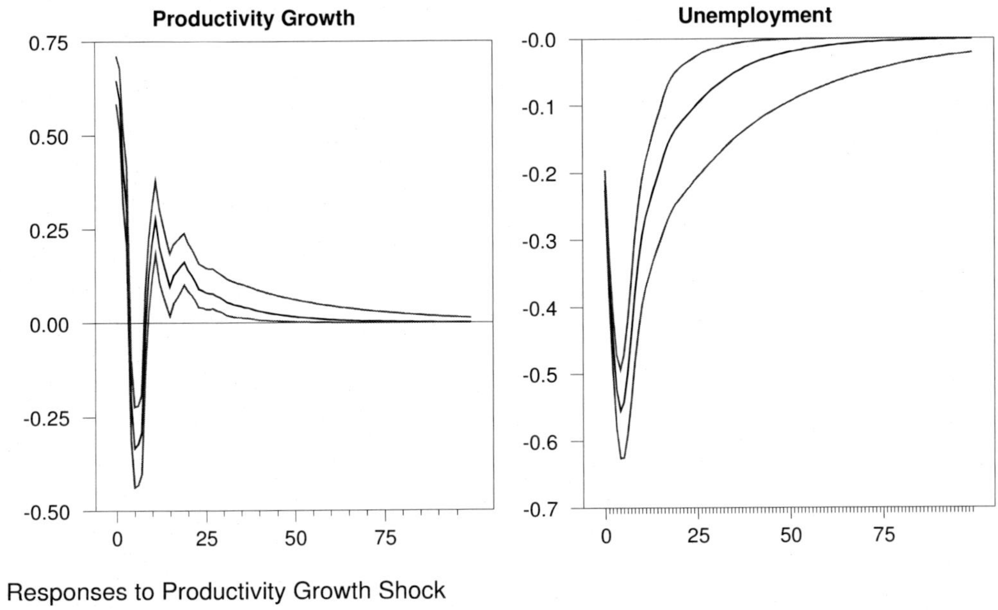

Figure 3. Responses of variables to a productivity growth shock identified by sign restrictions.

We calculate the confidence bands by using the Bayesian approach proposed by Sims and Zha (1999)[2]. The assumption is that VAR errors are normal and that both prior and posterior density belong to the Normal-Wishart family. We take 10000 draws from the posterior, where each draw is subject to the numerical minimization associated to the penalty function.

Thus we recover the structural disturbance by imposing that an unexpected increase in productivity causes a reduction in the rate of unemployment for some quarters.

In Figure 3 the response of the rate of unemployment to the productivity growth shock is reported. More precisely, we report the median responses of the variables to the identified shock, together with the 16th and 84th percentiles.

Instead Figure 4 presents the results concerning the variance decomposition analysis.

There are some interesting features of this analysis which deserve attention.

The most important is represented by the confirmation of the qualitative profile of the dynamics effects exert by productivity growth shocks on unemployment, in line with the results obtained in the previous section, by imposing a recursive structure to the VAR model.

The second, quite interesting feature of the response of the unemployment rate to a productivity growth shock, concerns the increase in the persistence detected by adopting a sign restrictions approach, since the effects exerted on the rate of unemployment become statistically non-significant only after 35 quarters.

[2]See also Doan, (2010).

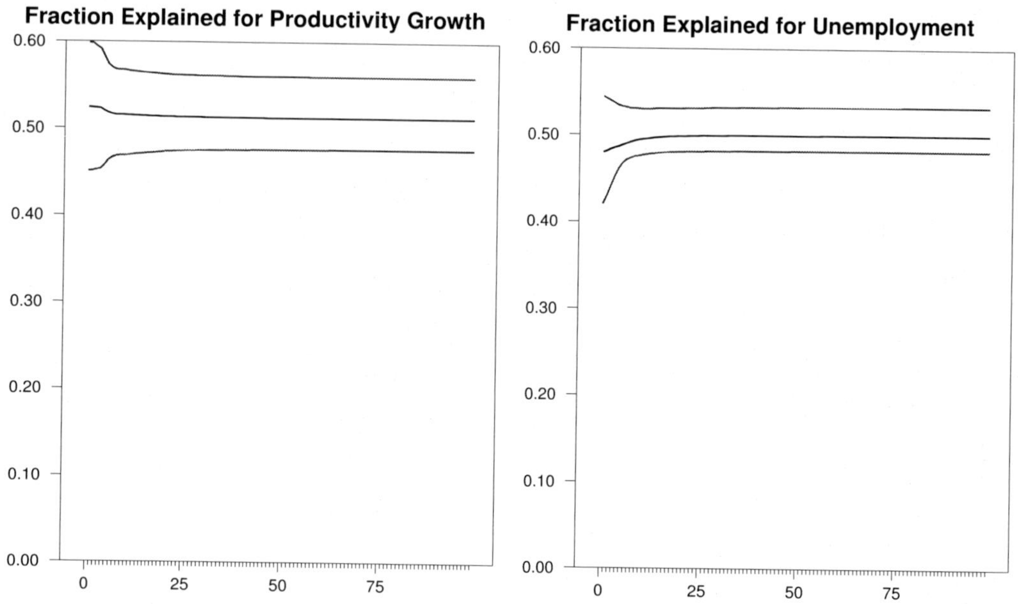

Figure 4. Fraction of the forecast error variance of the variables attributable to productivity growth shocks at different horizons.

Further, this conclusion is reinforced if we concentrate attention on the median response of unemployment, which shows a decrease in the unemployment rate following a productivity shock which lasts for 65 periods.

Thus there is also some evidence of long-run effects of productivity growth on unemployment.

Summing up: the sensitivity analysis conducted in this section points to the confirmation of the relevant role played by productivity growth in shaping the evolution of the unemployment rate in the US economy in the last 50 years.

The variance decomposition analysis, based on the sign restrictions approach and reported in figure 4, shows that the productivity growth shock explains a relevant part of the variability in the rate of unemployment, both at business cycle frequencies and at lower frequencies.

Indeed, it is important to notice that by adopting a more agnostic approach to the identification of the structural shocks, the relative importance of productivity in composing the variability of unemployment at different horizons increases, in comparison to the recursive identification strategy previously adopted. For, the productivity growth shock, according to this analysis, explains around 50 percent of the forecast-error variance of unemployment at almost all frequencies.

Moreover, we point out that, as shown in figure 4, the estimated confidence bands do not add particular uncertainty in the interpretation of the main results, given their relatively moderate amplitude.

However, it is worth stressing that our results, at least in this bivariate context, imply that both shocks, on the supply side and on the demand side, play a relevant role in driving unemployment rate fluctuations.

Summing up the conclusion concerning the forecast error variance analysis: from a qualitative point of view, the results of this section confirm that the productivity growth shocks have played a significant role in shaping the evolution of the rate of unemployment in the postwar period and that there is a large convergence of results provided by the two alternative identification strategies.

5. Conclusion

In this empirical investigation we have tried to shed some light on the dynamic relation between productivity growth and unemployment in the postwar US economy. We have used a bivariate structural VAR model and our main finding is that productivity growth shocks have represented an important, exogenous source of fluctuations of the unemployment rate, both in the short and in the medium run in the last fifty years. More precisely, a positive productivity growth shock causes a persistent decrease of unemployment and this contraction in the rate of unemployment remains significant for many quarters.

This result revealed itself to be robust to alternative identification strategies of the structural shocks, since the results obtained by imposing a recursive structure with productivity growth ordered first are similar to those obtained by imposing sign restrictions on the responses of the unemployment rate.

Although the variance decomposition analysis has shown that a relevant role in shaping the evolution of unemployment has been played by productivity shock, unexpected movements on the aggregate demand side are also an important source of fluctuations of unemployment. In particular, by adopting a sign restrictions approach to the identification of the productivity growth shock, we find that there is a very persistent effect of this disturbance on unemployment and, moreover, that around fifty percent of the variability of unemployment at various horizons is explained by productivity growth shocks.

As far as long-run effects of productivity growth shocks are concerned, by adopting a sign restrictions identification strategy clear evidence emerges of a long-run effect exerted on the rate of unemployment, since 65 quarters are required before the dynamic effects of the structural shock vanish.

It is important to stress that our results point to an important distinction between the dynamic effects exerted on the two variables by shocks originated on the aggregate supply side and, alternatively, on the aggregate demand side. For, we find that in the first case productivity growth and unemployment move in opposite directions whereas, in the second, they move in the same direction.

Thus, as a whole, on the basis of the evidence presented in this chapter, we are led to conclude that one-single explanation of the fluctuations of unemployment at different frequencies in the postwar US economy, relying on monetary or alternatively real factors, does not fit the data well.

Instead, according to our empirical investigation, it seems that theoretical frameworks need to incorporate an explanation of the channels through which unexpected changes in productivity growth translate their persistent effects in a decrease in the rate of unemployment, at medium and low frequencies.

References

Ball, L. and Mankiw G.N. (2002). The NAIRU in Theory and Practise. *Journal of Economics Perspectives*, 16, 115 – 136.

Ball, L. and R. Moffitt, (2002). Productivity Growth and the Phillips Curve. In A. B. Krueger and R. Solow, eds., The Roaring Nineties: Can Full Employment Be Sustained? (New York: Russell Sage Foundation).

Benigno, P., Ricci, L.A. and Surico P. (2015). Unemployment and Productivity in the Long Run: The Role of Macroeconomic Volatility. *Review of Economics and Statistics*, 97, 698 – 709.

Berentsen, A., Menzio, G. and Wright R. (2011). Inflation and Unemployment in the Long Run. *American Economic Review*, 101, 371 – 398.

Beyer, A. and Farmer R. (2007). Natural Rate Doubts. *Journal of Economics Dynamics and Control*, 79, 1146 – 1164.

Blanchard, O. (1989). A Traditional Interpretation of Macroeconomic Fluctuations. *American Economic Review*, 101, 371 – 398.

Doan, T.A. (2010). RATS User's Manual, Version 8, Estima, 1560 Sherman Avenue, Suite 510, Evanston, IL 60201.

Friedman, M. (1977). Inflation and Unemployment. *Journal of Political Economy*, 85, 451 – 472.

Gomis-Porqueras, P., Julien, B. and C. Wang (2013). Optimal Monetary and Fiscal Policies in a Search-Theoretic Model of Money and Unemployment. *Macroeconomic Dynamics*, 17, 1330 – 1354.

Grubb, D., Jackman R. and Layard R. (1982). Causes of Current Stagflation. *Review of Economic Studies*, Special Issue, 707 – 730.

Hatton, T.J. (2007). Can Productivity Growth Explain the NAIRU? Long-Run Evidence from Britain, 1871-1999. *Economica*, 74, 475 – 491.

Haug, A.A. and King I. (2014). In the Long Run, US Unemployment Follows Inflation like a Faithful Dog. *Journal of Macroeconomics*, 41, 42 – 52.

Ireland, P.I. (1999). Does the time-consistency problem explain the behaviour of inflation in the United States? *Journal of Monetary Economics*, 44 279 – 291.

Mountford, A. and H. Uhlig (2009). What Are the Effects of Fiscal policy Shocks? *Journal of Applied Econometrics*, 24, 960 – 992.

Ribba, A. (2003). Short-run and Long-run Interaction between Inflation and Unemloyment in the USA. *Applied Economics Letters*, 10, 373 – 376.

Ribba, A. (2006). The Joint Dynamics of Inflation, Unemployment and Interest Rate in the Unites States since 1980. *Empirical Economics*, 31, 497 – 511.

Ribba, A. (2007) Permanent Disinflationary Effects in a Small Open Economy: Italy 1979-1995. *Economic Modelling*, 24, 66 – 81.

Sims, C.A. and Zha, T. (1999) Error Bands for Impulse Responses. *Econometrica* 67, 1113 – 1156.

Uhlig, H. (2005). What Are the Effects of Monetary Policy on Output? Results from an Agnostic Identification Procedure. *Journal of Monetary Economics, 52*, 381 – 419.

In: Unemployment
Editor: Tabitha Fletcher

ISBN: 978-1-63485-181-7

Chapter 3

FINITE SAMPLE INFERENCE FOR UNEMPLOYMENT-INFLATION TRADEOFF

H. D. Vinod*
Economics Department, Fordham University, NY, US

Abstract

Under the simultaneous presence of identification, endogeneity and non-spherical regression error problems, the choice between ordinary least squares (OLS) and generalized method of moments (GMM) should depend on finite sample evaluation of 'convergence in probability' and 'almost sure convergence.' We offer new simulation tools for this purpose. The new Keynesian Phillips curve (NKPC) estimation for US data finds little endogeneity-induced inconsistency and that using GMM seems to worsen it. The potential 'lack of identification' problem is attributed to possibly zero standard errors in the denominators of Wald pivots. We replace it by the Godambe pivot, leading to superior confidence intervals for deep parameters of the NKPC model.

PACS: 05.45-a, 52.35.Mw, 96.50.Fm

Keywords: bootstrap, simulation, convergence, inflation inertia, sticky prices

1. Introduction

Unemployment and inflation arise mostly because of the inability of agents to to optimally set prices and wages under dynamically changing market conditions. Study of unemployment in Economics often involves a study of trade-offs. The well-known Phillips curve originally studied a trade-off between unemployment and inflation, which appears to have faded away in the recent data. Another trade-off is between job vacancies and unemployment, called the Beveridge curve, which yields the "natural" unemployment rate at its intersection with the job creation curve. Vinod (2012) fits a multiplicative nonhomogenous function for industrial production to estimate distinct scale elasticities, marginal elasticities and elasticities of substitution of unemployment and vacancies under Bush and Obama

*E-mail address: vinod@fordham.edu.

administrations. He finds that the Beveridge curve trade-off mostly disappears during the Obama years.

This paper considers a related macroeconomic model by Galí and Gertler (1999)(hereafter "GG99") known as the new Keynesian Phillips curve (NKPC). It involves microeconomic foundations by estimating the fraction ϕ of firms fail to adjust prices to optimal levels. GG99 has inspired several papers cited in Kleibergen and Mavroeidis (2009), (hereafter "KM09"), followed by discussion in the same journal. More recently, Mavroeidis et al. (2014) survey of over 100 papers deals with single equation estimation of the NKPC model. A typical model regresses inflation on past and future inflation and a proxy variable x_t for real marginal cost. Why marginal cost? Assuming Cobb-Douglas production technology, marginal cost is proportional to the ratio of 'nominal wage' to 'nominal output' and also proportional to the 'output gap' (between actual and potential output under fully flexible prices and wages).

Almost all authors use the generalized method of moments (GMM) for estimation of NKPC, without even considering OLS. Mavroeidis et al. (2014) complain that (a) seemingly innocuous specification changes in instruments lead to big differences in point estimates, and (b) that inference using vector autoregressions (VAR) "can be spurious when identification is weak." Hence they call for "new identification approaches." This paper is an attempt to provide a new approach which avoids both instrumental variables and VAR. We use numerical tools to quantify convergence in probability (and almost sure convergence) at the actual sample size n, rather than when $n \to \infty$ for both GMM and OLS or generalized least squares (GLS).

We use KM09's US quarterly data for 1947-2007, where x_t are real marginal costs based on the share of labor in the nonfarm business sector, and inflation π_t is measured by the deflator for gross domestic product (GDP) as a part of Federal Reserve Economic Data (FRED). Although one can choose even longer data series to achieve better asymptotics, underlying macroeconomic notions might become too stretched. For example, the operational meaning of the inflation variable (GDP deflator) to economic agents cannot be assumed to be constant, while the quality and content (product mix) of the GDP change dramatically over time. Thus, many economic time series must remain intrinsically short to remain meaningful.

Since most macroeconomic series are intrinsically short (finite), Leamer (2010) coined 'asymptopia' to describe the unrealistic focus on asymptotic econometrics to explain the failure to predict the great recession of 2008. The asymptotic theory relies on Slutsky's theorem, which in turn assumes the continuity theorem. Inapplicability of these theorems in finite samples means that instrumental variables can seriously distort the evidence. Leamer explains this informally by appealing to a case where the ratio of two sample means $(\bar{y}/\bar{x})$ is a distorted estimate of $(E(y)/E(x))$ when the denominator drifts close to zero at finite sample sizes.

Instead of asymptotic theory, we use computer intensive simulations described in greater detail in Section 3. We create 999 simulated sample paths of partial sum sequences for OLS and GMM in the finite range of the last few (=100 here) observations. Next, we compute the 'relative frequency' with which these sample paths stay inside a suitably defined ($\pm\epsilon$) bound for each coefficient of interest, allowing us to report numerical approximations to the probability of 'convergence in probability' (p_n) and of 'almost sure convergence' (a_n).

These new tools make our conclusions context-dependent, but allow us to be less sensitive to statistical assumptions, (e.g., applicability of the Slutsky theorem), since wandering sample paths are specific to the data and estimators at hand. Even though our results for KM09 data favor OLS over GMM, we cannot claim that this would hold in general. However, we argue that it is better to provide general tools allowing the data to guide the choice between estimators.

If E_t denotes expectation conditional on information at time t, our NKPC model is given by:

$$\pi_t = \lambda x_t + \gamma_f E_t(\pi_{t+1}) + \gamma_b \pi_{t-1} + u_t. \tag{1}$$

Economists are more interested in three deep parameters: β the discount factor, α the probability that prices remain fixed, and ϕ the fraction of rigid (backward looking) price setters in the economy. The deep parameters are related to the parameters of (1) by the following four nonlinear equations in three unknowns derived by GG99.

$$\begin{aligned} A &= \alpha + \phi\,(1 - \alpha\,(1 - \beta)) \\ \lambda &= (1-\phi)(1-\alpha)(1-\beta\,\alpha)/A \\ \gamma_f &= \beta\,\alpha/A \\ \gamma_b &= \phi/A \end{aligned} \tag{2}$$

We shall see that numerical estimates of the deep parameters β, α and ϕ can be obtained even though simple explicit expressions are unavailable. We simply use the R Development Core Team (2008) package 'rootSolve' and a suitable set of estimates of parameters $\{\lambda, \gamma_f, \gamma_b\}$ for the left sides.

Since prices are observable while marginal costs or other information used by price setters are not available to the econometrician, it is convenient to replace the $E_t(\pi_{t+1})$ in eq. (1) by $\pi_{t+1} - \eta_{t+1}$, where η_t denotes the one-step ahead forecast error for inflation. Upon substitution in (1) we merge the forecast error into the equation error and include an intercept to yield the equation for estimation as:

$$\pi_t = \gamma_0 + \lambda x_t + \gamma_f \pi_{t+1} + \gamma_b \pi_{t-1} + \epsilon_t, \tag{3}$$

where the endogeneity problem arises from possible correlation of ϵ_t errors with the regressors. GG99 among others assume that $\gamma_0 = 0$, that is, force the line of regression through the origin. A recent version by Cogley and Sbordon (2008) can be used to justify our inclusion of the intercept.

Section 2 discusses newer tools for assessing exogeneity of the right hand side variables in equation (3). Section 3 reviews some notions from the maximum entropy (ME) bootstrap for time series and some tools in R for learning mathematical theory of convergence concepts. We use these tools to approximately evaluate the consistency of OLS and GMM estimates of (3). Section 4 contains our numerical example for NKPC and Section 5 contains efficient (GLS) estimation of the NKPC model. Section 6 considers identification of the three deep parameters by using Godambe pivot instead of Wald's. We report corresponding confidence intervals for and Section 7 contains our final remarks.

2. Generalized Correlation Coefficients and Exogeneity of Regressors

This section considers the exogeneity of regressors in equation (3). Koopmans (1950) defined exogenous variables as those *approximately causing* the dependent variables. If the regressors are not exogenous (causal), we run the risk of inconsistency of the OLS. Koopmans favors treating lagged variables as exogenous because they are predetermined. This section briefly explains how to check the possible endogeneity of x_t and π_{t+1} in eq. (3) by using newer generalized correlation coefficients to assess if they approximately cause the dependent variable π_t.

It is convenient to use generic notation for exogeneity assessment. Consider two nonparametric kernel regression of Y on X and vice versa. Zheng et al. (2012) have named the two distinct R^2 values as generalized measures of correlation, GMC(Y—X) versus GMC(Y—X), and proved their asymptotic consistency. Since R^2 is always positive, GMC's provide no information regarding the direction of the relation. Hence, Vinod (2014) [Sec. 7.1] defines:

$$r^*(Y|X) = \mathrm{sign}(\mathrm{r_{XY}})\sqrt{\mathrm{GMC(Y|X)}}], \tag{4}$$

where its square root is assigned the sign of the Pearson correlation coefficient. Similarly, $r^*(X|Y) = \mathrm{sign}(\mathrm{r_{XY}})\sqrt{\mathrm{GMC(X|Y)}}$, generally distinct from the one in eq. (4).

Vinod (2015b) reports extensive simulations showing that when

$$|r^*(Y|X)| > |r^*(X|Y)| \tag{5}$$

one can conclude that X is the approximate "cause" of Y rather than vice versa. By Koopmans' criterion we want to make sure that the right hand variables x_t and π_{t+1} approximately cause the dependent variable π_t.

Table 1. Generalized correlations, r^*, Pearson correlations r and p-values for testing the null true r being zero: $\rho = 0$. Causal direction is indicated by the inequality between two r^* values from equation (5).

	Y	X	Cause	r*x|y	r*y|x	r_{xy}	p-value
1	π_t	x_t	π_t	0.2469	0.4657	0.2192	6e-04
2	π_t	π_{t+1}	π_t	0.7639	0.7941	0.7484	0

The results in Table 1 show that both regressors are potentially endogenous, since the dependent variable can cause their values to change. Hence the possible lack of consistency of the OLS (sometimes called the simultaneous equations bias) is a potential problem in estimating eq. (3).

3. Simulations to Avoid Asymptotics Using 'meboot' and 'ConvergenceConcpets' Packages in R

Efron's bootstrap for independent and identically distributed (iid) data readily creates simulated versions (resamples) of stationary time series. Singh (1981) pointed out the inadequacy of the iid bootstrap for stationary but dependent time series (m-dependent). Liu

(1988) and Lahiri (2003) study block bootstrap for non-iid but stationary situations in detail. Vinod and López-de-Lacalle (2009) (hereafter "VL09") provide an R package called 'meboot' for implementing the maximum entropy bootstrap from Vinod (2004) for strongly time-dependent non-stationary (possibly long memory) data which remains applicable despite structural changes, as shown in Vinod (2015a).

The meboot package is designed to avoid the following three properties of traditional iid bootstrap (iid-boot), letting x_t denote a generic series for which we seek bootstrap resamples, not to be confused with the real marginal cost of eq. (3).

- The iid-boot shuffles with replacement, which repeats some x_t values while not using as many others. It never admits nearby data values in a resample. In many applications there is no reason why values near the observed x_t are impossible. While the first quarter 1967 GDP deflator was 23.612, there is no justification for excluding nearby values of say 23.6124 and 23.6119.
- The iid-boot resamples must lie in the closed interval $[\min(x_t), \max(x_t)]$.
- The iid-boot shuffle loses all dependence information in the sequence $(x_1, \ldots x_n)$. Reordering will end up with essentially the original set x_t, except that some dropped x_t values are replaced by the repeats. Hence, it is impossible to generate a large number J of sensibly distinct resamples with the iid-boot without admitting nearby values, which is what 'meboot' does.

VL09 explain the 'meboot' computer intensive algorithm with a detailed list of steps, examples and graphics. Given a time series x_t, where $t = 1, 2, \ldots T$, the algorithm creates $j = 1, 2, \ldots J$ random resamples: $x_{t,j}$.

When only the range of the random variable is known, and we wish to be maximally non-committal about its functional form, the maximum entropy (ME) principle suggests the uniform density. In our context the ME density is a patchwork of uniform densities residing in the domain of magnitudes or values defined over 'small' neighborhoods around each ordered observation. Joag-dev (1984) surveys the literature on stochastic dependence and notes that dependence between two random measurements X and Y is high when their order statistics match. The algorithm matches the order statistics of each resample $x_{t,j}$ with the order statistics $x_{(t)}$ of the original data. Various examples in VL09 show that the algorithm is easy to use in practice. Vinod (2015a) describes simulations showing good performance of meboot.

The meboot package allows us to create a large number ($J = 999$) of reincarnations of π_t, x_t variables which are similar to the data series, but not too similar. Their autocorrelation and partial autocorrelation functions (acf, pacf) are also similar, without imposing identical parameters. See VL09 for an illustration of plots of (original and resampled) airline passenger series with acf, pacf and power spectra. The plots show that 'meboot' resamples are plausible representations of what might happen to the series, despite the presence of shifting seasonalities and regime changes.

Statistical inference for time series assumes that the observed series is one realization ω from the infinite dimensional ensemble $\omega \in \Omega$ of all possible series. The 'meboot' package provides a computer intensive approximation to Ω. Khintchine's "law of iterated logarithm" provides that assuming bounded means and variance, iid distributions, paths of partial sum sequences can fluctuate within a bound $\pm\sqrt{[2\sigma^2 nlog\,(log(n))]}$, where n is sample size and σ^2 is the variance.

Now we review the R package called 'ConvergenceConcepts,' Lafaye de Micheaux and Liquet (2009) (hereafter, CC) intended for learning asymptotic theory by allowing students to work with concrete examples. The CC package directly studies similar paths of partial sum sequences $(X_{n,\omega} - X_\omega)$ based on n observations as $n \to \infty$. We write convergence in probability for sample size n as: $X_n \xrightarrow{p} X$ whenever

$$\forall \epsilon > 0 \;\; p_n = P[\omega; |X_{n,\omega} - X_\omega| > \epsilon] \to 0 \text{ as } n \to \infty. \tag{6}$$

The CC package explicitly evaluates p_n as a relative frequency. It counts the sample paths that wander outside the $\pm\epsilon$ bound among a large number J(=999) of sample paths indexed by ω.

Almost sure convergence means that the limit of $X_{n,\omega}$ equals X_ω for all paths as $n \to \infty$. The CC package also reports a similar relative frequency.

$$\forall \epsilon > 0 \;\; a_n = P[\omega; \exists k \geq n; |X_{k,\omega} - X_\omega| > \epsilon] \to 0 \text{ as } n \to \infty. \tag{7}$$

The relative frequency provides an approximation to the probability a_n for 'almost sure' convergence. More important, the CC package permits us to approximately evaluate whether the relative frequencies satisfying the inequality $p_n < a_n$ are individually decreasing as n increases, in the context of a particular problem.

Consider a bootstrap approximation to a pivotal regression statistic, assumed to be a smooth functional of the true unknown cumulative density, conditioned on the available sample. Hall (1992) describes mathematical details of bootstrap convergence concepts. Using a generic notation, let our pivotal statistic be b_i denoting the ordinary least squares (OLS) estimate of the i-th true unknown coefficient β_i. The bootstrap resampling here "conditions" on the observed sample to create J regression problems with bootstrap estimates denoted by b_i^*. The bootstrap is successful because the empirical distribution function of $b_i^* - b_i$ is often a good approximation to that of $b_i - \beta_i$. In a simulation study, β_i are known and we can directly study whether the bootstrap b_i^* converges to β_i as $n \to \infty$, provided we can vary n over a range of values, eliminating the middleman b_i, as it were. Thus b_i^* based on n observations play the role of $X_{n,\omega}$ and β_i play the role of X_ω in the notation of the CC package.

If one chooses $\epsilon > 0$ too large, then too many paths are likely to lie within the $\pm\epsilon$ bound, making the probability of a path going outside the bounds approach zero. Conversely, if $\epsilon > 0$ is too small, too many paths readily go outside the bound making the probability of a path going outside the bounds approach unity. Since we need to avoid both extremes, a fixed $\epsilon = 0.01$(say) for all coefficients does not work. Fortunately, the simulation allows us to choose our ϵ as $\bar{\epsilon} = \overline{(|b_i^* - \beta_i|)}$, where the average is over a large number of simulated sample paths admitting various sample sizes. These $\bar{\epsilon}$ values are expected to be different for each regression coefficient. I modified the 'meboot' package function 'checkConv' for convergence computations in regressions, to allow for leads and lags of inflation appearing in the NKPC model.

The following section illustrates our use of these packages for the NKPC example.

4. Numerical Comparison of OLS and GMM Paths

This section compares the finite sample paths of OLS and GMM coefficient estimates of $\gamma_0, \lambda, \gamma_f$ and γ_b appearing in eq. (3). We want to know if they converge 'in probability' and /or 'almost surely.'

We begin with the OLS regressions with and without the intercept. Since the intercept is statistically insignificant it might be appropriate to force the line of regression through the origin. However, the estimate of $\hat{\lambda}$ remains insignificant in both cases. Since the NKPC specification requires us to retain λ in the model, we have the option to retain the intercept.

Table 2 reports our OLS results. The adjusted coefficient of determination is: $R^2 = (0.6728, 0.8819)$ for the models with and without the intercept, respectively. The p-values for the F tests for significance of overall models are close to zero for both models.

Table 2. OLS regression results with intercept (upper panel) and without intercept (lower panel) for the NKPC model of equation (3)

Parameter	Estimate	Std. Error	t value	Pr(>|t|)
γ_0	7.4868	4.1674	1.80	0.0737
λ	6.4049	9.3445	0.69	0.4938
γ_f	0.4580	0.0497	9.21	0.0000
γ_b	0.4453	0.0498	8.94	0.0000
λ	8.9282	9.2824	0.96	0.3371
γ_f	0.4857	0.0475	10.22	0.0000
γ_b	0.4732	0.0475	9.95	0.0000

Next, we report the results based on the GMM, estimated with and without the intercept, and two choices of of instrumental variables. Notation 'gmm2' refers to the instrument choice π_{t-3}, π_{t-4}. Notation 'gmm3' refers to the choice x_{t-3}, x_{t-4}. Our GMM estimates use the R package 'gmm,' Chausse (2009) with (wmatrix="optimal") for the weight matrix appearing in the GMM objective function and also choosing the 'continuous updated GMM'.

Table 3. GMM results with and without intercept for the NKPC model of equation (3) where gmm2 has π_{t-3}, π_{t-4} as instruments and where gmm3 has x_{t-3}, x_{t-4} as instruments

estimator	$\hat{\gamma}_0$	$\hat{\lambda}$	$\hat{\gamma}_f$	$\hat{\gamma}_b$
gmm2.with.intercept	15.2830	15.5568	0.4879	0.3632
gmm2.NO.intercept		8.1709	0.4739	0.4921
gmm3.with.intercept	8.1363	6.5145	0.4564	0.4423
gmm3.NO.intercept		8.8153	0.4844	0.4747

KM09 impose $\beta = 1$ restriction on the discount factor, implying a strong prior assumption that economic agents do not discount. In eq. (2) the assumption implies that

$\gamma_f + \gamma_b = 1$, $A = \alpha + \phi$. It appears that in Table 3 where no restriction is imposed, the sum $(\hat{\gamma}_f + \hat{\gamma}_b) < 1$ always holds, questioning the validity of KM09 prior assumption.

The main motivation for using GMM is to remove possible inconsistency of OLS induced by the endogeneity of regressors. Now we use a slightly improved version of 'checkConv' function in the 'meboot' package to approximately check the convergence of OLS in our current situation. A modification is needed, since leads and lags of the dependent variable π_t are present on the right hand side of (3). The simulation needs to correctly use these leads and lags.

There are $N = 240$ observations in the data set for OLS and $N = 236$ after omitting suitable lagged values needed as instruments for GMM. We reserve the last 100 data points for the study of convergence properties and define 100 sample sizes: $n' = \{140, 141, \ldots 240\}$ for OLS and $n' = \{137, 138, \ldots 236\}$ for GMM. The simulation evaluates J paths for each $n \in n'$, separately for each regression coefficient. The bounds $(\pm\bar{\epsilon})$ for sample paths are chosen to be the grand means of $100\,J$ simulated errors.

The CC package counts the paths straying outside the bounds and evaluates the probabilities p_n defined in equation (6) for 'convergence in probability' and a similar probability a_n for 'almost sure convergence.' We have 100 evaluations of p_n, a_n for each $n \in n'$. Convergence means these probabilities should decline as n increases, or $(dp_n/dn) < 0$ and $(da_n/dn) < 0$. One can approximately evaluate these derivatives by running two regressions of p_n and a_n on $n \in n'$. If we have consistency, these regressions should have statistically significant negative slopes, indicated by the p-values of these slopes being 'small' (< 0.05) at the 5% level (say).

Table 4 reports estimates, t-values and p-values based on a regression of relative frequencies of sample paths p_n, a_n on sample sizes n' of those paths. In the column entitled 'Estimate' the first value for the intercept has the wrong sign (positive) suggesting a lack of convergence of the intercept. Other values in the Estimate column are all negative. Large values in the t-value column indicate statistically significant declining probabilities for the OLS estimator. All OLS slopes are significant.

Table 4. Table for convergence of OLS coefficients of NKPC model regressing both p_n and a_n on intercept and n'

	(p/a).coef.No	Estimate	Std. Error	t value	Pr(>|t|)
1	prob. $\hat{\gamma}_0$	0.001986	0.000363	5.463893	0
2	a.s. $\hat{\gamma}_0$	-0.001042	4.8e-05	-21.914181	0
3	prob. $\hat{\lambda}$	-0.001525	0.000277	-5.510934	0
4	a.s. $\hat{\lambda}$	-0.002853	0.000124	-22.989386	0
5	prob. $\hat{\gamma}_f$	-0.003682	0.000283	-13.004067	0
6	a.s. $\hat{\gamma}_f$	-0.004177	0.000185	-22.612834	0
7	prob. $\hat{\gamma}_b$	-0.003903	0.000317	-12.294969	0
8	a.s. $\hat{\gamma}_b$	-0.005923	0.000211	-28.087495	0

Figure 1 depicts convergence properties of the OLS $\hat{\lambda}$, showing that p_n in the upper panel and a_n in the lower panel reach zero over 100 simulated sample sizes from $n = 140$ to $n = 240$. Figures 2 and 3 are similar to Figure 1 except that they refer to different coefficients of the NKPC model.

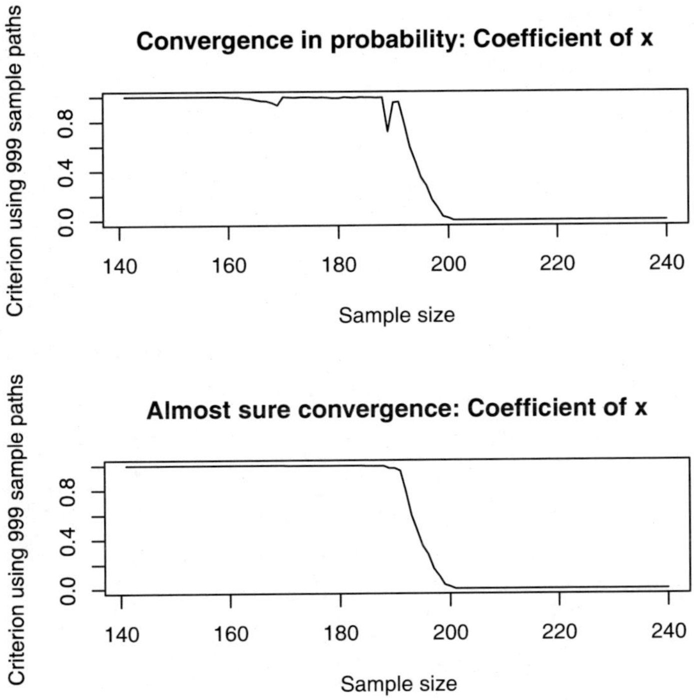

Figure 1. Convergence of OLS estimate $\hat{\lambda}$.

Since the figures show possibly nonlinear relations, we investigate what happens if we try to refine these results by considering quadratic regressions of p_n and a_n on $[1, n', n'^2]$, where 1 represents the intercept. Table for three coefficients (omitted for brevity) confirms what we see in the figures, namely that that OLS does approximately converge.

Next we evaluate the paths for the GMM estimator. As with the OLS, we let the simulation data help define the band $\pm\bar{\epsilon}$. It is interesting to compare the $\bar{\epsilon}$ values as average errors in our simulation for the four coefficients reported in Table 5. Note that the simulation error in the estimation of the intercept $\hat{\gamma}_0$ is very large along the row for GMM compared to the row for OLS. By contrast, the error for $\hat{\lambda}$ are large for OLS compared to GMM. The OLS error for $\hat{\gamma}_f$ and $\hat{\gamma}_b$ is much smaller than that of GMM in Table 5.

Table 5. A comparison of $\bar{\epsilon}$ values based on average of all simulation errors

Type	$\hat{\gamma}_0$	$\hat{\lambda}$	$\hat{\gamma}_f$	$\hat{\gamma}_b$
OLS	2.87	11.52	0.005	0.004
GMM	231.76	1.17	0.25	0.56

Of course, the magnitudes of distinct $\bar{\epsilon}$ values are not very important. We use them in the context of the CC package to numerically compute the proportion of paths going outside

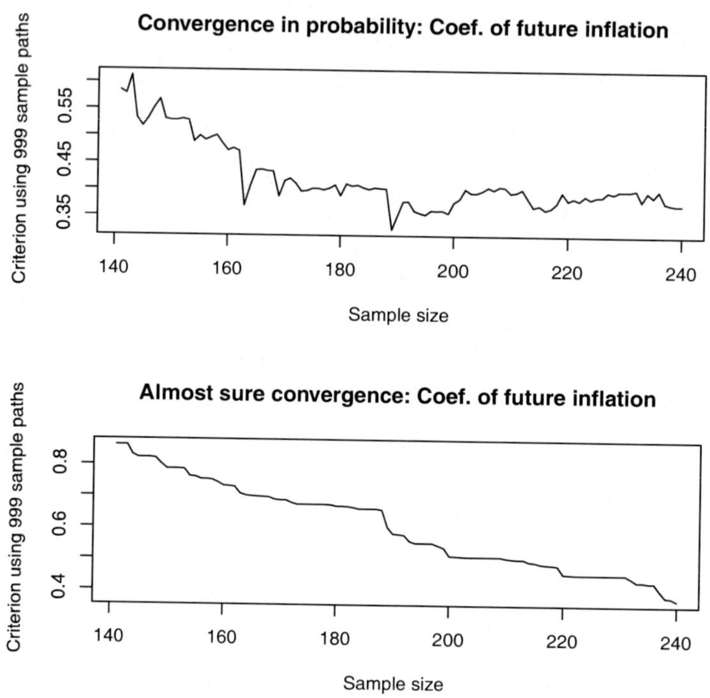

Figure 2. Convergence of OLS estimate $\hat{\gamma}_f$.

the band for OLS or GMM.

What about convergence of GMM? We evaluate equations (6) and (7) numerically to estimate p_n and a_n for each sample size in the range $n \in n' = \{137, 138, \ldots 236\}$. As before, we want to know if the estimated p_n and a_n of GMM are decreasing as n increases.

Table 6 is similar to Table 4. A study of Table 6 reveals that two values in the 'Estimate' column have the wrong sign (positive) along lines 1 and 5 showing a lack of convergence. Many t-values are not large enough to indicate statistically significantly declining probabilities for the GMM estimator. Note also that the p-values do exceed 0.05 along the first five rows of Table 6. Thus the convergence of GMM is more seriously in doubt compared to the convergence of OLS. We have implemented additional regressions of p_n or a_n on $[1, n', n'^2]$ and evaluated the partials of probabilities with respect of sample size n at suitable sample sizes, confirming the the results in Table 6 and the visual impression in our figures described next.

Figure 4 depicts convergence of the GMM estimate of $\hat{\lambda}$, showing that p_n in the upper panel slightly turns up instead of converging. The a_n in the lower panel reaches only about 0.4, instead of zero, within the range of simulated sample sizes from $n = 137$ to $n = 236$. Recall that we lose three observations due to three additional lags needed to construct instruments only for the GMM.

Figures 5 and 6 are similar to Figure 4 except that they refer to GMM coefficients of the future and lagged inflation variables in the NKPC model.

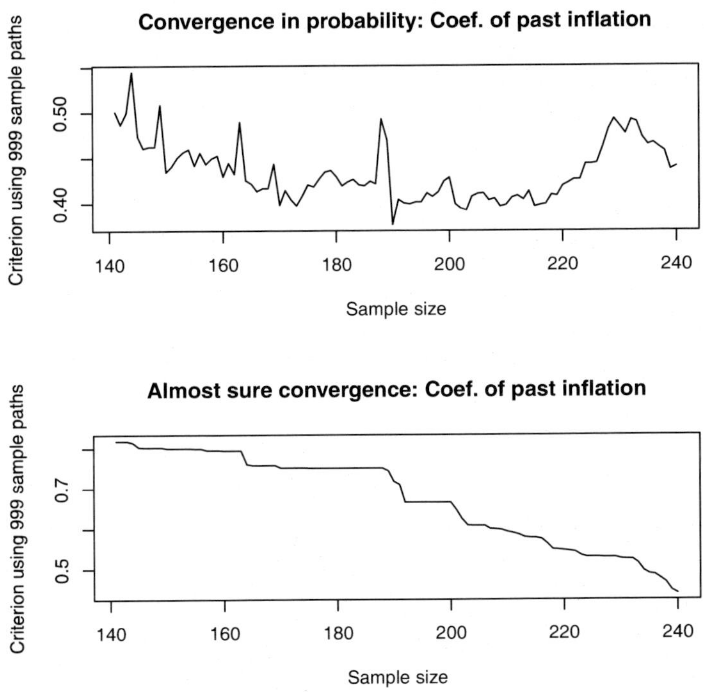

Figure 3. Convergence of OLS estimate $\hat{\gamma}_b$.

These figures, linear regressions in Table 4 and 6, along with unreported quadratic regressions further confirm that that the GMM estimator has no advantage over OLS in p_n, a_n convergence for our NKPC estimation in the relevant range of finite sample sizes $n \in n'$. If GMM happens to converge for very large values of n, it is of no practical relevance for the macroeconomic problem at hand.

When the available time series are close to a random walk (nonstationary, I(1): integrated of order 1), many econometrics texts, including page 187 of Vinod (2008), note that the OLS estimate converges to the true value at the fast rate n compared to the usual rate $\sqrt{n}$. This is called super-consistency of OLS. Our figures and tables showing that OLS has better convergence than GMM in the NKPC context is an observed fact, possibly due to several reasons. The approximate super-consistency property of OLS involving integrated variables (π_t, x_t) may be outweighing the endogeneity effects. Our Tailor-made evaluations of the actual functioning of the estimators using 'meboot' simulations show that OLS not only avoids possibly weak instruments, but has superior convergence properties than GMM in the present context. We argue that the choice between OLS and GMM should be guided by such contextual evidence near the actual sample size n, and not by (Slutsky theorem) asymptotics based on assuming $n \to \infty$.

In general, macroeconomic models can have a combination of proxy and instrument choices with potentially differing degrees of nonstationarity (possibly fractional d of $I(d)$) of variables and differing locations of structural changes. Asymptotic theory often focuses

Table 6. Table for convergence of GMM coefficients of NKPC model regressing both p_n and a_n on intercept and n'

	(p/a).coef.No	Estimate	Std. Error	t value	$\Pr(>\lvert t \rvert)$
1	prob. $\hat{\gamma}_0$	0.004905	0.003673	1.335426	0.274019
2	a.s. $\hat{\gamma}_0$	-0.001401	0.000504	-2.781518	0.068904
3	prob. $\hat{\lambda}$	-0.009309	0.004999	-1.862112	0.159496
4	a.s. $\hat{\lambda}$	-0.009109	0.003807	-2.392804	0.096497
5	prob. $\hat{\gamma}_f$	0.002603	0.008074	0.322358	0.76834
6	a.s. $\hat{\gamma}_f$	-0.013213	0.003861	-3.421941	0.041784
7	prob. $\hat{\gamma}_b$	-0.053053	0.011335	-4.68044	0.018428
8	a.s. $\hat{\gamma}_b$	-0.053053	0.011335	-4.68044	0.018428

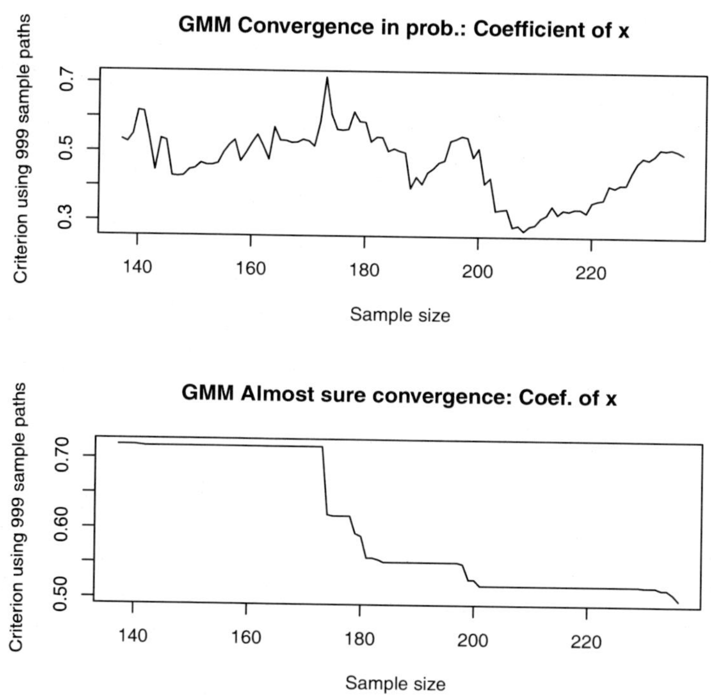

Figure 4. Convergence of GMM estimate $\hat{\lambda}$.

on nonstationarity, long-memory, endogeneity, structural change, and other prblems, only one or two at a time, wheras 'meboot' resamples faithfully incorporate all dependence properties of any observed series. The NKPC example has shown that meboot simulation can resolve ambiguities of asymptotic results in the practical context of a specific finite sample problem.

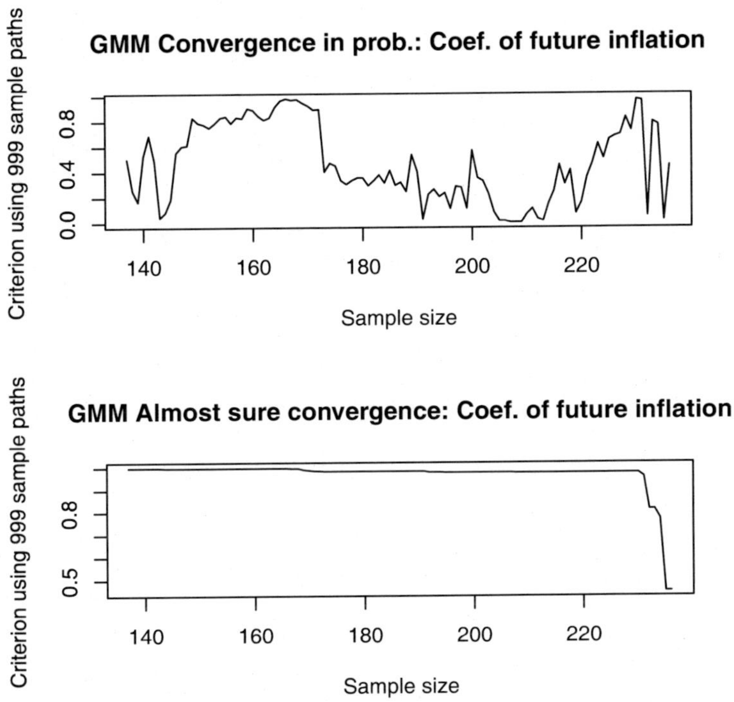

Figure 5. Convergence of GMM estimate $\hat{\gamma}_f$.

5. Efficient GLS Estimation of NKPC Model

While OLS may be converging, we know that the presence of autocorrelated regression errors can lead to inefficient estimates. Generalized least squares (GLS) estimation allows for non-spherical regression errors in eq. (3). Some R tools for this discussed in Vinod (2010) are applied in this section to the NKPC model. Leamer (2010) encourages efficient estimations instead of a 'whitewash' using Hal White's robust standard errors.

We use an R function called 'bestArma' which helps minimize the Akaike Information Criterion (AIC) for various ARMA(p,q) models. For annual data, one does not usually choose the AR order larger than 2. Since four lags make one year in *quarterly* data, we admit autocorrelations for lag order 4. The best model associated with the smallest AIC turns out to be ARMA(4, 2). Its coefficients with standard errors are:

	ar1	**ar2**	**ar3**	**ar4**	**ma1**	**ma2**
coef.	-0.6484	0.4989	0.6164	0.3980	-0.0349	-0.8096
s.e.	0.1021	0.0822	0.0724	0.0624	0.0958	0.0913

The GLS coefficient estimates for the NKPC model are: $\lambda = 0.1827763, \gamma_f = 0.5226623, \gamma_b = 0.5199869$. Correcting for the first order AR(1) serial correlation is fairly common. However, GLS correction for ARMA(4, 2) regression errors explained in Vinod

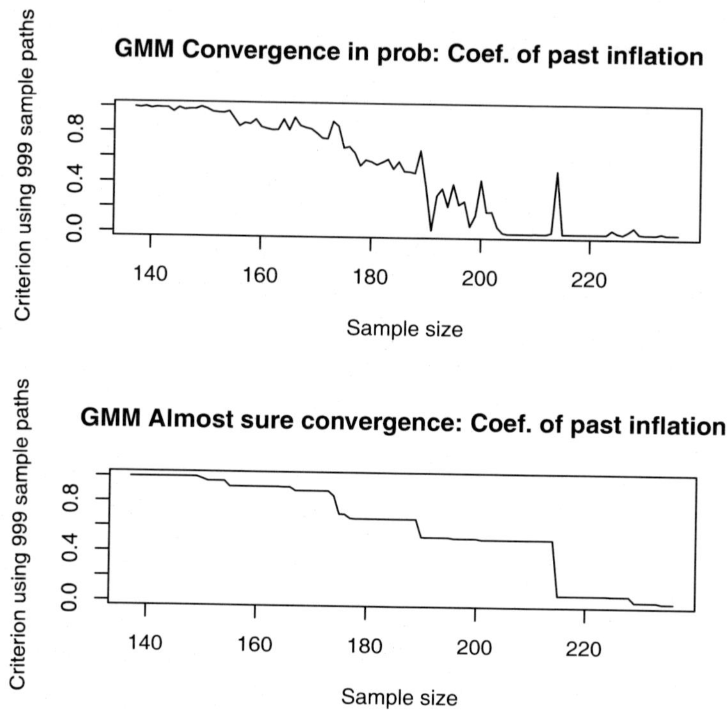

Figure 6. Convergence of GMM estimate $\hat{\gamma}_b$.

(2010) is less common. Section 2.3.2 of my textbook Vinod (2008) explains how this involves 4 roots of the characteristic polynomial.

6. Identification and Inference for Deep Parameters

Consider first the identification of structural (deep) parameters (α, β, ϕ) from (reduced form) coefficient estimates $\hat{\gamma}_b, \hat{\lambda}, \hat{\gamma}_f$, numerically solved by using the R package 'rootSolve'. Econometrics texts (e.g., Vinod(2008), sec.6.4.1) explain that there can be a lack of uniqueness of structural parameters. Fortunately, this identification problem is absent here, because of nonlinearity of eq. (2).

The second identification problem arises when expectational variables (e.g., expected inflation) are replaced by observable quantities, Vinod (2008, sec. 10.1.6), making the deep parameters "locally almost unidentifiable." Dufour (1997) (also cited by KM09) proves that Wald-type pivot (coefficient divided by standard error) is then fundamentally flawed due to unbounded confidence sets and zero coverage probability. Our solution to the second identification problem is to avoid Wald-type pivot altogether.

Wald type pivot leads one to use the Taylor series (delta) method needing partial derivatives of nonlinear functions giving highly conservative (asymptotic) standard errors and (wide) confidence intervals. Hence avoiding Wald-type pivot is worthwhile. Instead of Wald, we use Godambe (1985) pivot function (GPF) relying on his theory of estimating functions explained in Vinod (2008, Sec. 10.3).

The GPF is defined as

$$\text{GPF} = \sum_{t=1}^{n} g_t^* \Big/ \left[\sum_{t=1}^{n} E(g_t^*)^2\right]^{1/2}, \tag{8}$$

where g_t^* is the 'scaled quasi-score function' from the underlying quasi likelihood function also known as the optimal estimating equation.

Vinod (1997) extends the GPF to multivariate regression problems. When there are n observations, in the simpler scalar case he rewrites the GPF as a sum of n scaled quasi-scores:

$$\text{GPF} = \sum_{t=1}^{n} S_t/S_c = \sum_{t=1}^{n} \tilde{S}_t, \quad \text{where } S_c = \left[\sum_{t=1}^{n} E(S_t)^2\right]^{1/2}, \tag{9}$$

where we denote scaled quasi-score functions as: $\tilde{S}_t$. As a sum of n items, McLeash's dependent data central limit theorem from the 1970's assures us that GPF $\sim N(0,1)$, is asymptotically unit normal under certain conditions. The GPF is a pivot because its sampling distribution, $N(0,1)$, is independent of unknown parameters. More important, the GPF is not subject to the second identification problem.

Having solved the two identification problems, our statistical inference for deep parameters provides confidence intervals by using meboot resamples and R function 'gpf' available at Vinod (2008), pages 456–457. Even though (9) is univariate, we apply the Frisch-Waugh theorem to compute GPF confidence intervals for each regression coefficient in a sequence. Thus the R packages meboot, rootSolve along with 'gpf' solve the nonlinear equations for deep parameters in eq. (3) and provide their 95% confidence intervals fairly simply.

First two columns in Table 7 report OLS estimates of deep parameters for models with and without intercept respectively as: $\hat{\alpha} = (0.0751, 0.0532)$, $\hat{\beta} = (0.8166, 0.9184)$, and $\hat{\phi} = (0.0596, 0.0476)$, rounded to two digits. Table 7 also reports efficient estimates, of deep parameters (ie, after adjusting for ARMA(4, 2) regression errors, truncated for $\hat{\beta}$) in the column entitled 'GLS' as: $\hat{\alpha} = 0.47, \hat{\beta} = 1, \hat{\phi} = 0.58$. The last two columns in Table 7 entitled 'LoKM09' and 'UpKM09' include GMM confidence limit estimates copied from Table 3 of KM09 for comparison. Now we discuss them one by one.

Table 7. GPF confidence limits on deep parameters for OLS, OLS$_{no.int}$ (no intercept), GLS after correcting for ARMA(4, 2) regression errors and confidence limits copied from Table 3 from KM09

Parameter	OLS	OLS$_{no.int}$	GLS	Lower	Upper	LoKM09	UpKM09
α	0.08	0.05	0.47	0.21	0.99	0.56	1
β	0.82	0.92	1	0.00	1.00	NA	NA
ϕ	0.06	0.05	0.58	0.29	0.72	0	1

The probability that prices remain fixed is estimated by $\hat{\alpha}$. Bils and Klenow (2004) study frequency of price changes for 350 categories of goods and services covering about 70 percent of consumer spending, using unpublished 1995-97 data from the Bureau of

Labor Statistics (BLS). Even though they observe dramatic variation in the frequency of price changes across goods, they find that about half $\hat{\alpha} = 0.5$ of prices remain unchanged for 5.5 months or less. It is gratifying that $\hat{\alpha} = 0.5$ is inside our GLS limits [0.21, 0.99]. Unfortunately 0.5 is outside KM09 limits [0.56, 1]. Moreover, note that our GLS upper limit of 0.99 (although close to the KM09 upper limit of 1) is genuine, whereas the KM09 upper limit is binding (truncated range).

The GLS point estimate of the discount factor related to time preference by consumers, $\hat{\beta} = 1$ is obtained only after truncation to the acceptable range [0,1]. Our strictly binding range limit implies that we do not have enough information to accurately determine the discount factor β. This is perhaps not surprising, since our quarterly data on inflation π_t and labor income share x_t together may not have enough information about time preference of consumers. This is handled by KM09 by imposing the prior restriction $\beta = 1$ on NKPC before estimation begins. We are no worse off than KM09, since $\hat{\beta} = (\hat{\gamma}_f + \hat{\gamma}_b) < 1$ always holds in our tables.

The last deep parameter ϕ refers to the fraction of backward looking price setters in the economy. Christiano et al. (2005) have a model explaining the observed inertia in inflation and output such as ours. The GLS point estimate $\hat{\phi} = 0.58$ with a confidence range of 29% to 72% appears to be intuitively plausible to me than the OLS point estimate of only 8%. KM09 estimate the range to be [0, 1] with binding both limits implying inadequate information to determine ϕ.

The above discussion shows that GMM-based confidence limits for the NKPC model by KM09 are less plausible and less informative than our GLS confidence limits for both α and ϕ. We can also question the restriction $\beta = 1$ used by KM09. This section shows that the gpf function and 'meboot' resamples not only satisfy the ergodic theorem (time averages equal ensemble averages by construction), but provide meaningful confidence intervals for highly nonlinear functions (2) of estimated coefficients, without using the dubious Wald-type pivot and standard errors based on Taylor series (delta) methods.

7. Conclusion

A need for greater realism in macro-econometric work is obvious in light of recent failure to predict the great recession of 2008. A recent Mavroeidis et al. (2014) survey also calls for new approaches to overcome (a) sensitivity to instrumental variables and (b) unreliable inference using VAR models. Accordingly, this paper takes a fresh look at unique challenges arising from evolving dynamics, simultaneity, structural change of economic regimes and changing nonlinearities by using simulation tools from the free R software. In modern medicine, there is an attempt to tailor-make the medicines to individual patients using genetic and other specific information. We use the CC package in R to tailor-make an inference for the specific non-stationary time series with all their individual quirks, similar to the 'warts and all' of an individual patient.

Our illustration focuses on the New Keynesian Phillips Curve model of equation (1) specified for estimation as equation (3). An application of new causality tools from Vinod (2015b) confirms that the regressors are possibly endogenous, implying that OLS is subject to simultaneous equations bias. It is commonly estimated by GMM, with an array of possibly weak instrumental variables, despite the ever-present 'large dark shadow' of asymptotic bias mentioned by Leamer (2010). Using US data we find that the contextual finiteness of n matters in the choice between GMM and OLS or GLS.

The meboot (recently supported by extensive simulation in Vinod (2015a)) and CC packages in R allow us to evaluate sample path probabilities p_n for 'convergence in probability' and a_n for 'almost sure convergence' in the context of a simulation based on equation (3). Then we check whether the p_n, a_n probabilities indeed decline as n increases over the relevant range $n' = [140, 240]$ of the last 100 evaluations of 999 sample paths. A statistically significant slope coefficient of p_n, a_n regressed on $n \in n'$ should be negative for evidence of convergence. Also, the corresponding graphs should show a declining pattern approaching zero. Our six figures show a more convincing declining pattern and clearer reach to zero for OLS than GMM. Since our p_n, a_n are all evaluated at finite n, they are not subject to Leamer (2010)'s 'asymptopia' criticism.

The key reason for using GMM is the possible removal of inconsistency arising from endogeneity of regressors. A simulation reveals that a large number of GMM sample paths for relevant finite range $n' = [140, 240]$ diverge. Hence GMM offers no convergence advantage over OLS in the context of our model and data. Thus we have demonstrated that numerical evaluations of approximate convergence probabilities at finite n do matter and offer a fresh approach without using (a) weak instruments or (b) VAR inference.

Certain identification problems associated with deep parameters are known in the NKPC literature. We use Godambe's pivot function (GPF) from Biometrics to construct confidence intervals for our deep parameters of the NKPC model. The central limit theory implies that GPF as a sum of n scaled scores means its sampling distribution is $GPF \sim N(0, 1)$, a genuine pivot. It overcomes the Dufour (1997) identification problems by guaranteeing the scale factor to be strictly positive.

Our GPF confidence intervals have reasonable values for the most interesting two of the three deep parameters of the NKPC. Hence our GPF intervals associated with efficient GLS estimation in our Table 7 seem to offer a superior alternative to KM09. We offer meaningful confidence intervals without imposing KM09's intuitively unrealistic and empirically unsupported (no discounting) constraint $\beta = 1$.

References

Mark Bils and Peter J. Klenow. Some evidence on the importance of sticky prices. *Journal of Political Economy*, 112(5):947–985, 2004.

Pierre Chausse. *gmm: Generalized Method of Moments and Generalized Empirical Likelihood*, 2009. URL http://CRAN.R-project.org/package=gmm. R package version 1.1-1.

Lawrence J. Christiano, Martin Eichenbaum, and Charles L. Evans. Nominal rigidities and the dynamic effects of a shock to monetary policy. *Journal of Political Economy*, 113(1): 1–45, 2005.

Timothy Cogley and Argia M. Sbordon. Trend inflation, indexation, and inflation persistence in the new keynesian phillips curve. *American Economic Review*, 98(5):2101–2126, 2008.

J-M Dufour. Some impossibility theorems in econometrics with applications to structural and dynamic models. *Econometrica*, 65:1365–1387, 1997.

J. Galí and M Gertler. Inflation dynamics: A structural econometric analysis. *Journal of Monetary Economics*, 44:195–222, 1999.

V P Godambe. The foundations of finite sample estimation in stochastic processes. *Biometrika*, 72:419–428, 1985.

P. Hall. *The bootstrap and Edgeworth expansion*. Springer Verlag, New York, 1992.

Kumar Joag-dev. Measures of dependence. In P. K. Krishnaiah and P. K. Sen, editors, *Handbook of Statistics, Vol. 4*, pages 79–88. North Holland, New York, 1984.

F Kleibergen and S. Mavroeidis. Weak instrument robust tests in gmm and new keynesian phillips curve. *Journal of Business and Economic Statistics*, 27(3):293–311, 2009.

Tjalling C Koopmans. When is an equation system complete for statistical purposes. Technical report, Yale University, 1950.
URL http://cowles.econ.yale.edu/P/cm/m10/m10-17.pdf.

P. Lafaye de Micheaux and B. Liquet. Understanding convergence concepts: a graphical simulation based approach. *The American Statistician*, 63(2):173–178, 2009. URL http://www.biostatisticien.eu/ConvergenceConcepts/. Software: R Package, ConvergenceConcepts, version 0.5.

S. N. Lahiri. *Resampling Methods for Dependent data*. Springer Verlag, New York, 2003.

E. E. Leamer. Tantalus on the road to asymptopia. *Journal of Economic Perspectives*, 24 (2):31–46, 2010.

R. Y. Liu. Bootstrap procedures under some non-iid models. *The Annals of Statistics*, 16 (4):1696–1708, 1988.

Sophocles Mavroeidis, Mikkel Plagborg-Moller, and James H. Stock. Empirical evidence on inflation expectations in the new keynesian phillips curve. *Journal of Economic Literature*, 52(1):124–188, 2014.

R Development Core Team. *R: A Language and Environment for Statistical Computing*. R Foundation for Statistical Computing, Vienna, Austria, 2008. URL http://www.R-project.org/. ISBN 3-900051-07-0.

K Singh. On the asymptotic accuracy of efron's bootstrap. *The Annals of Statistics*, 9: 1187–1195, 1981.

H D Vinod. Using godambe–durbin estimating functions in econometrics. In I Basawa, V P Godambe, and R Taylor, editors, *Selected Proceedings of the Symposium on Estimating Equations*, volume 32 of *IMS Lecture Notes — Monographs Series*, pages 215–237, 1997.

H D Vinod. Ranking mutual funds using unconventional utility theory and stochastic dominance. *Journal of Empirical Finance*, 11(3):353–377, 2004.

H D Vinod. Superior estimation and inference avoiding heteroscedasticity and flawed pivots: R-example of inflation unemployment trade-off. In H D Vinod, editor, *Advances in Social Science Research Using R*, pages 39–63. Springer, New York, 2010.

H D Vinod. New bootstrap inference for spurious regression problems. *Journal of Applied Statistics*, 2015a. URL http://www.tandfonline.com/doi/full/10.1080/02664763.2015.1049939.

H D Vinod. Generalized correlation and kernel causality with applications in development economics. *Communications in Statistics - Simulation and Computation*, 2015b. URL http://dx.doi.org/10.1080/03610918.2015.1122048. Accepted Nov. 10, 2015.

H D Vinod and Javier López-de-Lacalle. Maximum entropy bootstrap for time series: The meboot R package. *Journal of Statistical Software*, 29(5):1–19, 2009. URL http://www.jstatsoft.org/v29/i05/.

Hrishikesh D. Vinod. *Hands-on Intermediate Econometrics Using R: Templates for Extending Dozens of Practical Examples*. World Scientific, Hackensack, NJ, 2008. URL http://www.worldscibooks.com/economics/6895.html. ISBN 10-981-281-885-5.

Hrishikesh D. Vinod. Unemployment reduction prowess under bush versus obama years. *SSRN eLibrary*, 2012. URL http://ssrn.com/abstract=2149316.

Hrishikesh D Vinod. Matrix algebra topics in statistics and economics using R. In M. B. Rao and C. R. Rao, editors, *Handbook of Statistics: Computational Statistics with R, Vol. 34*, pages 143–176. North Holland, Elsevier Science, New York, 2014.

Shurong Zheng, Ning-Zhong Shi, and Zhengjun Zhang. Generalized measures of correlation for asymmetry, nonlinearity, and beyond. *Journal of the American Statistical Association*, 107:1239–1252, 2012.

In: Unemployment
Editor: Tabitha Fletcher
ISBN: 978-1-63485-181-7

Chapter 4

The Great Recession and Health among Employed Workers*

Mark Tausig[1] and Rudy Fenwick[2]
[1]Lehman College/CUNY, Bronx, NY, US
[2]The University of Akron, Akron, OH, US

Abstract

This research focuses on understanding how the Great Recession of 2007-2009 and/or long-term labor market changes may have separately or jointly affected health among employed workers in 2010. In order to fully understand the impact of the Great Recession on employed worker health, we need to distinguish between the effects of on-going structural changes in the nature or work and its organization and the effects of labor market uncertainties directly related to the recession. Our results suggest that the Great Recession itself (as indexed by occupational unemployment and underemployment rates) had no direct effects and few indirect effects on the health of currently employed workers. Rather, social statuses as these affect occupation and exposure to labor market instability (both structural and recessionary) and, thereby, stressful work conditions appear to account for health among such workers. Employers may also shift regular, fulltime employees to contingent and part-time jobs that are more stressful- reflecting both long-term structural changes and employer responses to reduced product and service markets in the recession.

The Great Recession of 2007-2009 had a devastating effect on every sector of the U.S. economy including, of course, the labor market. The health-related effects of that labor market change on workers are just beginning to be documented. To date, most research has focused on either the effects of individual job loss on individual health or on the ecological effects of unemployment rates on the aggregate health of the general population (Stuckler et al. 2011; Stuckler et al. 2009; Bell & Blanchflower 2010; Katz 2010). However, the extent of the recession's effects on worker health could be underestimated if only the effects on those

* A previous version of this paper was presented at The APA/NIOSH Tenth International Conference on Occupational Stress and Health. Los Angeles, CA. May 2013.

losing their jobs are tabulated (Fenwick & Tausig 1994; Tausig & Fenwick 1999; Catalano & Dooley 1983). Because recessions squeeze corporate profits, for example, it is not unusual for corporations to both lay off employees (leading to decreased health among unemployed workers) and to restructure the jobs of remaining employees to increase efficiency and obtain better control over the production process, but increasing stress among "surviving" employees (Fenwick & Tausig 1994). A more complete estimate of the health effects of recession on workers should include a consideration of its effects on these employed workers.

There are a small number of studies that have focused on employed workers. And, while those studies have consistently found that increased work pressure and job insecurity during the recession are associated with increases in depression and anxiety symptoms among workers (Burgard, et al. 2012; Russell & McGinnity 2014), the relationship between indicators of the recession such as unemployment rates and health have only been assumed rather than measured and incorporated into the analysis. Lam et al. (2014) did show that the relationship between job insecurity and well-being among employed workers was contingent on the economic turbulence (national unemployment rate in 2010) represented by the Great Recession. That turbulence exacerbated the effect of insecurity on distress in 2010 compared to the insecurity-distress relationship in the more settled economy in 2006.

In order to more fully understand the impact of the Great Recession on employed worker health, we need to address several matters; to what extent did on-going structural changes in the nature of work and its organization affect worker health independently of changes in the labor market that reflect the recession; to what extent did the recession itself affect the health of employed workers and, how are these effects experienced by workers in different labor market positions? Long-term structural changes to the nature and organization of work have been linked to negative health outcomes and these changes were on-going during the recession. The Great Recession may have exacerbated those on-going structural changes or the recession could have independent effects on worker health. And, the notion that changes in the nature and organization of work might differentially affect workers based on labor market position has not been previously considered but is consistent with what we know about the labor market and what we know about health inequality.

We will examine these concerns by measuring and comparing the impacts of both occupational unemployment and underemployment rates in 2006 (pre-recession) and 2010 (post Great Recession) on conditions of work and subsequent health in the context of social status and occupational differences between workers. Examining the effects of these indicators on the health of employed workers is information important to understanding the full effects of the recession on the overall health and well-being of the American labor force.

Long-Term Structural Change, Extrinsic Job Conditions and Health

Prior assessments of the effects of recessions on employed workers' health have focused on the internal transformations of work conditions that reflect the way employers attempt to deal with economic uncertainty. For example, the impact on workers of the 1974-5 recession could be understood mostly in terms of the work organization's response to a declining product market which led to layoffs and/or the internal restructuring of jobs intended to increase productivity among remaining employees (Fenwick & Tausig 1994). Since those studies, however, there have been substantial changes to the forms and organization of work and these changes are on-going. As a result of long-term structural changes in the nature and organization of work, a more complex analysis is now required to understand how a recession might affect work-related stressors that can affect the health of employees. By 2006 and 2010 (the years of the surveys that will be analyzed) work and its labor market context were vastly different than in the 1970s. In 2006/2010 (and notwithstanding the Great Recession itself), the labor market was organized in light of global competitive factors, advanced technologies and macro-economic conditions that created new modes of employment including underemployment and contingent employment.

As a result of these factors, jobs have become generally more "precarious" for individual workers (Kalleberg 2009). Several authors have made an argument that emphasizes the permanent, structural state of "precarity" or generalized employment and financial insecurity that defines the modern labor market (Jacoby 2001; Hacker 2006; Fullerton & Wallace 2007; Kalleberg 2009; Kalleberg 2011; Kalleberg & Marsden 2012). Kalleberg and Marsden (2012) found that between 1972 and 2006, perceived job insecurity both tracked cycles of economic expansion and decline and, controlling for unemployment rates, the proportion of workers reporting high job insecurity increased by about 1.5 percent per year between 1977 and 2006.

Increases in job insecurity are related to lower worker well-being (Burgard, et al. 2009; Ferrie et al. 2004; Ferrie et al. 2005; Sverke et al. 2002). And, Burgard et al. (2012) have reported that perceived job insecurity was related to increased symptoms of major and minor depression among a sample of working-aged adults in Southeast Michigan in late 2009/early 2010 during the Great Recession.

Another way that work has become more insecure is through increases in "underemployment." The U.S. Bureau of Labor Statistics defines "underemployment" as working part-time for economic reasons, either because workers cannot find full-time employment or they have had their hours cut from full to part-time because of slack demand for their employer's products or services (Sum & Khatiwada 2010). Like the unemployment rate, the rate of underemployment is cyclical, rising and falling in rough synchrony with unemployment rates. For example, over the period of the Great Recession, the rate of unemployment rose from 4.4% in early 2007 to approximately 10% in the fourth quarter of 2009, while the rate of underemployment rose from 2.4% to 6.6% of the labor force (U.S. Bureau of Labor Statistics, 2008; Sum & Khatiwada 2010). But, as with unemployment, there has been a long-term increase in structural underemployment. The percentage of Americans working part-time increased more than 60% between the 1970s and the start of the Great Recession (Fenwick 2009). Moreover, almost all of the growth in part-time employment has been among those who prefer full-time employment but cannot find it. Thus, under the BLS definition, approximately 40% of all part-time workers would be considered underemployed (Tausig & Fenwick 2012).

The research into the effects of underemployment on worker health and well-being has shown that it increases depression symptoms as much as unemployment affects depression symptoms (e.g., Dooley et al. 2000; Friedland & Price 2003). There is also evidence from an Australian study that increases in suicide rates among younger male workers were significantly related to increasing rates of underemployment in this age cohort (Page et al. 2013).

The structural reorganization of work has entailed not only more involuntary part-time employment (underemployment), but also increased *non-standard,* or "contingent," employment that represents another form of job insecurity. Contingent employment denotes employment in which the worker is not a continuous employee of the firm for which work is done and who does not have an implicit or explicit contract for ongoing employment, for example, temporary, seasonal or contract workers (U.S. Bureau of Labor Statistics 2011). Virtanen, et al. (2003) found that contingent workers experienced higher rates of both physical and mental illness due to their higher levels of job and financial insecurity, although these rates were not as high as those among the low-income unemployed.

Thus, long-term structural changes have provided organizations with ways other than just layoffs to deal with the impact of slack demand for their products and this may be important for understanding organizational reactions to recessionary periods. Organizations can increase the use of contingent workers and/or employ individuals part-time when workers themselves desire full time employment (underemployment). The strategy gives work organizations "numerical flexibility" in the numbers and hours that workers are employed (Smith 1997; Kalleberg 2001).

LONG-TERM STRUCTURAL CHANGE, INTRINSIC JOB CONDITIONS AND HEALTH

The intrinsic organization of work has also changed. Workers are more likely to be working under conditions (e.g., high performance work systems-flexible work systems) that directly expose them to the external vicissitudes of labor markets-including unemployment and underemployment (Cappelli et al. 1997; Smith 1997) and to the internal challenge of work intensification (Green 2004; Hudson 2002). While some of these new high performance forms of work lead to greater organizational involvement and job satisfaction, they also have the potential to increase job stress and poor health among workers due to the increased intensity of the work (Macky & Boxall 2008; Berg & Kalleberg 2002).

Processes of work intensification reflect long-term, structural responses to a changed global economy (Green 2004). According to Green (2004:712), "work intensification has taken place quite broadly across occupations and sectors" but it is also related to economic cycles of recession and expansion. Russell and McGinnity (2014) reported that both job insecurity and work pressure increased among employed workers in Ireland between 2003 and 2009 with the Irish economy's entry into recession. Hudson (2002) connects work intensification to global competitive pressures but also to organizational strategies related to the "flexibalization" of work. Green (2004), Hudson (2002) and Lapido and Wilkinson (2002) suggest that work intensification reflects a process that passes organizational competitive pressures to workers. Numerous authors have observed that shifts to high performance work formats can result in increased work demands (intensification) and reduced decision latitude (job flexibilization) (Smith 1997; Cappelli et al. 1997; Berg & Kalleberg 2002; Macky & Boxall 2008; Barker 1993).

Organizations can use "functional flexibility" to intensify work and make continued employment contingent on market conditions. For workers these strategies increase the uncertainty of their employment and finances and may decrease well-being.

Increased work intensification and "precarity" have also made it more difficult for many workers to balance their work obligations with those of their families. On the one hand, work intensification requires more physical, psychological, and time commitment to the job, which often interferes with family relations and obligations, especially for the increasing numbers of dual earner and single parent households (Presser 2003). "Precarity," on the other hand, while not necessarily demanding more commitment to one's job, creates its own family stress by increasing financial uncertainties and hardships due to the uncertainties of continued employment and a steady number of work hours (Mishel, et al. 2009; Reynolds 2003; Young & Schieman 2012).

Overall, changes in the extrinsic conditions of employment and changes in the intrinsic organization of work that are a function of long-term structural changes may affect the health of employed workers in addition to any effects attributable to the Great Recession. What is not known is the extent to which these long-term structural effects might be accelerated by recession-related increases in the unemployment and underemployment rates or if recession-related labor market changes have independent effects on extrinsic and intrinsic work conditions. The answer to this latter unknown will help us understand the effect of the Great Recession itself on employed worker health. However, before we can proceed to make the relevant assessments, we need to also understand that workers are not equally exposed to any of these work-related changes.

Social Status and Recession-Related Labor Market Instability

One's exposure to the risk of unemployment or underemployment due to cyclical changes in the economy is partly a function of occupational position in the labor market. Occupational attainment is a function of not only human capital assets, such as education, but also ascribed characteristics such as gender, age, race and immigration status (Hudson 2007; Sum & Khatiwada 2010). These social status indicators are related to one's occupation and to the place of one's occupation in core or secondary labor markets that determine attainment of "good" versus "bad" jobs- jobs that pay well, offer benefits and opportunities for career advancement and are stable versus those that are not (Hudson 2007).

Exposure to recession-related labor market instability and subsequent stressful work-related experiences are, therefore, not equally distributed among workers. To the extent that human capital and social status characteristics determine position in the labor market, exposure to labor market-related instability will be a function of one's occupational standing. In turn, such variations in exposure to labor market changes (i.e., the Great Recession) are ultimately related to variations in the observed effects of work-related conditions on health. That is, it is possible that the impact on worker health of recession-related changes in work conditions map to social status inequality and health disparities.

In sum, to assess the effects of the Great Recession on the health of employed workers, we need to account for the ways that long-term structural changes continued to affect extrinsic and intrinsic aspects of work that may be stressful while we evaluate the effects of the recession itself. We also need to assess how worker social status characteristics affect exposure to labor market instability and then health via differences in labor market positions that are a function of social status. Figure 1 illustrates the expected relationships between all constructs.

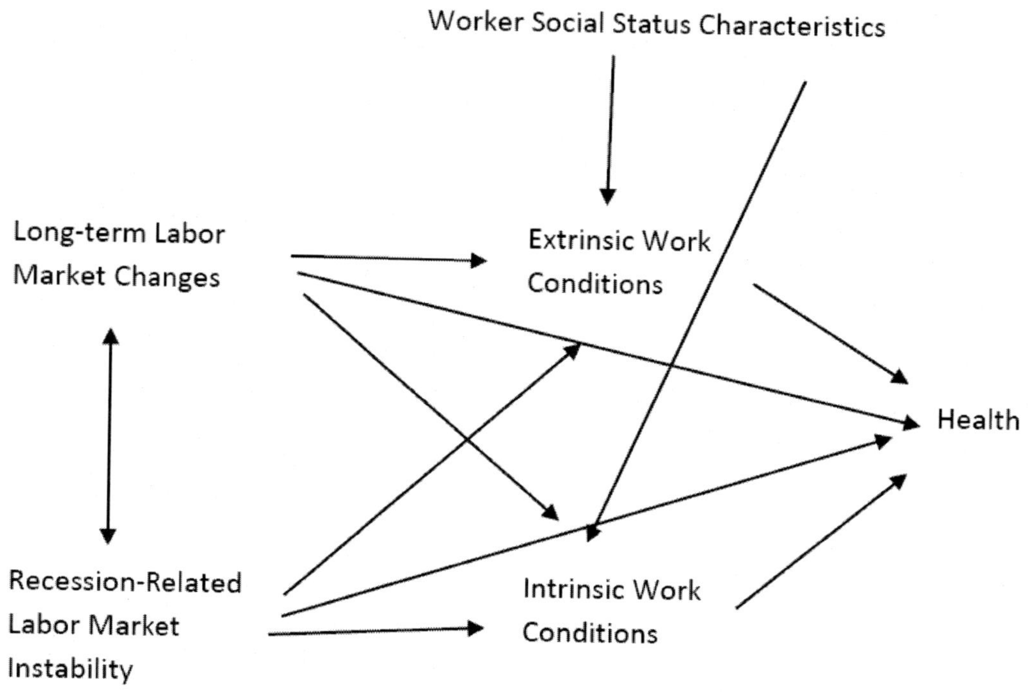

Figure 1. General Model to Evaluate Relationships between Long-term Labor Market-related Change, Recession-related Labor Market Instability, Extrinsic Work Conditions, Intrinsic Work Conditions and Health Outcomes.

Sample and Measures

Data used to test our argument come from the Quality of Work Life (QWL) modules of the 2006 and 2010 General Social Survey (GSS). The GSS is a representative sample of non-institutionalized English-speaking adults over the age of 18. The QWL module was completed by all currently-employed respondents in the GSS survey. Our analysis is based on respondents who reported working either fulltime or part-time at the time of the surveys and who were not self-employed, leaving a total of 2473 respondents. Because these are not panel data, our analyses cannot definitively establish causal relationships among variables.

Social status characteristics that we include are *gender* (male, female), *age, education* (in years), *race* (non-white, white), *marital status* (not-married, married) and *immigration status* (born in the U.S., not born in the U.S.).

Labor market instability is indexed by measures of both occupational unemployment rates and occupational underemployment rates in each survey year (i.e., as indicators of pre-recession and recession). Occupational *unemployment* rates for 2006 and 2010 were obtained from the U.S. Bureau of Labor Statistics *Current Population Survey* tabulations of "Employed and experienced unemployed persons by detailed occupation and class of worker" tables. These data are listed by SOC (Standard Occupational Codes) categories that were matched with GSS respondent SOC occupation codes. The appropriate occupationally-specific unemployment rate was then added to each GSS record (see Appendix). Occupational *underemployment* rates were computed from the *Current Population Survey* of February 2010 based on the compilation of economic reasons why workers were working part-time. The sum of workers working part-time because of slack work, poor business conditions or inability to find a full-time job were used to count those workers who are considered underemployed- the Bureau of Labor Statistics definition (Sum & Khatiwada 2010). The rate was computed by dividing the number of underemployed workers in each occupational category by the total number of employed workers in that occupational category. These occupation-specific rates are listed in the appendix. Unemployment and underemployment rates characterize the (in)stability of the labor market. These rates are aggregates by occupation and provide indicators of economic cyclic context. In 2006, unemployment and underemployment rates were comparatively low consistent with the characterization of that time as one of economic expansion. The rates in 2010 are fully descriptive of the Great Recession.

Extrinsic Work Conditions: We measured whether the respondent was employed as a *contingent or regular* (permanent) employee, whether the respondent was employed *fulltime or part-time* and whether the respondent had been *laid off* in the past year to represent extrinsic work conditions.

Intrinsic Work Conditions: We include two, often-studied measures of respondents' intrinsic work conditions. *Work intensity* is measured using a 4-item scale that corresponds to the original Karasek (1979) job demands scale. *Work flexibility* is measured as a three item scale also using items from the original Karasek measure of decision latitude. Some recent scholarship has used the concepts of "work intensification" rather than job demands (Berg & Kalleberg 2002; Green 2004; Macky & Boxall 2008) and "work flexibilization" instead of decision latitude (Green 2004). As with Karasek's (1979) original conceptualization of demand/control, "intensification" and "flexibilization" are conceptualized as independent but intersecting dimensions of work. Green argues that "high levels of effort (work intensity) are… assumed to be generated in the model of the high-commitment work organization but are also an ingredient of a more traditional Taylorist form of organization…" (2004:710). Further, the European Foundation for the Improvement of Living and Working Conditions, (2013:43) argues that: "when discussing work intensity and the impact of the crisis (Great Recession), Karasek's job demand-control model…can be very useful…".

To assess the potential impacts of the recession on work-family balance and, job and financial insecurity, we measured work-family balance as two separate dimensions by using the items that ask (1) the extent of *work-to family* and (2) the extent of *family-to work interference*. *Job insecurity* is measured by reversing the response categories to the statement: "the job security is good." This measure accounts for the conceptualization of job insecurity as a "classic chronic work stressor" (Barling & Kelloway 1996). We have no measure of insecurity as "precarity." *Financial insecurity* (dissatisfaction) is measured by two items: "We are interested in how people are getting along financially these days, pretty well-satisfied with your present financial situation, more or less satisfied, or not satisfied at all"; and, "During the last few years, has your financial situation been getting better, worse, or has it stayed the same?" Responses to the two items were ordered identically and summed so that higher scores indicate greater financial insecurity.

Health: Respondents' *mental health* is measured by the number of days in the last 30 when "your mental health was not good." Overall *general (poor) health* is measured by responses to the question: "In general, my health is; excellent, very good, good, fair or poor."

ANALYTIC STRATEGY

We will evaluate OLS regression models that predict exposure to higher occupational unemployment and underemployment rates as functions of social status characteristics that are known to predict occupation and labor market position (Table 2). Second, we will evaluate how labor market instability conditions (unemployment rates and underemployment rates) affect extrinsic and intrinsic work characteristics (Tables 2 and 3) and finally how all of these variables affect health status (Table 4). The impact of unemployment and underemployment rates on outcome variables assesses the extent to which higher or lower rates affect outcomes, regardless of the year in which they were observed. We will also include a term for sample *year* (0 = 2006, 1 = 2010) that will tell us if the survey year affects the predictor variables in a given equation independently of market instability. Finally, we will include interaction terms for year by unemployment rate and year by underemployment rate. These interaction terms tell us if the levels of unemployment and underemployment during the recession had independent effects on outcome variables. In other words, the work-related consequences and health effects of the recession are evaluated using these latter terms.

RESULTS

Table 1 compares variable means from the 2006 and 2010 GSS-QWL modules. The comparisons provide evidence concerning changes in the U.S. labor force over the course of the Great Recession. During this time the labor force became significantly older, whiter and, more educated. These changes reflect the differential consequence of increased rates of unemployment experienced by younger, less educated and non-white workers (Sum et al. 2009). The changes in the social status characteristics of the labor force suggest that the impact of the Great Recession was unevenly experienced by workers as a function of their social status, making some workers more or less likely to remain in the labor force. In analyses not shown, there were significant reductions in the proportion of workers in construction and extraction, installation, maintenance and repair, production and transportation and material moving occupations (the least skilled occupations) between 2006 and 2010. A further implication (not tested here) is that workers who are no longer in the labor force experience greater health concerns.

The reported rates of unemployment and underemployment shown are based on the actual distribution of occupations reported by GSS respondents and therefore do not precisely match national rates mentioned earlier. They represent aggregate rates in the sample. These indicators of the recession, rates of both unemployment and underemployment more than doubled: unemployment from 4.1 percent in 2006 to 8.8 percent in 2010; underemployment from 2 to 4.7 percent.

Table 1. Means and Standard Deviations for Measured Variables among Employed Persons: 2006 compared with 2010

	2006 N = 1516			2010 N = 957	
	Mean	s.d		Mean	s.d
Sex (0, male, 1, female)[b]	.52	0.5		.55	0.5
Age	41.2	12.7	a	42.7	13.5
White (0 non-white, 1 white)[b]	.71	0.5	a	.77	0.4
U.S. born[b]	.86	0.4		.87	0.3
Education (years)	13.8	3.1	a	14.1	3.0
Marital Status (0 not, 1 married)[b]	.49	0.5		.47	0.5
Unemployment Rates	4.1	1.9	a	8.8	4.2
Underemployment Rates	2.0	1.2	a	4.7	2.0
Laid off in last year[b]	.07	0.3	a	.09	0.3
Part-time Worker[b]	.16	0.4		.18	0.4
Contingent Worker[b]	.12	0.3		.12	0.3
Work interferes with family	2.2	1.0	a	2.3	1.0
Family interferes with work	2.0	0.8		2.0	0.8
Financial Status-worse	3.7	1.2	a	4.1	1.3
Job Insecurity	1.7	0.8	a	1.8	0.9
Work Intensity	5.1	2.1		5.2	2.2
Job Flexibilization	9.8	1.7		9.9	1.7
Poor Mental Health Days	3.0	6.5	a	3.8	7.3
Poor General Health	2.3	1.0		2.4	1.0

[a] = significant difference 2006 vs. 2010.
[b] = percentage in category.

Changes in the extrinsic and intrinsic conditions of work show that the percentage of respondents who experienced layoffs during the preceding year increased from 7 to 9 percent, but there were no significant changes in the overall proportion of respondents employed part-time or on a contingent basis. Not surprisingly, both job and financial insecurity levels increased significantly, as did work interference with families. Neither the levels of work intensity (demands) nor work flexibilization (decision latitude) changed significantly.

The average number of days of poor mental health increased by nearly one day, from 3 to 3.8 days per month, but there was no change in the level of overall poor general health.

Table 2 summarizes our findings regarding year by year associations between social status characteristics of workers and exposure to occupational unemployment and underemployment levels. Equation 1 (2006 and 2010) indicates that social status characteristics were strongly associated with exposure to unemployment rates and in roughly the same way in 2006 and 2010. Younger workers, those with lower education and males were more likely to work in occupations with higher unemployment rates. Although the results are much the same for the explanation of underemployment exposure (Equation 2, 2006 and 2010), it was females (rather than males) and unmarried individuals, as well as younger and less educated workers who were more likely to work in a context of higher underemployment. These findings are consistent with the dual labor market explanation for the distribution of good and bad jobs. Thus, exposure to labor market instability as represented by occupational unemployment and underemployment rates is seen to vary by social status characteristics. Workers face unequal amounts of employment instability that may also affect work conditions and health.

Table 2. OLS Regressions for Labor Market Instability and for Extrinsic Work Conditions (N = 2331)

Dependent Variable	Occupational Unemployment Rates (Eq. 1)		Occupational Underemployment Rates (Eq. 2)		Contin-gent	Part-time	Laid off in last year
	2006	2010	2006	2010	Eq. 3	Eq. 4	Eq. 5
Age	-.01** (.00)	-.02* (.01)	-.01* (.00)	-.02*** (.01)	.00** (.00)	.00* (.00)	-.00*** (.00)
Education (years)	-.30*** (.01)	-.70*** (.04)	-.13*** (.01)	-.31*** (.03)	..01 (.00)	-.00 (.00)	-.00 (.00)
Married	-.15 (.09)	-.39 (.21)	-.08 (.06)	-.53** (.18)	.03* (.01)	-.01 (.01)	.01 (.02)
Born in the U.S.	.10 (.13)	.07 (.33)	.03 (.09)	.03 (.27)	.07** (.02)	-.04 (.02)	-.03 (.03)
White	-.23* (.10)	-.09 (.26)	-.19** (.07)	-.21 (.21)	-.00 (.02)	-.04** (.01)	-.04 (.02)
Female	-.60*** (.08)	-1.48*** (.21)	.17** (.06)	.59 ** (.17)	.05** (.01)	-.04** (.01)	-.05* (.02)
Occupational Unemployment					.01 (.01)	-.04*** (.00)	.02** (.01)
Occupational Under-employment					-.02 (.01)	.10*** (.01)	-.01 (.01)
Year					.09** (.03)	.03 (.04)	.01 (.03)
Year x Unemployment Rate					-.02* (.01)	.03*** (.01)	.00 (.01)
Year x Under-employment Rate					.022 (.01)	.07*** (.01)	-.01 (.01)
Intercept	9.68*** (.25)	21.41*** (.68)	3.88*** (.18)	9.78*** (.56)	.74*** (.06)	.92*** (.12)	.23*** (.05)
Adjusted R^2	.30	.35	.14	.17	.03	.06	.05

Note: Values are unstandardized B's (standard error in parens).
*p < .05; **p < .01; ***p < .001.

In the second part of Table 2, we review findings intended to explain extrinsic work conditions and how these are related to worker social status characteristics and market instability. We focus on the market-related findings here. In Equation 3, we see that in 2010 workers were more likely to be employed in contingent jobs. Moreover, these contingent jobs were more likely to be observed in 2010 in occupational categories in which unemployment rates were lower. Contingent employment reflects one way in which firms achieve numerical flexibility. And, contingent employment is not counted as unemployment. It would appear that contingent employment in 2010 represented an alternative to unemployment in otherwise low unemployment occupations and furthers the suggestion that the recession accelerated the longer term shift of employment to more precarious forms. In equation 4, part-time employment decreased in the context of higher unemployment rates and increased in the context of higher underemployment rates. This makes sense in light of the fact that some component of part-time employment is considered a form of underemployment. Part-time employment increased in 2010 in consequence of higher unemployment and underemployment rates. We see, therefore, that part-time employment accelerated as a result of the recession. Finally, in equation 5, the likelihood that, although currently employed, one experienced a lay off in the previous year increased with the occupational unemployment rate regardless of survey year. As we have no information on the employment histories of respondents, we interpret this finding to reflect the possibility that a currently employed worker in a relatively unstable occupation will experience periods of both employment and unemployment.

Table 3. OLS Regressions for Intrinsic Work Conditions (N = 2264)

Dependent Variable	Work Intensity Eq. 6	Work Flexibility Eq. 7	Job Insecurity Eq. 8	Financial Insecurity Eq. 9	Work Interferes w/ Family Eq. 10	Family Interferes w/Work Eq. 11
Age	-.01*** (.00)	.00 (.00)	-.00 (.00)	.01*** (.00)	-.00* (.00)	-.00** (.00)
Education (years)	.07*** (.02)	.07*** (.01)	-.01 (.01)	-.06*** (.01)	.03** (.01)	.02** (.00)
Married	.01 (.01)	.23** (.07)	-.04 (.04)	-.17** (.05)	.14** (.04)	.22*** (.04)
Born in the U.S.	-.16 (.16)	.17 (.11)	.03 (.06)	.13 (.09)	.17* (.07)	.00 (.06)
White	.45*** (.11)	.09 (.08)	-09* (.04)	-.10 (.06)	.16** (.05)	.03 (.04)
Female	.16 (.10)	.06 (.07)	.04 (.09)	.13* (.06)	-.11* (.04)	.05 (.04)
Occupational Unemployment	-.01 (.06)	-.24*** (.04)	.04 (.02)	.01 (.03)	-.06* (.03)	.01 (.02)
Occupational Under-employment	-.10 (.09)	.03 (.06)	-.03 (.03)	.04 (.05)	.04 (.04)	-.06 (.03)
Laid off last year	.17 (.18)	-.10 (.13)	.51*** (.07)	.72*** (.10)	.16* (.08)	.07 (.07)
Part-time Job	-.70*** (.13)	-.41 *** (.09)	.02 (.05)	.14* (.07)	-.32*** (.06)	-.08 (.05)
Contingent Employment	-.05 (.15)	.24* (.11)	.10** (.06)	-.18* (.08)	.09 (.07)	.11 (.06)
Year	-.02 (.22)	.02 (.16)	-.01 (.09)	.12 (.13)	.06 (.10)	.08 (.09)
Year x Unemployment Rate	-.01 (.06)	.19*** (.04)	-.04 (.02)	0.2 (.03)	.05* (.03)	-.02 (.02)
Year x Under-employment Rate	.11 (.09)	-.10 (.06)	.06 (.04)	-.00 (.05)	-.05 (.04)	.04 (.03)
Intercept	3.79*** (.46)	9.16*** (.33)	1.64*** (.18)	3.75*** (.26)	1.81*** (.21)	1.76*** (.18)
Adjusted R^2	.04	.13	.04	.09	.05	.03

Note: Values are unstandardized B's (Standard error in parens).
*p <.05; **p< .01; *** p< .001.

Table 3 reports analysis of the predictors of intrinsic work conditions as a function of social status characteristics, labor market instability, extrinsic work conditions and, year. The results show that occupational unemployment and underemployment rates have few effects on intrinsic work conditions nor did the recession have much effect on intrinsic work conditions. Greater work flexibility (decision latitude) is, however, associated with working in an occupation with a lower unemployment rate. But, in 2010 this relationship was reversed. Working in an occupation with a higher unemployment rate increased work flexibility following the recession. Working in an occupation with a lower unemployment rate increased work-to-family interference. Here too, we see that in 2010 this relationship is reversed and that working in an occupation with a lower unemployment rate decreased work-to-family interference. This suggests that employed workers in the recession are willing to make adjustments to their perceptions of work in light of the ongoing higher unemployment and underemployment rates. It is also notable that job insecurity is predicted exclusively from working in a contingent job and having been laid off in the last year. Job insecurity does not seem to be related to general labor market instability but to personal employment instability. Financial insecurity is increased when the worker experienced a lay off in the previous year and decreased with regular employment. Neither market instability nor the recession affects this relationship.

Table 4. OLS Regressions for Poor General Health Status and Days of Poor Mental Health (N = 1474)

Dependent Variable	Poor Health Eq. 12	Poor Mental Health Eq. 13
Age	.01* (.00)	-.03* (.01)
Education (years)	-.06*** (.01)	-.28*** (.07)
Married	-.04 (.05)	-1.45*** (.36)
Born in the U.S.	.06 (.09)	.02 (.60)
White	-.11 (.06)	.73 (.43)
Female	.02 (.05)	.57 (.37)
Occupational Unemployment	.03 (.03)	.17 (.22)
Occupational Underemployment	-.03 (.05)	-.56 (.32)
Laid off last year	-.15 (.10)	-.44 (.71)
Part-time Job	.00 (.07)	.19 (.49)
Contingent Employment	-.01 (.08)	.36 (.56)
Work Intensity	.03* (.01)	.37*** (.09)
Work Flexibility	-.04* (.02)	.00 (.11)
Job Insecurity	.01 (.02)	.42*** (.11)
Financial Insecurity	.14*** (.02)	.77*** (.15)
Work to Family Interference	.06 (.03)	.63** (.20)
Family to Work Interference	-.01 (.03)	.28 (.23)
Year	.04 (.12)	.46 (.84)
Year x Unemployment	-.04 (.03)	-.24 (.22)
Year x Underemployment	.05 (.05)	.59 (.33)
Intercept	2.52*** (.33)	-.59 (2.23)
Adjusted R^2	.09	.10

Note: Values are unstandardized B's (standard errors in parens).
*$p < .05$; ** $p < .01$; *** $p < .001$.

Working part-time is associated with reduced work intensity, less work flexibility and less work-to family interference. This finding is certainly consistent with expectations. Finally, we continue to see that social statuses that strongly affect occupational labor market status are also predictive of intrinsic work conditions. For instance, younger, better educated white workers report greater work intensity while older, less educated, unmarried and female workers report greater financial insecurity.

Table 4 presents the regression equations predicting poor general health and number of poor mental health days. Market instability (including the recession) did not predict health outcomes. Unemployment and underemployment rates per se and the escalation of those rates during the recession did not directly affect health outcomes. Poor health is explained by higher age, less education, greater work intensity, less work flexibility and greater financial insecurity. There does not appear to be much evidence to support the notion that the recession had any effect on general health. A greater number of poor mental health days, likewise was not explained by indicators of market instability. More poor mental health days are predicted by social status characteristics and intrinsic work conditions. Younger workers, those with less education and who are unmarried reported more poor mental health days. Workers in jobs with greater job intensity, higher job insecurity and financial insecurity and higher levels of work-to-family interference report more days of poor mental health.

DISCUSSION AND CONCLUSION

This research has focused on understanding how the Great Recession of 2007-2009 and long-term labor market changes may have separately or jointly affected health outcomes among employed workers. Research findings related to the health effects of the recession of 1974-75 suggested that, aside from being laid off and the consequent health effects of unemployment, workers who retained employment were affected by the restructuring of their jobs, and in particular experienced increased job demands and reduced decision latitude that reflected organizational responses to unstable markets (Fenwick & Tausig 1994).

Since then research on the work-health relationship has suggested that long term trends in both the organization of work and in employment relations have shifted the sources of work-related distress to consider the greater work intensity and commitment required for many jobs (Green 2004) and also to assess the role played by increased job precarity and financial insecurity (Kalleberg 2009). These newer sources of work-related stress have been conceptualized as "structural" trends tied to long term changes in global markets. But the relationship between these trends and more "cyclical" economic changes such as recessions has not been assessed. Some researchers suggest that the nature of work in high performance work organizations includes more direct worker exposure to market instability (Cappelli et al 1997; Vallas 1999). If this argument is correct it may be that, even without any recession-related changes in work conditions, workers will be more vulnerable to the health effects of work organization, and that the recession will have few effects on work conditions because workers are already exposed to market uncertainty in the current form of their work. Likewise, the nexus between work and family has also undergone significant changes since the 1970s: the increased participation of women in the labor force and the increased numbers of both dual career and single parent families has increased the relevance of work-family intersections. The evidence is substantial that the increasingly fragile work-family nexus is strained by trends both toward work intensification and work precarity (e.g., Presser 2003). But, as with the trends themselves, there has been no test of whether "cyclical" downturns add to these work-family strains.

Although our results are based on cross-sectional rather than panel data, they suggest that the Great Recession itself (as indexed by occupational unemployment and underemployment rates) had no direct effects and few indirect effects on the health of currently employed workers. Rather, social statuses as these affect occupation and exposure to labor market instability and, thereby, stressful intrinsic work conditions appear to account for reports of poor health. Too, the effect of unemployment rates on health among employed workers may have been attenuated because those in occupations or statuses prone to poorer health were still out of the labor force in 2010. One difference between the labor market in 1974-75 and the years of the Great Recession is that, in the latter period contingent and part-time employment forms are more prominent (and permanent?) employment options. That is, employers during the Great Recession may have "retained" workers by shifting them to contingent and part-time jobs. If that is the case, the unemployment rates observed might understate some shifts in the labor market. Our analysis shows that labor market instability was related to more contingent and part-time employment (underemployment but not unemployment). And, contingent and part-time employment is related to decreased work flexibility and increased job insecurity, factors related to negative health outcomes.

The data we analyzed relates to currently employed workers and it may well be that current employment itself "neutralizes" much of the potentially negative effects of generalized unemployment and underemployment rates on individual health. Having a job during this Great Recession may have offset work-related factors that might ordinarily increase ill health. There is ample research evidence that the health effects of unemployment, for example, are largely reversed by re-employment (Kessler et al. 1989; Liem & Liem 1988; Payne & Jones 1987; Turner 1995; Warr & Jackson 1985). Between 2006 and 2010, more currently employed workers reported having been laid off in the previous year and so it may be the case that such workers felt better with any form of employment. Our analysis also shows that "intrinsic" work conditions were more directly related to health conditions and so another interpretation of our overall findings is that the immediate stressful (or not) context of day-to-day work, regardless of how those conditions arose, is more important to health status.

Yet another important outcome of our research is the recognition that social status characteristics are importantly related to work-related ill health. It is clear that individuals are exposed to different levels of economic instability and work-related stressful conditions as a function of social status characteristics and the way these are related to occupation. This recognition is consistent with the social statuses as fundamental causes of illness argument (Link & Phelan 1996). Social statuses clearly affect occupational attainment and, therefore, exposure to both recessionary and work-related stressors. The recession is not the same event to all workers because they will be differentially exposed to recession-related stressors as a function of social statuses (i.e., labor market positions). Our findings are thus consistent with those reported by Lam et al. (2014: 69) who also note that their findings "may reflect selection into particular kinds of occupations that may promote job insecurity and/or mental health…" Our findings, then, are more evidence for the argument that social inequality causes health inequality.

Clearly, recessions affect well-being among those who lose work (and their families). But what does it mean that workers who have jobs during periods of very high unemployment and underemployment do not seem to be adversely affected by the recession? One possibility is that the critics of new forms of work (Smith 1977; Vallas 1999) are correct that workers are now more directly exposed to variations in product and labor markets and so the effects of the recession are "built in" to their jobs. Another possibility is that employers have changed their strategy for dealing with the threat to their organization of a recession from internal reorganization to a strategy of numerical flexibility that relies on creating contingent or involuntary part-time work. While these forms of employment are related to distress, the effects on health of the recession are masked by long-term shifts to these forms of employment.

What is needed at this point is panel data that includes individual employment history. Of course it is also possible that we have not successfully represented the recession with our aggregate (at the occupational categorical level) measure. And using aggregate and individual data in the same models poses statistical and interpretative problems.

That we did not show many direct health-related effects of the Great Recession on employed workers is not to say that the Great Recession had no effects on worker health. In addition to the effects of unemployment on health, the recession changed the composition of the work force and thus, exposure to labor market and work-related stressors that already were related to worse health. Moreover, the Great Recession may have accelerated long-term shifts to less secure forms of employment that also have negative effects on health.

APPENDIX: OCCUPATIONAL EMPLOYMENT AND UNDEREMPLOYMENT RATES, 2006 AND 2010

	Unemployment Rate		Underemployment Rate	
	2006	2010	2006	2010
SOC Occupational Category				
Management	1.8	4.8	0.6	1.8
Business and Financial Operations	2.4	5.6	0.8	1.6
Computer and Mathematical Science	2.4	5.2	0.4	1.0
Architecture and Engineering	1.7	6.2	0.3	1.2
Life, Physical, and Social Service	1.8	4.6	1.0	1.7
Community and Social Service	2.3	4.6	1.0	2.7
Legal	1.3	2.7	0.2	1.3
Education, Training, and Library	2.4	4.2	1.7	3.4
Arts, Design, Entertainment, Sports and Media	4.0	8.9	2.7	5.3
Healthcare Practitioner and Technical	1.4	2.5	0.8	2.4
Healthcare Support	4.6	7.6	3.1	7.5
Protective Service	3.4	5.9	0.6	2.8
Food Preparation and Serving Related	7.2	12.4	4.9	12.6
Building and Grounds Cleaning and Maintenance	7.0	12.8	4.8	8.0
Personal Care and Service	4.7	8.7	4.2	8.1
Sales and Related	4.7	9.4	2.8	6.6
Office and Administrative Support	4.2	8.7	1.9	4.5
Farming, Fishing, and Forestry	9.5	16.3	3.8	4.7
Construction and Extraction	6.8	20.1	2.0	6.5
Installation, Maintenance, and Repair	3.7	9.3	1.4	2.4
Production	5.5	13.1	1.5	3.3
Transportation and Material Moving	6.2	12.4	2.7	5.8

Source: U.S. Bureau of Labor Statistics.

References

Barker, J. R. (1993). Tightening the Iron Cage: Concertive Control in Self-managing Teams. *Administrative Science Quarterly, 38*, 408-437.

Barling, J., & Kelloway, E. K. (1996). Job Insecurity and Health: The Moderating Role of Workplace Control. *Stress Medicine, 12*, 253-259.

Bell, D. N., & Blanchflower, D. G. (2010). UK Unemployment in the Great Recession. *National Institute Economic Review, 214*, R3-R25.

Berg, P., & Kalleberg, A. L. (2002). The Effects of High Performance Work Practices on Job Stress: Evidence From a Survey of U.S. Workers. *Conference on Work Intensification.* Paris.

Burgard, S. A., Brand, J. E., & House, J. S. (2009). Perceived Job Insecurity and Worker health in the United States. *Social Science and Medicine, 69*, 777-785.

Burgard, S. A., Kalousova, L., & Seefeldt, K. S. (2012). *Perceived Job Insecurity and Health: The Michigan Recession and Recovery Study.* National Poverty Center Working Paper Series. Retrieved from http://www.npc.umich.edu/publications/working_papers/.

Cappelli, P., Bassi, L., Katz, H., Knoke, D., Osterman, P., & Useem, M. (1997). *Change at Work.* New York: Oxford University Press.

Dooley, D., Prause, J., & Ham-Rowbottom, K. A. (2000). Financial Stress, Employment and Mental Health Underemployment and Depression: Longitudinal Relationships. *Journal of Health and Social Behavior, 41*, 421-436.

European Foundation for the Improvement of Living and Working Conditions. (2013). *Impact of the Crisis on Working Conditions in Europe.* Available in electronic format only, www.eurofund.europa.eu.

Fenwick, R. (2009). Flexible Work Arrangements. In Carr, D. (Ed.) *Encyclopedia of the Life Course and Human Development* (Vol.2, p. 144-152). Detroit: Macmillan Reference.

Fenwick, R., & Tausig, M. (1994). The Macroeconomic Context of Job Stress. *Journal of Health and Social Behavior, 35*, 266-282.

Ferrie, J. E., Shipley, M. J., Newman, K., Stansfeld, S. A., & Marmot, M. (2005). Self-reported Job Insecurity and Health in the Whitehall II Study: Potential Explanations of the Relationship. *Social Science and Medicine, 60*, 1593-1602.

Friedman, D.S. and Price, R.H. (2003). Underemployment: Consequences for the health and well-being of workers. *American Journal of Community Psychology*, 32:33-45.

Fullerton, A. S., & Wallace, M. (2007). Traversing the flexible turn: US workers' perceptions of job security, 1977-2002. *Social Science Research, 36*, 201-221.

Green, F. (2004). Why Has Work Effort Become More Intense? *Industrial Relations: A Journal of Economy and Society*, 43, 701-741.

Hacker, S.J. (2006). *The Great Risk Shift.* New York: Oxford University Press.

Hudson, K. (2007). The New Labor Market Segmentation: Labor Market Dualism in the New Economy. *Social Science Research, 36*, 286-312.

Hudson, M. (2002). Flexibility and the Reorganization of Work. In B. Burchell, D. Lapido & Wilkinson, F, *Job Insecurity and Work Intensification* (pp. 39-60). London: Routledge.

Jacoby, S. M. (2001). Risk and the Labor Market: Societal Past as Economic Prolougue. In I. Berg, & A. L. Kalleberg, *Sourcebook of Labor Markets: Evolving Structures and Processes* (pp. 31-60). New York: Kluwer Academic/Plenum Publishers.

Kalleberg, A. L. (2001). Organizing Flexibility: The Flexible Firm in a New Century. *British Journal of Industrial Relations, 39*, 479-504.

Kalleberg, A. L. (2009). Precarious Work, Insecure Workers: Employment Relations in Transition. *American Sociological Review, 74*, 1-22.

Kalleberg, A. L. (2011). *Good Jobs, Bad Jobs.* New York: Russell Sage Foundation.

Kalleberg, A. L., & Marsden, P. V. (2012). Labor Force Insecurity and U.S. Work Attitudes, 1970s-2006. In P. V. Marsden, *Social Trends in American Life: Findings from the General Social Survey Since 1972* (pp. 315-337). Princeton: Princeton University Press.

Karasek, R. (1979). Job Demands, Job Decision Latitude and Mental Strain: Implications for Job Redesign. *Administrative Science Quarterly, 24*, 285-307.

Katz, L. F. (2010, April 29). Long-term Unemployment in the Great Recession. Washington, DC.

Kessler, R. C., House, J. S., & Turner, J. B. (1987). Unemployment and Health in a Community Sample. *Journal of Health and Social Behavior, 28*, 51-59.

Kessler, R.C., House, J.S. & Turner, J.B. (1989). Unemployment, reemployment, and emotional functioning in a community sample. *American Sociological Review*, 54: 648-657.

Lapido, D., & Wilkinson, F. (2002). More Pressure, Less Protection. In B. Burchell, D. Lapido & Wilkinson, F, *Job Insecurity and Work Intensification* (pp. 8-38). London: Routledge.

Lam, J., Fan, W., & Moen, P. (2014). Is Insecurity Worse for Well-being in Turbulent Times? Mental Health in Context. *Society and Mental Health*, 4,55-73.

Liem, R., & Liem, J. H . (1988). Psychological eeefects of unemployment on workers and their families. *Journal of Social Issues, 44*, 87-103.

Link, B. G. & Phelan, J. (1995). Social conditions as fundamental causes of disease. *Journal of Health and Social Behavior, 35*, 80-94.

Macky, K. & Boxall, P. (2008). High-involvement Work Pressures, Work Intensification and Employee Well-being: A Study of New Zealand Worker Experiences. *Asia Pacific Journal of Human Resources,* 46, 38-55.

Mishel, L. R., Bernstein, J., & Shierholz, H. (2009). *The State of Working America: 2008-2009.* Ithaca: ILR Press.

Page, A., Milner, A., Morrell, S., & Taylor, R. (2013). The Role of Under-Employment and Unemployment in Recent Birth Cohort Effects in Australian Suicide. *Social Science and Medicine*, 93, 156-162.

Payne, R & Jones, J. G. (1987). Social class and re-employment: Changes in health and perceived financial circumstances. *Journal of Occupational Behavior, 8,* 175-184.

Presser, H. (2003). *Working in a 24/7 Economy: Challenges for the American Family.* New York: Russell Sage.

Reynolds, J. (2003). You Can't Always Get What You Want: Mismatches between Actual and Preferred Working Hours in the U. S. *Social Forces* 81 (4), 1171-1199.

Russell, H., & McGinnity, F. (2014). Under Pressure: The Impact of Recession on Employees in Ireland. *British Journal of Industrial Relations, 52*, 286-307.

Smith, V. (1997). New Forms of Work Orgainzation. *Annual Review of Sociology*, 315-339.

Stuckler, D., Basu, S., Suhrcke, M., Coutts, A., & McKee, M. (2009). The Public Health Effect of Economic Crises and Alternative Policy Responses in Europe: An Empirical Analysis. *The Lancet, 378* (9786) 124-125.

Stuckler, D., Basu, S., Suhrcke, M., Coutts, A., & McKee, M. (2011). Effects of the 2008 Recession on Health: A First Look at European Data. *The Lancet, 378*(9786), 124-125.

Sum, A., Beard, A., McLaughlin, J., & Khatiwada, I. (2009). *The Labor Market Impacts of the Great Recession of 2007-2009: Impacts on Unemployment and Labor Underutilization.* Boston: Northeastern University, Center for Labor Market Studies.

Sum, A., & Khatiwada, I. (2010). The Nation's underemployed in the "Great Recession" of 2007-09. *Monthly Labor Review*(November), 3-15.

Sverke, M., Hellgren, J., & Naswall, K. (2002). No Security: A Meta-analysis and Review of Job Insecurity and its Consequences. *Journal of Occupational Health Psychology, 7*, 242-264.

Tausig, M., & Fenwick, R. (1999). Recession and Well-being. *Journal of Health and Social Behavior, 40*, 1-16.

Tausig, M., & Fenwick, R. (2012). *Work and Mental Health in Social Context.* New York: Springer.

Turner, J. B.(1995) . Economic context and the health effects of unemployment. *Journal of Health and Social Behavior, 36*, 213-229.

U.S. Bureau of Labor Statistics. (2008). *Involuntary Part-Time Work on the Rise. Summary.* 08-08.

U.S. Bureau of Labor Statistics. (2011). The employment situation- December 2010. USDL-11-002.

U. S. Bureau of the Census. (1978). *Statistical Abstracts of the Unived States.* Washington, D.C.: U. S. Government Printing Office.

Vallas, S.P. (1999). Rethinking Post-Fordism: The meaning of workplace flexibility. *Sociological Theory, 17*, 68-101.

Virtanen, P., Liukkonen, V., Vahtera, J., Kivimaki, M., & Koskenvuo, M. (2003). Health Inequalities in the Workforce: The Labour Market Core-Periphery Structure. *International Journal of Epidemiology, 34*, 1015-1021.

Warr, P. & Jackson, P. (1985). Factors influencing the psychological impact of prolonger unemployment and of re-employment. *Psychological Medicine, 15,* 795-807.

Young, M & Schieman, S. (2012). When Hard Times Take a Toll: The Distressing Consequences of Economic Hardship and Life Events Within the Family-work Interface. *Jouranl of Health and Social Behavior,* 53, 84-98.

In: Unemployment
Editor: Tabitha Fletcher

ISBN: 978-1-63485-181-7

Chapter 5

EVALUATING PERSISTENCE IN THE UNEMPLOYMENT RATE OF EMERGING EUROPEAN ECONOMIES

Zorica Mladenovic* and Aleksandra Anic
University of Belgrade, Faculty of Economics, Belgrade, Serbia

ABSTRACT

Alternative unemployment theories imply different dynamic characteristics of the unemployment rate time-series. Therefore, time-series econometric methods provide a methodological framework for testing the validity of the two most important theories of unemployment: the theory of unemployment hysteresis and the theory of the natural rate of unemployment. Discrimination between the two theories is based on the empirical assessment of whether unexpected random shocks have a long-lasting effect on unemployment.

The purpose of this paper is to evaluate the persistence of the unemployment rate in the following emerging European countries: Slovenia, Slovakia, the Czech Republic, Poland, Hungary, Cyprus, Malta, Estonia, Latvia and Lithuania. The unemployment rate in the EU15 is also analyzed. Monthly time series are collected from 2004 when these countries joined the EU. The sample ends in mid-2015.

The econometric analysis has three steps. First, ordinary unit-root tests are employed, showing that almost all series are non-stationary. Second, the Lee-Strazicich unit-root test designed to handle up to two structural breaks is applied, providing results opposite to those first reached. Third, given that a linear specification may be inadequate to capture the true dynamics in the unemployment rate, the Markov-switching autoregressive model is used. The model outperforms a standard linear specification in several economies.

Persistence in the unemployment rate was found to be at a relatively high level, in some cases exceeding the degree of persistence in EU15. No unique pattern was found in respect to the level of persistence associated with either a rising or a falling trend in the unemployment rate.

Keywords: unemployment rate, persistence, unit-root, structural break

* Faculty of Economics, University of Belgrade, Kamenicka 6, 11000 Belgrade, Serbia, Email: zvujos@ekof.bg.ac.rs, zorima@eunet.rs.

INTRODUCTION

Unemployment is one of the key variables for implementing economic policy. This stems from the significant impact unemployment has on macroeconomic variables, primarily inflation. Evaluating the persistence of unemployment may provide relevant information for policy makers to understand the path and dynamics of important macroeconomic variables.

Time-series econometric methods provide a methodological framework for testing the validity of the two most important theories of unemployment: the theory of unemployment hysteresis and the theory of the natural rate of unemployment. The Blanchard-Summers (Blanchard and Summers (1987) and Barro (1988)) theory of unemployment hysteresis implies an extremely high level of persistence, so that influences of unexpected random shocks to unemployment have long-lasting effects. Using econometric terminology, the existence of a unit-root in the unemployment rate would support the theory of unemployment hysteresis. The Friedman-Phelps (Friedman (1968) and Phelps (1967, 1968)) natural rate of unemployment theory is based on the assumption that in the long-run the unemployment rate is determined by macroeconomic fundamentals, so that unexpected shocks only have temporary influence. Hence, the unemployment rate should fluctuate around a stationary equilibrium level, which may have a deterministic trend. For the natural rate of unemployment theory to be accepted as empirically valid, no unit-roots are supposed to be found in the unemployment rate time-series.

Naturally, unit-root tests emerge as the first statistical tool useful in making discrimination between the two competing theories. However, these tests cannot properly take into account several features of unemployment frequently found in empirical papers. Non-linear behavior and structural break presence, for example, represent important characteristics of this time-series. Therefore, modified unit-root tests that control for one or two structural breaks are often implemented in applied work. Also, different models designed to deal with specific aspects of non-linear dynamics are also employed.

The purpose of this paper is to evaluate the persistence of the unemployment rate in the following emerging European countries: Slovenia, Slovakia, the Czech Republic, Poland, Hungary, Cyprus, Malta, Estonia, Latvia and Lithuania. The unemployment rate in the EU15 is also analyzed. Monthly time series are considered over the period: January, 2004 – July 2015. Our sample begins in 2004, when the selected countries acceded to the EU. Over the 2004-2015 period these economies were struck by several economic shocks, giving rise to the question of how the unemployment rate reacted to them.

Econometric analysis is conducted in three steps. First, a set of ordinary unit-root tests is employed, showing that almost all series are non-stationary. Second, the Lee-Strazicich unit-root test designed to handle up to two structural breaks is applied, providing results opposite to those first reached. In fact, stationarity around the broken trend was detected as the dominant feature of most time-series considered. Third, linear specification cannot explain the smooth adjustments of the unemployment rate to the shocks, which is a feature described in literature (for example: Cuestas and Ordonez (2011), Fosten and Ghoshray (2011), Ghoshray and Stamatogiannis (2015)). Hence, models with time-varying parameters seem preferable for describing changes due to frequent and huge shocks. We use the Markov-switching autoregressive model (Hamilton (1989, 1990)). This specification assumes that the mean, variability, and persistence of the unemployment rate change randomly across different regimes. The superiority of this specification over the standard linear autoregressive model was confirmed for several economies.

The contribution of this paper is twofold. First, it includes the recent period, enabling the assessment of the influence the 2008-2009 crisis has had on the unemployment rate dynamics. Second, our econometric approach combines frequently used techniques with some of the methods mostly neglected in this type of empirical investigation for emerging European countries.

The rest of the paper is organized as follows. Section 2 reviews the recent empirical literature that econometrically tested the two competing unemployment theories. The results of unit-root testing in our sample are given in Section 3, while Section 4 describes the results of the Markov-switching autoregressive models. Concluding remarks are summarized in Section 5.

2. Literature Review

The empirical validity of the unemployment hysteresis hypothesis was assessed for a number of countries and regions. The methodological framework was used according to the development and achievements in time-series and panel econometrics. Contrary to the literature for developed economies, empirical investigation for emerging economies, including those in Europe, has not been performed often.

Leon-Ledesma and McAdam (2004) has quantified the degree of persistence in 12 countries from Central and Eastern Europe (including Croatia and Russia). Results were benchmarked against the EU. Data are considered over the period of early transition: 1992-2001. Standard univariate and panel unit-root tests were employed, along with the unit-root test that allows for one break. The latter test rejected the unemployment hysteresis hypothesis. To take into account the multiple equilibrium patterns in the unemployment rate, the Markov switching regression model was estimating, suggesting the presence of a high and low unemployment equilibrium towards which the economy fluctuates when large shocks occurred. For almost all economies the speed of adjustment was estimated to be greater than in the EU.

In Camarero, Carrion-i-Silvestre and Tamarit (2005, 2008) 9 European economies were considered that joined the EU in 2004. The unemployment rate time-series are analyzed for the time span of 1991-2003. The hysteresis hypothesis is tested versus the natural rate hypothesis on unemployment using univariate and panel unit-root tests that account for the presence of level shifts. The results rejected the hysteresis hypothesis and indicated up to four structural breaks that can be explained by institutional changes due to the implementation of market-oriented reforms. The estimated degree of persistence in unemployment differs significantly across countries, reflecting the stage reached in the transition process and the institutional set-up of the labor market.

Cuestas and Ordonez (2011) investigated the unemployment rate dynamics of 8 emerging European economies over the period 1998-2007. A nonlinear unit-root test was implemented showing that in five countries unemployment is a stationary process with highly persistent structural changes. Additionally, evidence was presented showing the possibility of a time varying equilibrium unemployment rate for four countries that shared a common nonlinear component. The same data set is analyzed in Cuestas, Gil-Alana and Staehr (2011) along with the unemployment rate for EU15. The econometric methodology was based on unit-root tests that account for structural changes, non-linearities and fractionally integrated alternatives. The model that assumes fractional integration showed that the unemployment rate does not contain a unit-root in any of the 8 economies. However, the level of persistence is estimated to be high, although it differs substantially among countries in the sample. Findings in this paper indicate that a future crisis would have an effect on the unemployment rates in some of the Central and Eastern European economies similar in magnitude to that experienced by the EU-15.

Furuoka (2015) examined the level of unemployment persistence in Estonia using annual data from 1993 to 2011 for five different regions. Panel data methods are applied revealing that data are well described as being mean-reverting processes. Thus, the natural rate in unemployment hypothesis is empirically supported by these data in Estonia.

3. Empirical Results of Unit-Root Testing

Our data set comprises monthly observations on the unemployment rate for the following emerging European countries: Slovenia, Slovakia, the Czech Republic, Poland, Hungary, Cyprus, Malta, Estonia, Latvia and Lithuania. The unemployment rate in EU15 is also taken into account. All data cover the sample period from January, 2004 to July, 2015 (139 observations). Data are collected from EUROSTAT. Empirical results are obtained by Oxmetrics9.1, RATS and EViews9.

Data are depicted in Figure 1. We may notice that series exhibit a changing trend suggesting that the sample covers intervals of both a decrease and an increase in the unemployment rate. In order to find out if the trend is of a stochastic or deterministic nature we apply several unit-root tests with the results given in Table 1. It is evident that the unemployment rates are unit-root processes in all economies. Thus, persistence is estimated to be extremely high. For three countries (Poland, Latvia and Lithuania) some of the tests even implied two unit-roots. However, we argue that such a result is probably due to unaccounted structural breaks.

To capture unemployment dynamics in a more accurate way, unit-root tests should explicitly take into account the possibility that structural breaks exist. Thus, we further calculated the values of the Lee-Strazicich (LS) unit-root test (Lee and Strazicich, 2003), widely used to incorporate up to two structural breaks. The test that assumes changes in both intercept and slope of the deterministic trend function is applied. Results are reported in Table 2. Non-stationarity is confirmed only for the unemployment rate in Cyprus and Hungary. In other countries, including the EU-15, we found strong evidence of stationary movements that follow the broken deterministic trend component. One structural break was identified within the second half of 2008 in almost all cases. This finding indicates the significant influence the start of the Great recession has had on the unemployment rates in most of the countries analysed.

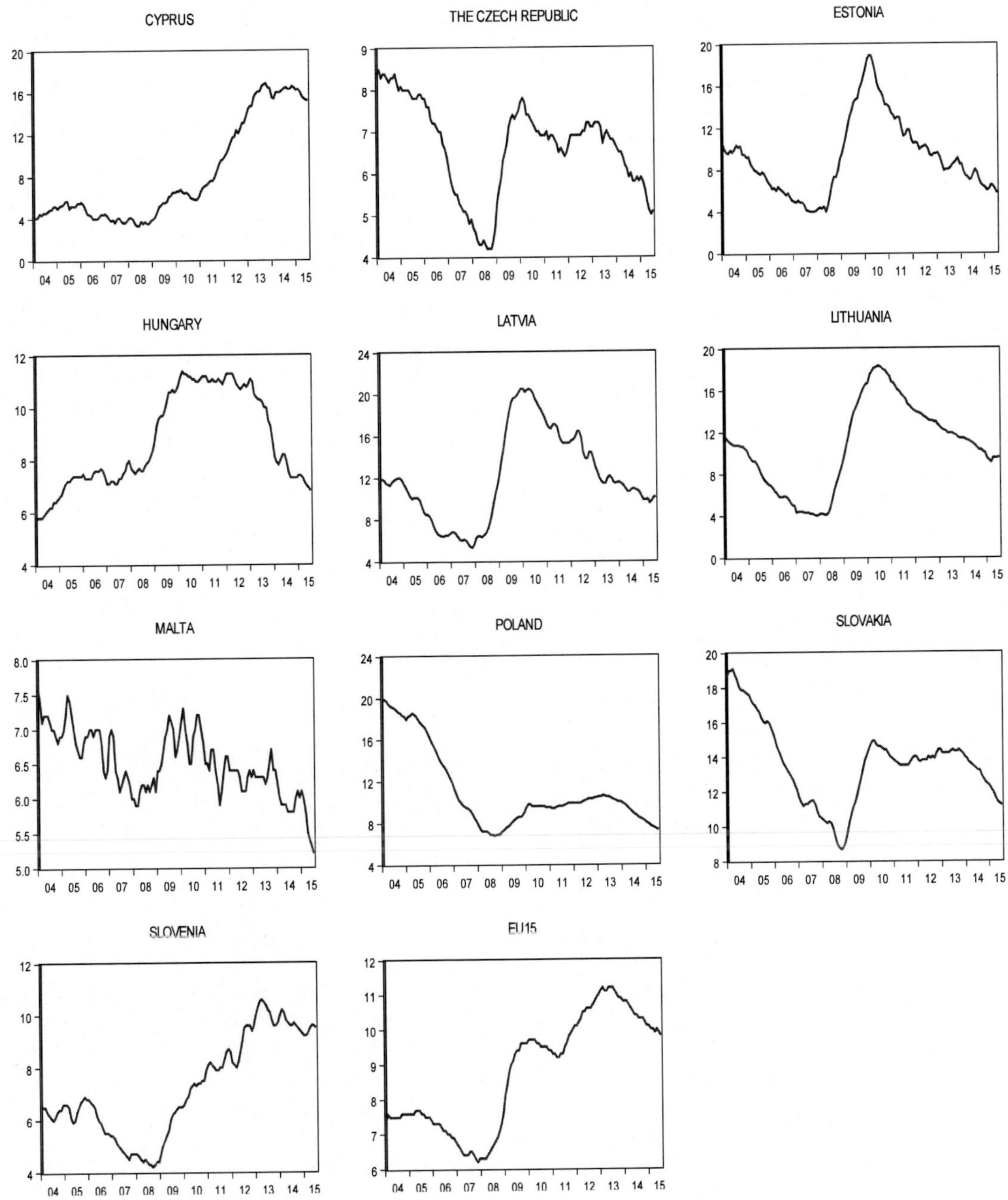

Figure 1. The unemployment rate in select economies.

The identified breaks actually show that huge shocks have a significant impact on the unemployment rate. Therefore, short-lived temporary shocks, along with a few permanent shocks described by structural breaks, seem like a plausible explanation for the unemployment rate in most of the emerging European economies. In addition, this result implies that unemployment reverts to its constant or average level upon a sudden change due to a break. This clearly rejects the unemployment hysteresis hypothesis in the following countries: Slovenia, Slovakia, the Czech Republic, Poland, Malta, Estonia, Latvia and

Lithuania Contrary to this, the hypothesis is accepted as empirically valid for Cyprus and Hungary.

Table1. Results of unit-root testing

Country	Test for unit-root in	ADF	Number of lags	Unit-root	KPSS	Unit-root	ERS	Unit-root
Cyprus	Level	0.27	1	Yes	1.11	Yes	1.18	Yes
	1st difference	-8.33	0	No	0.31	No	-7.27	No
The Czech Republic	Level	-1.88	2	Yes	0.76	Yes	-0.85	Yes
	1st difference	-4.90	1	No	0.30	No	-3.87	No
Estonia	Level	-1.21	1	Yes	1.06	Yes	-1.22	Yes
	1st difference	-6.48	0	No	0.40	No	-6.33	No
Hungary	Level	-1.40	1	Yes	3.16	Yes	-0.69	Yes
	1st difference	-6.30	0	No	0.70	No	-6.32	No
Latvia	Level	-2.21	4	Yes	0.70	Yes	-2.21	Yes
	1st difference	-2.63	3	Yes	0.27	No	-2.64	No
	2nd difference	-12.02	2	No	-	-	-	-
Lithuania	Level	-2.24	2	Yes	1.53	Yes	-2.21	Yes
	1st difference	-2.32	1	Yes	0.74	Yes	-2.09	No
	2nd difference	-18.73	0	No	0.04	No	-	No
Malta	Level	-1.51	4	Yes	1.46	Yes	0.91	Yes
	1st difference	-9.21	3	No	0.06	No	-6.02	No
Poland	Level	-2.47	4	Yes	1.56	Yes	-0.26	Yes
	1st difference	-2.39	3	Yes	0.83	Yes	-2.19	No
	2nd difference	-10.19	2	No	0.04	No	-	-
Slovakia	Level	-2.85	1	Yes	0.31	No	-0.26	Yes
	1st difference	-4.13	0	No	-	-	-2.19	No
Slovenia	Level	-0.79	1	Yes	0.99	Yes	-0.65	Yes
	1st difference	-5.83	0	No	0.28	No	-5.08	No
EU-15	Level	-1.40	2	Yes	1.08	Yes	-1.02	Yes
	1st difference	-3.13	1	No	0.14	No	-3.37	No

Note: The model with a constant is used. The 5% critical values are -2.88, 0.46 and -1.94 respectively for the ADF, the KPSS and the ERS test. The number of lags refers to a number of correction elements included in the application of the ADF and the ERS test. The truncation parameter in calculating the Newey-West correction for KPSS test is either set to 8 or 9, or it corresponds to the number of corrections in the ADF test.

Table 2. Results of the LS unit-root testing that accounts for up to two structural breaks

Country	Number of lags	Dates of breaks	LM test statistics
Cyprus	14	-	-4.42
The Czech Republic	13	October, 2008. June, 2011.	-5.98*
Estonia	13	September, 2006. November, 2009.	-5.69*
Hungary	18	-	-4.90

Country	Number of lags	Dates of breaks	LM test statistics
Latvia	17	August, 2008. May, 2012.	-6.39*
Lithuania	15	September, 2006. December, 2009.	-7.64*
Malta	15	November, 2008. September, 2011.	-4.99**
Poland	12	November, 2006. February, 2011.	-7.39*
Slovakia	18	November, 2008. November, 2011.	-5.81*
Slovenia	18	December, 2007. August, 2008.	-5.27*
EU15	13	September, 2008. February, 2012.	-5.82*

Note: * and ** respectively denote the values of the test-statistics that are less than the critical values for the significance level of 5% and 10%.

4. Modelling the Unemployment Rate Dynamics

Some empirical results for OECD countries (for example: Fosten and Ghoshray (2011) and Ghoshray and Stamatogiannis (2015)) and economies in the early phase of transition (Leon-Ledesma and McAdam, 2004) indicate that the unemployment rate dynamics is characterized by at least two different regimes during which it supports either hysteresis or natural rate hypothesis of unemployment. Such a behaviour cannot be discovered by the unit-root tests applied above. The Markov-switching (MS) model appears as the relevant framework, because it can associate different degrees of persistence, mean and variability in the unemployment rate with different regimes over time. We have found only one paper that addressed this approach in quantifying the degree of persistence in emerging European countries (Leon-Ledesma and McAdam, 2004).

We will undertake the estimation of MS specification for all data except for those countries (Hungary and Cyprus) where all unit-root tests indicate non-stationarity of the unemployment rate.

The basic idea of the MS model, upon which empirical results will be provided, will briefly be reviewed. The baseline method in time-series analysis to measure the persistence in time- series x_t is the sum of autoregressive coefficients, $\sum_{i=1}^{p}\phi_i$, from the autoregressive model of order p, $x_t = \alpha_0 + \sum_{i=1}^{p}\phi_i x_{t-i} + e_t$. This can be rewritten as: $x_t = \alpha_0 + \rho x_{t-1} + \sum_{i=1}^{(p-1)}\delta_i \Delta x_{t-i} + e_t$, so that the parameter $\rho = \sum_{i=1}^{p}\phi_i$ contains information about the sum of autoregressive parameters and thus provides a measure of persistence in the unemployment rate. The error term, e_t, is Gaussian white noise.

This specification can be modified in a number of different ways to take account of possible regime changes and nonlinearity in a given time series. To allow for changes in some parameters we employ the Markov-switching autoregressive model assuming that mean, variability and persistence may differ between two regimes. The relevant specification is of the following form (Hamilton (1989, 1990)):

$$x_t = (\alpha_0 + \alpha_1 S_t) + (\rho + \rho_1 S_t)x_{t-1} + \delta_1 \Delta x_{t-1} + \ldots + \delta_{p-1}\Delta x_{t-p+1} + (h_0 + h_1 S_t)e_t \quad (4.1)$$

S_t is the unobserved random variable that follows a Markov chain defined by transition probabilities between two states. The full matrix of transition probabilities for two states reads as follows:

State at *t+1*	Condition at *t*	
	S_t=0	S_t=1
S_{t+1}=0	$q=p_{0/0}$	$f=p_{0/1}$
S_{t+1}=1	$p_{1/0}$	$P_{1/1}$

Shifts of the economy from state 0 to state 1 are governed by the introduced random variable S_t. Under this specification we have two different regimes: regime 0 (i.e., S_t =0) and regime 1 (i.e., S_t =1). The parameters α_1, ρ_1, h_1 capture the changes in the mean of the unemployment rate, the persistence of a shock to the unemployment rate and the variance during regime 1 relative to regime 0.

Satisfactory models were estimated for all emerging economies and the EU-15. The results are given in Tables 4.1-4.7 and relevant graphs are depicted in Figures 4.1 - 4.6. Since the results are similar for the three Baltic countries, only the results for Estonia are presented.

The Czech Republic

The two-state MS model fits well to the dynamics of the unemployment rate in the Czech Republic. Two different persistence regimes have been detected. Regime 0 has an extremely high persistence characterized by the estimated magnitude of $\hat{\rho} = 0.994$. This is also a regime of a lower mean level. Regime 1 is found to have a smaller persistence: the estimate is 0.839. During regime 1 the unemployment rate exhibited a higher mean value. Statistically, persistence does not differ from 1 in regime 0, suggesting unit-root presence. Therefore, this specification explains two statistically different regimes in the unemployment persistence. Economic implications also vary across the two regimes.

The probability *q* of remaining in the regime of higher persistence, while being in that regime is 0.98. The probability *f* of switching from the regime of lower to the regime of higher persistence is small and is equal to 0.02, implying that the probability of staying in the regime of lower persistence is also high, 0.98. The economy remains in the regime of extremely high persistence in unemployment 57% of the time, while the remaining 43% is associated with the regime of lower persistence in unemployment. The average duration of the regime of high persistence is 38 months, while the average duration of the regime of lower persistence is 57 months.

A visual inspection of the regimes, from Figure 2, indicates that the regime of extremely high persistence (regime 0) is closely related to a strong downward trend in the unemployment rate. The regime of lower persistence is estimated for time intervals during which the unemployment rate exhibited either an upward or a mild downward trend. We may conclude that there is an asymmetric reaction of unemployment to positive or negative shocks. In general, persistence is higher when strong negative shocks occur.

Table 3. Estimated model for the Czech Republic

Parameter	α_0	$(\alpha_0+\alpha_1)$	ρ	$(\rho+\rho_1)$	h_0	Q	F
Estimate	-0.002	1.12	0.994	0.839	0.12	0.98	0.02
p-value	0.98	0.00	0.00	0.00	0.00	0.00	0.36

Parameter	δ_1	δ_5	δ_7
Estimate	0.17	0.20	0.12
p-value	0.09	0.02	0.07

$Linearity\,test:\ \chi_4^2 = 20.29(0.00);\ Box-Pierce\ Q(36)\ \chi_{36}^2 = 24.91(0.92),$
$ARCH1\ F = 0.84(0.36);\ Normality\chi_2^2 = 0.60(0.74)$

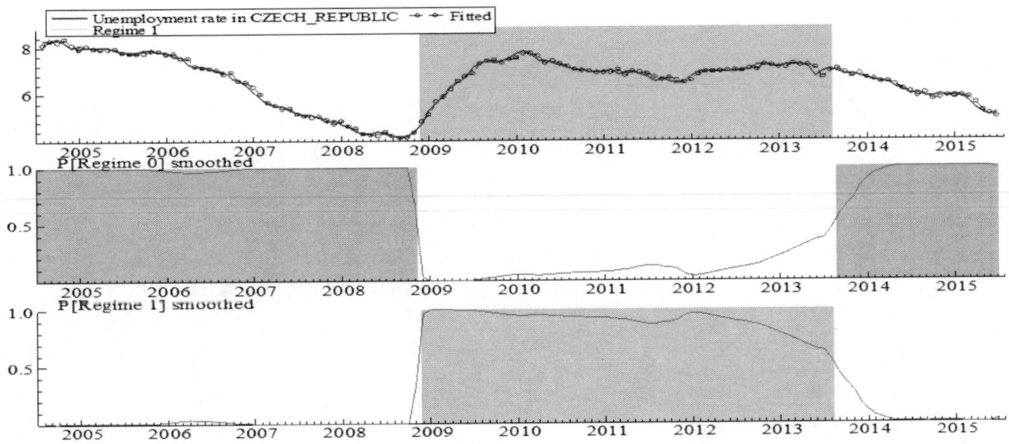

Figure 2. Two regimes of persistence in the Czech Republic.

Estonia

The two-state MS model performs well for the unemployment rate in Estonia. Regime 0 has a smaller unemployment persistence, estimated to be 0.933. Regime 1 is described as having a slightly higher persistence (the estimate is 0.961). These measures of persistence differ significantly at the 10% level (according to the Wald test), but they imply stationarity in both cases. The average duration of regime 0 is about 10 months, taking up 61% of the sample. The remaining 39% belongs to regime 1, lasting 7 months on average (Figure 3). The period of up to mid-2010 is split almost equally between the two regimes, such that the regime of smaller persistence covers a strong downward trend, while the regime of higher persistence describes a rapid growth in the unemployment rate over the period June 2008 - April 2010. After that, switches between regimes occurred more often, but sharp decreases in unemployment rate were again closely related to a lower level of persistence.

The probability of staying in the regime of lower persistence when already in that regime is q=0.90, while the probability of staying in the regime of higher persistence while being in that regime is 0.83 (1-f).

Similar results were found for Latvia and Lithuania. In the case of Latvia, one of the two regimes was estimated to have a unit-root in unemployment rate, but it covers only one-third of the sample.

Table 4. Estimated model for Estonia

Parameter	α_0	$(\alpha_0+\alpha_1)$	ρ	$(\rho+\rho_1)$	h_0	Q	F
Estimate	0.36	0.67	0.933	0.961	0.26	0.90	0.17
p-value	0.00	0.00	0.00	0.00	0.00	0.00	0.05

Parameter	δ_1	δ_5	δ_8
Estimate	0.20	0.15	0.34
p-value	0.02	0.01	0.00

$Linearity\ test:\ \chi_4^2=12.89(0.01);\ Box-Pierce\ Q(36)\ \chi_{36}^2=42.10(0.22),$
$ARCH1\ F=0.57(0.45);\ Normality\ \chi_2^2=0.98(0.61)$

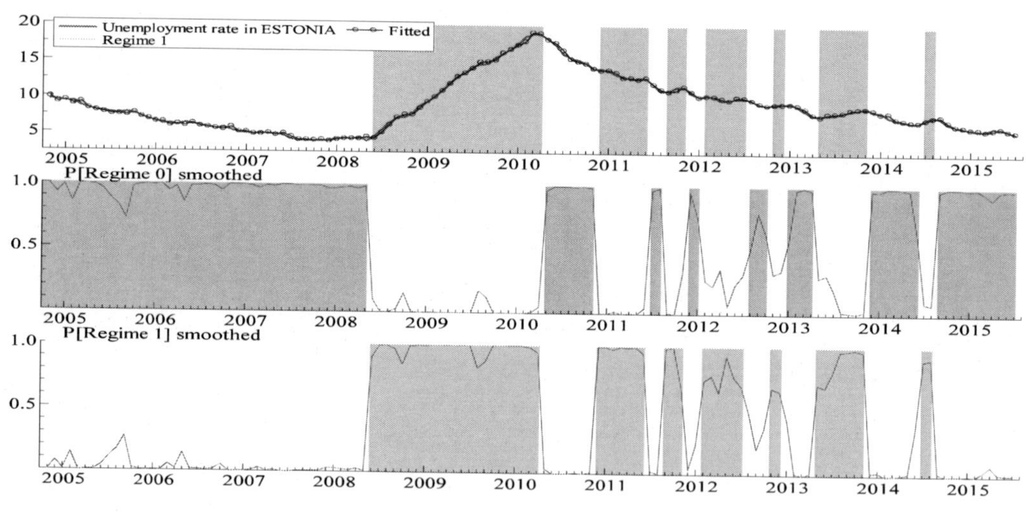

Figure 3. Two regimes of persistence in Estonia.

Malta

The estimated two-state MS model for the unemployment rate in Malta reveals specific properties of this time-series. Regime 0 is found to have a lower degree of persistence estimated at 0.95. Regime 1 is estimated to be of a higher persistence that suggests unit-root presence (the estimate is 1). The probability q of staying in the regime of lower persistence, while being in that regime is 0.87. The probability 1-f of remaining in the regime of higher persistence is low, 0.09.

The economy spent about 87% of the time in the lower persistence regime 0. Its average duration was 7 months. The remaining 13% is described by a unit-root regime 1 with an average duration of 1.13 month. Unit-root behaviour is short-lived. Due to transitory shocks, persistence has a tendency to increase, but it rapidly returns to its mean value (Figure 4).

Table 5. Estimated model for Malta

Parameter	α_0	$(\alpha_0+\alpha_1)$	ρ	$(\rho+\rho_1)$	h_0	(h_0+h_1)	Q	F
Estimate	0.26	0.19	0.953	1.006	0.13	0.006	0.87	0.91
p-value	0.19	0.00	0.00	0.00	0.00	0.00	0.00	0.00

Parameter	δ_1	δ_2	δ_3	δ_4	δ_5
Estimate	0.42	0.26	-0.54	-0.18	0.43
p-value	0.00	0.00	0.00	0.00	0.00

$Linearity\,test: \chi^2_5 = 31.8{,}5(0.00); Box-Pierce\ Q(36)\ \chi^2_{36} = 47.06(0.10),$

$ARCH\,1\ F = 0.02(0.87); Normality\chi^2_2 = 0.51(0.78)$

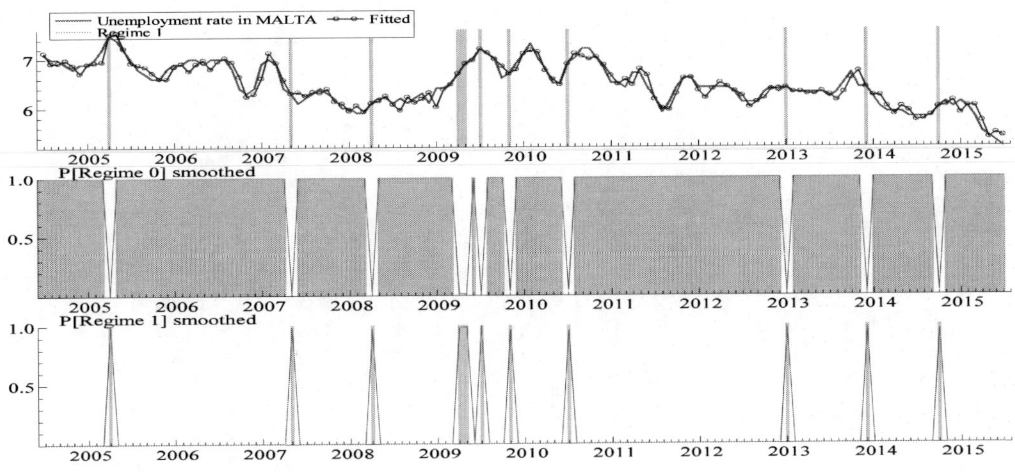

Figure 4. Two regimes of persistence in Malta.

Slovenia

The estimated two-state MS model performs statistically well. Regime 0 has a smaller persistence, estimated to be 0.992. Regime 1 is described as having a higher persistence (the estimate is 1.025). Unit-root presence was statistically found in regime 0 even showing mild explosive behaviour in regime 1. The average duration of regime 0 is about 10 months, covering 85% of the sample. The rest of the sample is associated with regime 1 that on average lasts 1.9 months (Figure 5). We may notice that mild explosive behaviour is displayed over short subperiods of substantial increase in the unemployment rate. The probability of staying in the regime of unit-root persistence, when already in that regime is q=0.89. The probability of staying in the mild explosive regime while being in that regime is lower (0.44).

These results indicate an extremely high unemployment persistence in Slovenia that is captured either by the unit or the small explosive root.

Table 6. Estimated model for Slovenia

Parameter	α_0	ρ	$(\rho+\rho_1)$	h_0	Q	f
Estimate	0.03	0.992	1.025	0.09	0.89	0.56
p-value	0.51	0.00	0.00	0.00	0.00	0.01

Parameter	δ_1	δ_8
Estimate	0.48	0.12
p-value	0.00	0.04

Linearity test : $\chi_3^2 = 11.43(0.01)$; *Box – Pierce* $Q(36)$ $\chi_{36}^2 = 34.49(0.54)$, *ARCH* 1 $F = 0.20(0.66)$; *Normality* $\chi_2^2 = 4.79(0.09)$. *Model contains two impulse dummy variables for the following months : January, 2012 and April, 2015.*

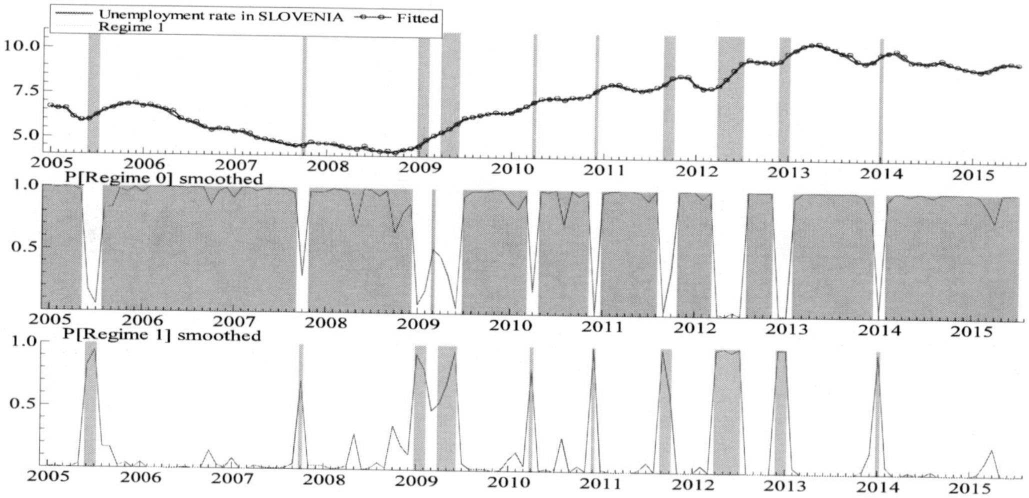

Figure 5. Two regimes of persistence in Slovenia.

Slovakia

Again the two-state MS model fits well with the changes to the unemployment rate. Regime 0 is characterized by the persistence estimate of 1.067. Regime 1 has a persistence estimate of 0.975. Regime 0 describes mild explosive behaviour in the unemployment rate associated with its lower mean level. In fact, as depicted in Figure 6, this regime is extracted only during a systematic decrease in the unemployment rate at 16% of the sample and thus revealing the lasting impact of systematic negative shocks. Regime 1 implies stationarity of the unemployment rate during most of the sample, 84%. The average duration of the higher persistence regime is about 3 months, while the average duration of the lower persistence regime is 15 months.

The probability q of remaining in the regime of higher persistence, while being in that regime is 0.63. The probability f of switching from the regime of lower to the regime of higher persistence is only 0.08, meaning that the probability of staying in the regime of lower persistence is 0.92.

Table 7. Estimated model for Slovakia

Parameter	α_0	$(\alpha_0 + \alpha_1)$	ρ	$(\rho + \rho_1)$	h_0	$(h_0 + h_1)$	Q	F
Estimate	-0.91	0.33	1.067	0.975	0.04	0.12	0.63	0.08
p-value	0.00	0.00	0.00	0.00	0.00	0.00	0.00	0.02

Parameter	δ_1
Estimate	0.82
p-value	0.00

$Linearity\,test:\ \chi_5^2 = 18.13(0.00);\ Box-Pierce\ Q(36)\ \chi_{36}^2 = 41.96(0.23),$

$ARCH1\ F = 0.53(0.47);\ Normality\chi_2^2 = 2.75(0.25)$

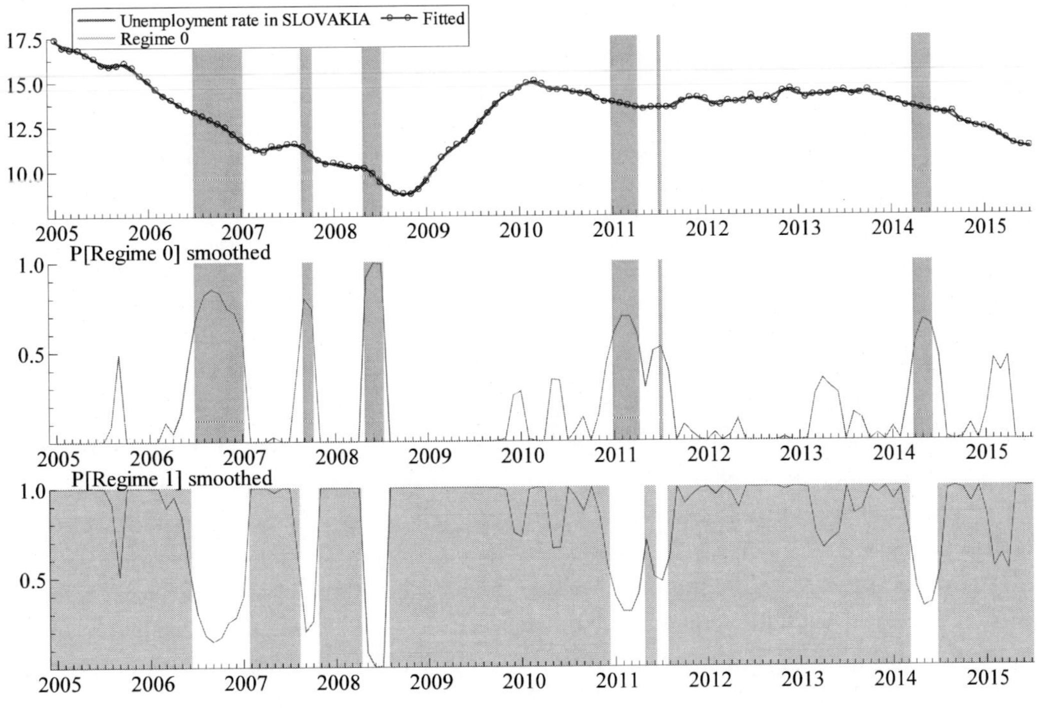

Figure 6. Two regimes of persistence in Slovakia.

Poland

The two-state MS model describes the unemployment rate dynamics in Poland well. Specifically, all parameters of the model, including short-run dynamics, were estimated for two regimes. Regime 0 was found to capture a higher persistence in unemployment with an estimate of 0.993. However, the parameter is statistically different from 1, implying stationarity. The persistence of regime 1 is quantified as 0.977. This estimate is lower than the one in regime 0, but still points to the high sensitivity of the unemployment rate to external shocks. The economy spent 75% of the time in the regime of higher persistence and 25% in the regime of lower persistence. Average durations were 3.5 and 1.2 months, respectively.

The probability q of remaining in the regime of higher persistence, while being in that regime is 0.7, about the same as the probability f of switching from the regime of lower to the regime of higher persistence. A visual presentation is omitted due to limitations of space.

Table 8. Estimated model for Poland

Parameter	α_0	$(\alpha_0+\alpha_1)$	ρ	$(\rho+\rho_1)$	h_0	(h_0+h_1)	q	F
Estimate	0.05	0.26	0.993	0.977	0.07	0.04	0.70	0.71
p-value	0.10	0.00	0.00	0.00	0.00	0.00	0.00	0.00

Parameter	δ_1	δ_2	δ_3	δ_4	δ_7
Estimate	0.85	0.26	-0.45	0.13	0.15
p-value	0.00	0.00	0.00	0.07	0.01

Linearity test : $\chi^2_{10} = 24.05(0.01)$; *Box – Pierce* $Q(36)$ $\chi^2_{36} = 33.75(0.59)$, *ARCH* 1 $F = 0.18(0.67)$; *Normality* $\chi^2_2 = 1.08(0.58)$, *Estimates of the shorth - run parameters refer to regime 0 and they are also significant for regime 1, buth they are not reported in order to save space.*

The EU15

As a benchmark case, the two-state MS model was fitted to the unemployment rate in the EU15. Again, two different persistence regimes have been detected. Regime 0 has a higher persistence estimated to be $\hat{\rho} = 0.991$. At the same time, this is a regime with a lower mean level and variability. Regime 1 is estimated to have a lower persistence (0.942), but higher mean value and variability. In both cases degrees of persistence are significantly lower than 1. Thus, no unit-root was formally found in any of the two regimes.

The economy stays in the regime of higher persistence in unemployment 73% of the time and in the regime of relatively smaller persistence 27% of the time. The average duration of the regime of higher persistence is 33 months, while the average duration of the regime of lower persistence is 19 months. Both probabilities of staying in one regime while being in that regime are high (0.98 and 0.94 respectively for regimes 0 and 1).

We may observe a strong correlation between the regimes and the type of trend exhibited by the data. Namely, a higher persistence is found for subsamples during which unemployment tends to fall or remains relatively stable (March, 2004 - September 2008, October 2009-April 2011, July, 2013 – July, 2015). A slightly lower persistence is associated with the upward trend in the unemployment rate.

The composite unemployment rate of the EU15 shows a relatively high persistence, but not an extreme one. This time-series appears to be more sensitive to negative than to positive shocks.

Summary

We will now summarize the results of Section 4 (see also Table 10). The estimated models reveal that persistence is relatively high in the EU15. Formally, no unit-root was estimated. Similar behaviour was found for the following economies: Poland, Estonia and Lithuania.

Unit-root presence was detected within one regime in the Czech Republic (57% of the sample), Latvia (32%), Malta (13%) and Slovenia (85%). However, the unemployment rate dynamics exhibits a different pattern during the unit-root regime across different economies. For example, unit-root presence is closely associated with the fall of unemployment rate in the Czech Republic, highlighting long-lasting effects of those shocks that have reduced unemployment. The unit-root in the case of Malta is of a transitory and probably seasonal nature. The unit-root regime in Slovenia covers most of the sample and indicates a persistent response of the unemployment rate to external shocks during the entire period considered.

In the cases of Slovakia and Slovenia, mild explosive behaviour was even determined in one of the two regimes. As already discussed, the other regime in Slovenia has a unit-root. In Slovakia another regime describes stationarity. Both explosive episodes are of short duration, but they have different implications. Namely, the explosive regime in Slovakia has been estimated for subsamples during which unemployment strongly declines. Contrary to that, explosive episodes in Slovenia occurred during a systematic increase of the unemployment rate.

Table 9. Estimated model for the EU15

Parameter	α_0	$(\alpha_0+\alpha_1)$	ρ	$(\rho+\rho_1)$	h_0	(h_0+h_1)	q	F
Estimate	0.06	0.67	0.991	0.942	0.06	0.08	0.98	0.06
p-value	0.12	0.00	0.00	0.00	0.00	0.00	0.00	0.07

Parameter	δ_1
Estimate	0.18
p-value	0.03

$Linearity\ test:\ \chi_5^2 = 33.16\,(0.00);\ Box-Pierce\ Q(36)\ \chi_{36}^2 = 34.7(0.53),$

$ARCH1\ \ F = 1.78(0.19)\ ;\ Normality\ \chi_2^2 = 3.04\,(0.21)$

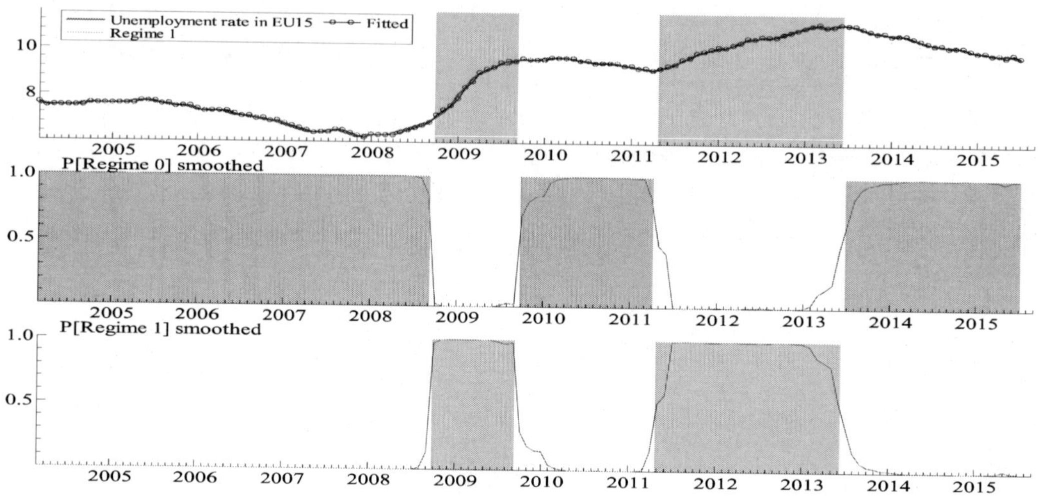

Figure 7. Two regimes of persistence in the EU15.

Table 10. Summary of estimated two-state MS models

Country/Region	Lower persistence estimate	Higher persistence estimate	Time spent in the unit-root/ mild explosive regime
EU15	<1	<1	-
The Czech Republic	<1	=1	57%
Estonia	<1	<1	-
Latvia	<1	=1	32%
Lithuania	<1	<1	-
Malta	<1	=1	13%
Poland	<1	<1	-
Slovakia	<1	>1	16%
Slovenia	=1	>1	85%/15%

Conclusion

The persistence of the monthly unemployment rate was estimated for ten emerging European economics and for the EU15 from the beginning of 2004 until mid-2015. Several conclusions can be derived.

An extremely high level of persistence described by unit-root presence, even when the modelling accounts for structural breaks, is detected for Hungary and Cyprus. For other countries in the sample the hysteresis hypothesis has been strongly rejected.

However, to allow for a more sophisticated approach that provides the possibility of splitting unemployment rate dynamics into the hysteresis and the natural rate theory hypothesis, the Markov-switching autoregressive model is implemented. This estimation has enabled further insight into the unemployment rate persistence.

Two regimes of high unemployment persistence without unit-roots have been found for the EU15. Similar behaviour was observed for the unemployment rates in Poland, Estonia and Lithuania.

Unit-root presence was detected within one regime, and stationarity within the other regime in the Czech Republic, Latvia and Malta. In Slovakia, stationarity was also found in one regime, while mild explosive behaviour was estimated in another regime. Given the duration and prevailing trend behaviour of the unemployment rate over the unit-root (or explosive) regime, we may argue that the degree of the unemployment persistence in these countries is of a similar magnitude as in the EU15.

A combination of unit and mild explosive root was determined for the Slovenian unemployment rate. Since Slovenian data were mostly covered by the unit-root regime, while explosive behaviour was connected with a strong upward trend, our final conclusion points to the extremely high level of persistence in Slovenia. Overall, our quantifications show that the estimated unemployment persistence in Hungary, Slovenia and Cyprus is of greater magnitude than in the EU15. The level of persistence can be taken to be of similar magnitude in the other economies considered.

Our empirical results are not in line with findings previously reported in Cuestas, Gil-Alana and Staehr (2011) that considered data for sample that ends in 2007. Since our sample captures dynamics during and after the Great Recession, we may argue that unemployment rate persistence has changed dramatically as a consequence of the 2008-2009 crisis. In fact, the LS unit-root test identifies the second half of 2008 as a break date for most time-series.

Returning to the behaviour of the unemployment rate dynamics explained by the Markov-switching autoregressive model, some additional points can be made. First, the frequency of regime switching differs substantially across countries. For example, the unemployment rate in the EU15 went through one regime twice and through the other regime once. The same holds for the Czech Republic. A shorter duration of regimes (more frequent regime switching) is estimated in other countries. This finding suggests that unemployment rates do not adjust with a similar speed to new equilibrium levels across different economies. Second, short-run dynamics vary significantly across estimated models because they are represented by different numbers of lagged changes in the unemployment rate that range from one to five. Such a result emphasizes a different degree of inertia in the unemployment rates. Third, no unique conclusion can be drawn concerning the correlation between level of unemployment persistence and its mean level or variability. It is evident that the dynamics of unemployment rates are characterized by different patterns indicating that country-specific measures of economic and employment policy should be implemented.

REFERENCES

Barro, R. (1988). The natural rate theory reconsidered: The persistence of unemployment. *American Economic Review, 78*, 32-37.

Blanchard, O. J., & Summers, L.H. (1987). Hysteresis in unemployment. *European Economic Review, 31,* 288-295.

Camarero, M., Carrion-i-Silvestre, J.L., & Tamarit, C. (2005). Unemployment dynamics and NAIRU estimates for accession countries: A univariate approach. *Journal of Comparative Economics, 33,* 584-603.

Camarero, M., Carrion-i-Silvestre, J.L., & Tamarit, C. (2008). Unemployment hysteresis in transition countries: Evidence using stationarity panel tests with breaks. *Review of Development Economics, 12,* 620-635.

Cuestas, J. C., & Ordonez, J. (2011). Unemployment and common smooth transition trend in Central and Eastern European Countries. *Economic Issues, 16,* 39-52.

Cuestas, J. C., Gil-Alana, L.A., & Staehr, K. (2011). A further investigation of unemployment persistence in European transition economies. *Journal of Comparative Economics, 39,* 514-532.

Friedman, M. (1968). The role of monetary policy. *American Economic Review, 58*, 1-17.

Furuoka, F. (2015). Unemployment hysteresis in the "Nordic Kitten": Evidence from five Estonian regions. *Panoeconomicus, 62*, 631-642.

Fosten J., & Ghoshray, A. (2011). Dynamic persistence in the unemployment rate of OECD countries. *Economic Modelling, 28,* 948-954.

Ghoshray, A. & Stamatogiannis, P. (2015). Centurial evidence of breaks in the persistence of unemployment. *Economics Letters, 129,* 74-76.

Hamilton, J.D. (1989). A new approach to the economic analysis of nonstationary time series and the business cycle. *Econometrica, 53,* 357-384.

Hamilton, J.D. (1990). Analysis of time series subject to changes in regime. *Journal of Econometrics, 45,* 39-70.

Lee, J., & Strazicich, M.C. (2003). Minimum Lagrange multiplier unit root test with two structural breaks. *The Review of Economics and Statistics, 85*, 1082- 1089.

Leon-Ledesma, M.A., & McAdam, P. (2004). Unemployment, hysteresis and transition. *Scottish Journal of Political Economy, 51,* 377-401.

Phelps, E.S. (1967). Phillips curve, expectations of inflation and optimal unemployment over time. *Economica, 34,* 254-281.

Phelps, E.S. (1968). Money-wage dynamics and labour-market equilibrium. *Journal of Political Economy, 76,* 678-711.

In: Unemployment
Editor: Tabitha Fletcher

ISBN: 978-1-63485-181-7

Chapter 6

ON THE POLITICAL ASPECTS OF UNEMPLOYMENT: THE CASE OF ELECTION RESULTS

António Bento Caleiro*
Department of Economics, University of Évora, Portugal

ABSTRACT

Unemployment is related to economic, political and social aspects. One of the least analysed political aspects is the relationship that, from a partisan or ideological perspective, should exist between the election results and the aging level of the voters, which is to be reflected in different electoral costs of unemployment. This chapter updates previous work on the subject, using a spatial econometrics methodology to estimate the relationship between the levels of aging and the election results that were obtained in the most recent elections that took place in Portugal, i.e., the October 2015 legislative elections. The results confirm the hypothesis that the level of unemployment involves a higher (resp. lower) electoral cost the less (resp. more) aged is the electorate.

Keywords: election results, Portugal, spatial econometrics, unemployment

1. INTRODUCTION

Unemployment is related to economic, political and social aspects. One of the least analysed political aspects is the relationship that, from a partisan or ideological perspective, should exist between the election results and the aging level of the voters, which is to be reflected in different electoral costs of unemployment.

As is known, the general decline in the retirement age -- despite some recent setbacks -- is a fact empirically proven (Auer & Fortuny, 2000). The decrease in the retirement age accompanied by an increase in life expectancy and decreasing fertility thus results in an increase of the electoral importance of older people and, in particular, pensioners. This

* Corresponding author: caleiro@uevora.pt.

becomes, in practice, even more relevant given that the electoral abstention on the part of the eldest appears to be lower than that associated to the younger electorate (Rubenson et al., 2004).

The electoral consequences of that phenomena, at least in theory, are thus evident. [1] An aging population is expected to implicate an increased electoral advantage of the parties that prove, or claim, to be the best in defending the interests of the elderly, in general, and pensioners, in particular. That parties, in principle, are supposed to be those that, in accordance to their ideology, consider unemployment relatively less important than inflation. As recognized, for example by Easterly & Fischer (2001), in fact, as the pensions of retirees are not usually fully indexed to inflation, this reduces the real purchasing power of their pensions.[2]

In other words, at least from a theoretical viewpoint, the more conservative parties, that is those on the right part of the political spectrum, appear thus to be privileged with this phenomenon of population aging, given their higher degree of (relative) aversion to inflation vis-a-vis unemployment.[3] Of interest to this assumption is the result of Scheve (2004) that inflation and unemployment have indeed a considerable impact on the public's economic objectives in a way that is generally consistent with the specification of utility/loss functions in the theoretical political economics literature.[4]

In turn, the electoral consequences of an aging population end up also having economic consequences. This is certainly the case because elections are political events with an evident economic importance, as, for instance, if we admit that, in ideological terms, the economic policies of different parties, when in power, are those that most defend the interest of their electorate basis.[5] This fact is particularly relevant in the models of the so-called partisan cycles, whether considering rational expectations (Alesina, 1987) or not (Hibbs, 1977).

Simply put, according to the vision of partisan cycles, there may be, for simplicity, two types of incumbents: one from the right-wing, *R*, for example, Republican ones in the US or Conservatives in the UK, and another of the left-wing, *D*, for example, Democrat ones in the United States or Labor in the UK, which differ in the economic objectives that are most

[1] Being certain that population aging alone should cause changes concerning the voting decisions, it is also apparent that the older population groups have become the target of specific election campaigns, especially by right-wing parties, as seems to be the case in Portugal and Italy, for example.

[2] It is certainly interesting to note that Welsch & Kühling (2015) conclude that unemployment aversion does not depend on income, whereas inflation aversion does depend on income.

[3] Note that even though the unemployment rate is relevant to an elderly -- though less relevant than the inflation rate -- especially if still of working age, the unemployment rate assumes generally higher proportions in the younger generation, and therefore should be considered more unpleasant by the youngest (Auer & Fortuny, 2000). Clearly, when the elderly are also retired, the unemployment rate seems that should loose even more (even if already lower) importance.

[4] See also Gandelman & Hernández-Murillo (2009), who found that both inflation and unemployment have a negative and similar effect on individuals' assessments of past and present well-being for themselves and their country.

[5] In this regard it is nonetheless interesting to note that some youth organizations, e.g., the US National Youth Rights Association (http://youthrights.org/issues/voting-age/, accessed on January 26, 2016) call out for lowering the voting age as it is considered that only in this case, the interests of young people would be properly taken into account as they will be relevant for policy. Going to the extreme defense of suffrage literally universal, some German associations have advocated that all children, regardless of their age, should have the right to vote in national elections, for such parents voting on their behalf (http://www.dw.com/en/germany-ponders-giving-children-the-right-to-vote/a-3470938-1, accessed on January 26, 2016). This would also be a way to combat electoral pressure put by pensioners against cutting pensions, considered to be exaggerated generous (http://www.dw.com/en/former-president-germany-turning-into-pensioner-democracy/a-3259871, accessed on January 26, 2016).

pursued. More specifically, it is considered the existence of objective functions by the possible types of incumbents as being: $L = \lambda_i\pi^2 + u^2$, $(i = R, D)$ or $U = -\lambda_i\pi^2 + y$, where π, u, and y, respectively represent the inflation rate, the unemployment rate and the product level, and λ_i is parameter such that: $\lambda_R > \lambda_D$. The argument usually considered to justify this assumption of a higher degree of inflation aversion on the part of right-wing incumbents is that there are more capital holders and more pensioners among the right-wing electorate. In economic terms, the consequences are thus evident. For such a model, lower inflation levels are to be associated to right-wing incumbents than those associated with left-wing incumbents, whereas a cycle in the output level may exist, in particular when there is an anticipated change of the incumbent's supporting party.[6]

In the tradition of Hibbs (1977) and Alesina (1987), the (former) hypothesis that the right parties are more averse to inflation is based precisely, even if in partial terms, in the fact that pensioners, traditionally more conservative in economic and political terms, are (the) most affected by inflation and not so much by unemployment, so preferring to vote for the party with a higher degree of aversion to inflation (relative to unemployment).

In terms of empirical evidence, there is also some support to the hypothesis that unemployment (relative to inflation) is of less (resp. more) concern to the elder (resp. younger) part of the electorate. As a matter of fact, the hypothesis that older voters, particularly pensioners, should favor the right-wing parties, has been effectively supported by some empirical studies as those presented below.

According to a multi-national study by Easterly & Fischer (2001), all age groups appeared more worried about inflation that young people up to 19 years. The age group most concerned about inflation consisted of the sixties immediately followed by the seventies and older (such that there are no significant difference between those groups). In accordance to the authors, the explanation for this lies in the fact that individuals in those ages tend to spend their accumulated resources and therefore do not appreciate the inherent uncertainty to inflation.

Also from a multi-country study by Van Lelyveld (1999), it was concluded that age is negatively related to the degree of aversion to unemployment. This inverse relationship also exists between the age of respondents in Germany, France, Ireland and the United Kingdom and the probability of unemployment being considered the major economic problem. This result is in agreement with the findings of Shiller (1997), which point to the fact that the elderly, particularly in Germany, are more concerned with inflation.

More recently, Jayadev (2006), also for a group of countries, has shown that young people under 20 years are those with a lower degree of aversion to inflation as well as that the right-wing supporters clearly have a greater degree of aversion to inflation. These results are broadly in accordance to those of Berlemann (2012) that, using data from 11 waves of the Eurobarometer survey, found age and political orientation to have significant effects (as theoretically expected) on the revealed preferences towards fighting inflation. Also Jayadev (2008, 2009) found that the so-called working class is more likely to consider combating unemployment rather than inflation as the economic policy's priority.

---

[6] All the legislative elections that took place in Portugal, from 1987 until 2011, were analyzed in Caleiro (2013), from a self-organizing map perspective, being precisely pointed out the especial importance of the elections that resulted in a change of the party in power.

That being said, the rest of the chapter is structured as follows: in section 2 the data is presented and briefly analyzed; section 3 offers the spatial statistics methodology, which is applied in section 4, where the results are discussed; section 5 concludes.

2. THE DATA

The legislative election that took place in Portugal in October 2015 is the one that will be considered in this chapter. Figure 1 shows the distribution of figures corresponding to the elections, according to the perspective of residents and non-residents in Portugal.

Having regard to Figure 1, a short explanation becomes necessary. Indeed, it is often stated that the electoral rolls are out of date, which is evident.[7] For example, it was estimated that the number of residents in Portugal, in late 2014, was about 10 million and 370 thousand individuals, of course not all being Portuguese. Given that only aged 18 or over are eligible to vote, i.e., electors, the number of 9 682 553 electors considered in the election under analysis seems to be clearly exaggerated. Thus, having voted 5 408 805 electors – the vast majority being residents in Portugal – it can not be considered to be trustworthy the total number of abstentionists, i.e., those that are practitioners of not getting involved politically, as being 4 273 748.

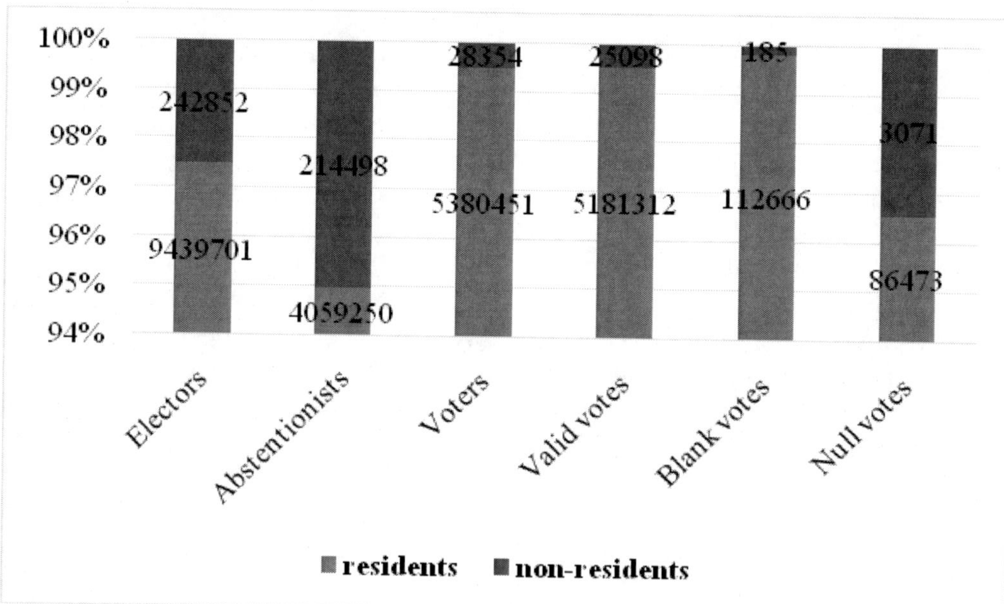

Figure 1. An overview of the numbers corresponding to the elections.

[7] Indeed, there appear to be few reasons to 'justify' this outdating on the electoral rolls, which are related to the fact that the number of members of parliament [MP] for each district is proportional to the number of registered electors enrolled in it. Also to the so-called emigration circle, i.e., the non-resident electors, reducing the number of electors could bring down the number of elected MP, which is 4 by now. Moreover, one of the criteria for a location to be considered city is the existence of a minimum of 8000 electors.

That being said, the variable of interest corresponds to the percentage of ballots obtained by each party (of those that obtained parliamentary representation) relative to the total of ballots.[8] Having this in mind, a brief explanation of the parties that will be considered in this chapter becomes necessary. Of the 20 parties or coalitions that participated in the October 2015 legislative election, only 5 of them elected members in the Parliament, and these are the subject of our study.

The coalition "Portugal Ahead" was formed by two parties, the PPD/PSD [Popular Democratic Party/Social Democrat Party] and the CDS/PP [Democratic Social Centre/People's Party]. The PPD/PSD is a liberal-conservative party. Its political position is in the centre-right. The CDS/PP is a Christian democratic and national-conservative political party. Its political position is in the centre-right to right-wing. This coalition obtained 36.86% of the ballots, with 102 members of parliament [MP, henceforth] elected. Having run isolated in the autonomous regions of the Azores and Madeira, the PPD/PSD obtained 1.50% of the ballots and elected 5 MP. The PS [Socialist Party] is a social(ist)-democratic party. Its political position is in the centre-left. It obtained 32.31% of the ballots and elected 86 MP. The BE [Left(ist) Block] is a left-wing party. It obtained 10.19% of the ballots and elected 19 MP. The CDU [Unitary Democratic Coalition] is a left-wing coalition between the PCP [Portuguese Communist Party] and the PEV [Ecologist Party "The Greens"]. It obtained 8.25% of the ballots, having elected 17 MP. The PAN [People-Animals-Nature] is a party that defends human and animal rights, also having environmental concerns. It obtained 1.39% of the ballots, having elected 1 MP.[9]

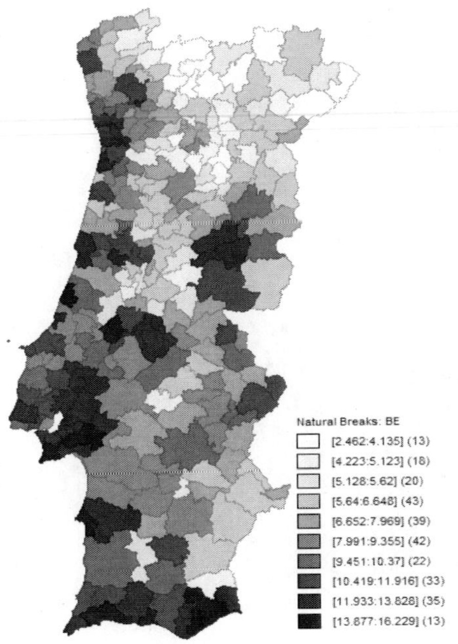

Figure 2. The BE results.

[8] Total is the sum of non-null and non-blank ballots, i.e., the sum of votes in the several parties.

[9] From now on, in the presentation of results, it will be used the alphabetical order of the name (in Portuguese) of the parties.

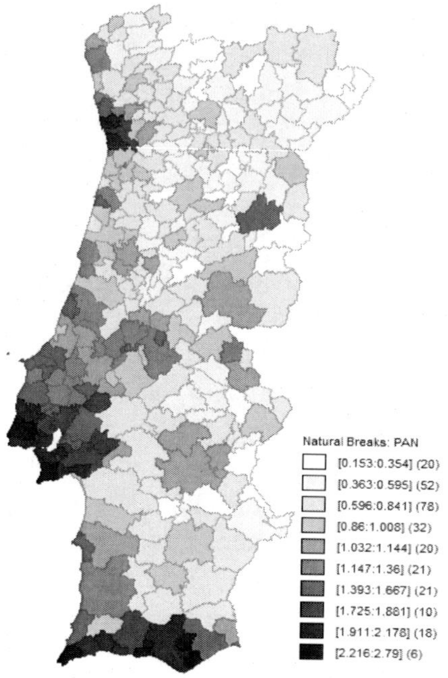

Figure 3. The PAN results.

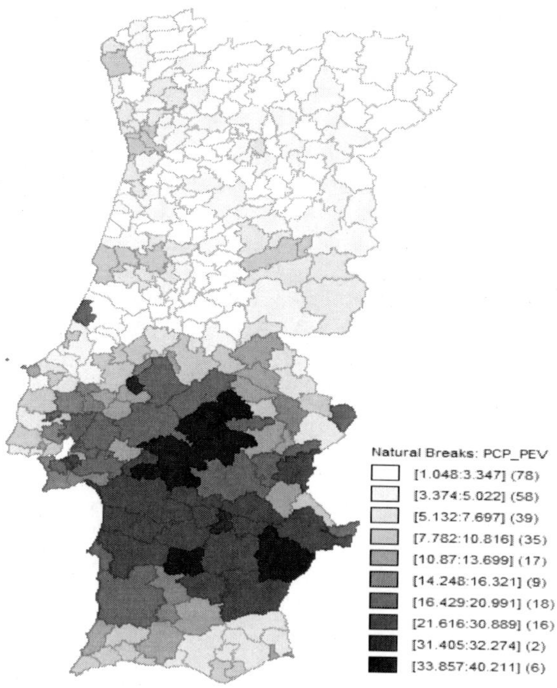

Figure 4. The PCP/PEV results.

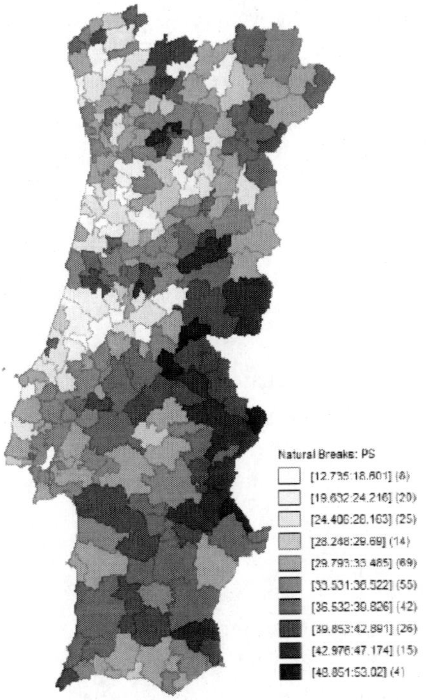

Figure 5. The PS results.

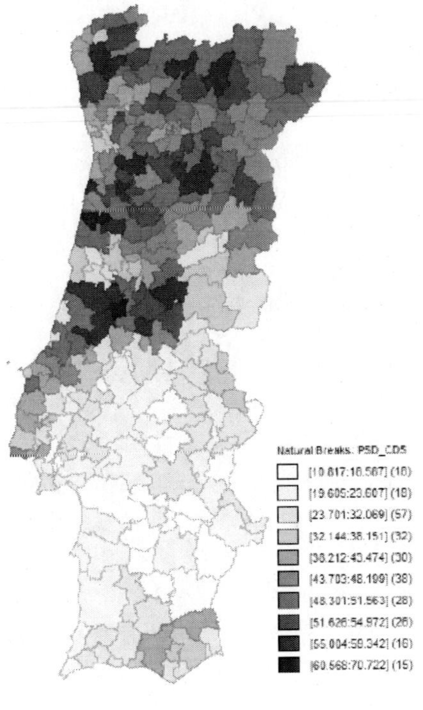

Figure 6. The PSD/CDS results.

Figures 2 to 6 present the results obtained by those parties in the municipalities of Portuguese mainland.

A visual inspection of Figures 2-6 show clear evidence of the existence of spatial clusters in the election results of all parties, eventually excluding the PS. This fact immediately calls out for the need of considering, as for the methodology, a spatial one.

3. The Spatial Statistics Methodology

If the values assumed by a given variable reflect a spatial dimension, using statistical techniques that properly reflect this dimension is advisable [see the pioneering article of Ord (1975) and/or, the so often referred manual of spatial econometrics of Anselin (1988)]. A spatial dimension can exist because, for instance due to 'contagion effects', there is a systematic spatial dependence between geographically neighboring variables.[10]

The spatial dependence may thus occur when the value assumed by the variable of interest, at a given location, depends on the value assumed by the same variable in neighboring locations. Generally speaking, that dependence relates to the existence of spatial autocorrelation, i.e., spatial clusters of similar values of the variable to be explained. In this case, this will happen when, for example, the election results obtained by the various parties in multiple locations depend on the values of those results in neighboring locations. If this is the case, the so-called spatial lag models are to be estimated, i.e.,

$$y = \mathbf{X}\beta + \rho\mathbf{W}\mathrm{y} + \varepsilon,$$

where y denotes the vector of the values assumed by the explained variable, $\mathbf{X}$ is the matrix of the values assumed by the exogenous explanatory variables, β is the vector of parameters to be estimated, ρ is the so-called spatial autoregressive parameter (also to be estimated), $\mathbf{W}$ is a matrix of spatial weights (see details further below), and ε is a vector of i.i.d. residuals.

That spatial dependency, in turn, may also result from a process of spatial diffusion of effects in the explanatory variable(s) and/or spatial dependence in the residuals, leading to some form of spatial errors model as follows

$$y = \mathbf{X}\beta + u, \text{ with } u = \lambda\mathbf{W}\mathrm{u} + \varepsilon,$$

where λ is the spatial error autocorrelation parameter.

In short, spatial dependence can assume several forms [see, among others, Anselin (2002; 2003)]. In any of these forms, the use of spatial statistical techniques may be necessary:

1. When there is a (theoretical) model that supports the existence of that kind of spatial dependence, as theoretically expected to happen with the election results (Caleiro & Guerreiro, 2005); and/or

[10] Apart from this type of spatial dependence, also the so-called spatial heterogeneity requires the use of spatial statistical techniques. Spatial heterogeneity refers to a spatial pattern in the data that results in instability, over space, of the parameters in the relationship between the variables under study. In other words, the relationship between the explained variable(s) and the explanatory variable(s) is 'location-specific' given that may vary significantly throughout the space.

2. When the spatial autocorrelation, detected at the level of spatial clusters, is confirmed by particularly suitable tests. Unfortunately, in most cases, a visual detection of spatial clusters is not an easy task. In this case (and, indeed, in any other cases) statistical tests of spatial correlation must be applied as, for example, the so-called Moran' I test, which is based on the computation of a statistic that is approximately the correlation coefficient between the values of variable under analysis, by location, and the average values that this variable assumes in neighboring locations.

In the calculation of spatial autocorrelation levels, the definition of neighborly relations is, therefore, essential. It is for example possible to define a neighborhood matrix as follows: $W = [w_{ij}]$, where $w_{ij} = 0$, if location j is not a neighbor of location i (and if $j = i$) and $w_{ij} = 1$ if location j is a neighbor of location i. Hence, an approximation to the so-called Moran's I will be given by the correlation coefficient between the values of the variable under analysis and its spatial lags, such as, for example, the average value of the neighboring observations, i.e., for all $j \neq i$ such that $w_{ij} = 1$.

In arithmetical terms, the Moran's I statistic is calculated as follows:

$$I = \frac{n}{\sum_i \sum_j w_{ij}} \frac{\sum_i \sum_j w_{ij} (x_i - \bar{x})(x_j - \bar{x})}{\sum_i (x_i - \bar{x})^2},$$

where n represents the number of spatial units/locations, identified by subscripts i and j, w_{ij} represents the spatial weights, and x represents the variable of interest, being $\bar{x}$ its average.[11]

Having regard to the aspect that the spatial distribution of election results seem to indicate, as shown in Figures 2-6, it proves to be of obvious interest to calculate the Moran's I for those election results. In terms of values, and its significance, the Moran's I assume results that confirm the impression from the visual analysis of the figures 2-6. In fact, for all parties, the value is significantly positive, being evident the existence of positive spatial autocorrelation. The values obtained were as follows:[12]

- BE Moran's $I = 0.6382$*** (z value = 18.3069)
- PAN Moran's $I = 0.7256$*** (z value = 19.8270)
- PCP-PEV Moran's $I = 0.7563$*** (z value = 18.2238)
- PPD/PSD-CDS/PP Moran's $I = 0.7384$*** (z value = 17.6647)
- PS Moran's $I = 0.4950$*** (z value = 13.0870)

These values, by confirming the existence of (positive) spatial autocorrelation require that any model that is to be statistically estimated must take account the spatial dimension of the data. This direction is reinforced by the fact that, given the nature of the variable of interest,

[11] A value close to the expected value of the Moran's I in the absence of autocorrelation, that is $-(n - 1)^{-1}$, exactly indicate this fact, given that a sufficiently high positive value indicates the existence of positive spatial autocorrelation.

[12] Since 278 municipalities are being considered, the expected value of Moran's I is $-(278-1)^{-1}$, i.e., approximately -0.0036.

there are empirical reasons for expecting the presence of a spatial dimension in the data. In what concerns these reasons, let us consider the following cases:

- First, let us consider the following motivating example indeed generally considered in detecting electoral cycles at the municipal level where the level of municipal expenditures over the mandate as decision variable is used for electoral purposes. Being those expenses associated with events covering more than one municipality, unless in case of a strategic coordination of all municipalities involved, a spatial correlation in that variable should be evident. This statistical phenomenon, observable depending on the nature of the variable of interest, cannot obviously be ignored when producing an empirical analysis of a possible election cycle, based on that decision variable at the level of these geographical units;
- Second, another motivating example based on geographical proximity as an element allowing for the occurrence of a phenomenon associated with, say, voting by comparison. Taking into account the situation in Portugal, especially with regard to municipal elections, it does not seem possible to rule out that a partial explanation of the election results in each municipality is a result of the comparison that voters make of the performance of their municipality compared to neighboring municipalities (especially when 'governed' by a different party);
- Third, another motivating example consist of the recognition that, in particular when legislative elections are to take place, the concentration of election campaigns nationwide around the major population centers or at locations of higher partisan influence, can generate spatial autocorrelation.

4. THE RESULTS

There are, of course, a variety of explanations (i.e., cultural, economic, political, social, etc.) to the results obtained by the various parties in the elections.[13] In any one of those types of explanations for the election results, the literature increasingly recognizes that the spatial location of observations corresponding to those results is a (crucial) factor to be taken into account (Beck et al., 2006; Caleiro & Guerreiro, 2005; Darmofal, 2006; O'Loughlin, 2002; 2003; Franzese & Hays, 2007; Sauerzopf & Swanstrom, 1999). Among those types we would like to point out those explanations based on demographic factors. Lesthaeghe & Neidert (2006) show that the so-called second demographic transition, for its differentiated effects throughout the territory, presents itself as explanatory of the spatial patterns of election results in the United States. Caleiro (2007) presents an analysis of the electoral consequences of population aging.

[13] For this kind of data there is a controversy, usually known as Galton's problem (Agnew, 1996; Anselin & Cho, 2002; King, 1996; 1997; and Kramer, 1983).

So, in the line of those authors, in order to achieve the objective proposed in this chapter we proceed with the (spatial) econometric estimation of a model considering as variable of interest the election results, obtained by the 5 coalitions/parties in the October 2015 election that took place in Portugal. As regards the explanatory variable, we will consider the aging index, x_1, i.e., the ratio between the number of seniors (65 and over population) and young people (0-14 years population), for the year 2014.[14]

To put clearer, it is our assumption that the aging index is a proxy for the unemployment rate, in the sense that, by hypothesis, the level of unemployment involves a higher (resp. lower) electoral cost the less (resp. more) aged is the electorate.[15] In order to make this hypothesis acceptable, Figures 7 and 8 show the unemployment rate and the aging index for the last year of data that is available.

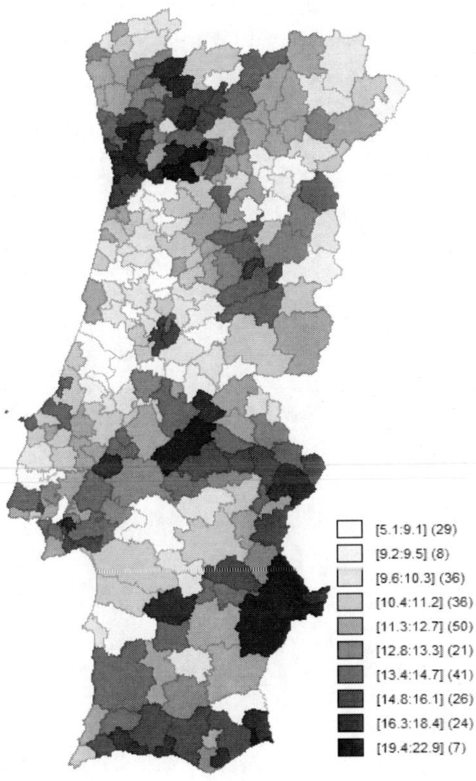

Figure 7. The unemployment rate (2011).

[14] The source of the data is the Instituto Nacional de Estatística.

[15] Note that this hypothesis also overcomes the problem due to the inexistence of data for the unemployment rate, by municipality, around October 2015. As a matter of fact, to the best of our knowledge, the last available data corresponds to that obtained at the Census 2011.

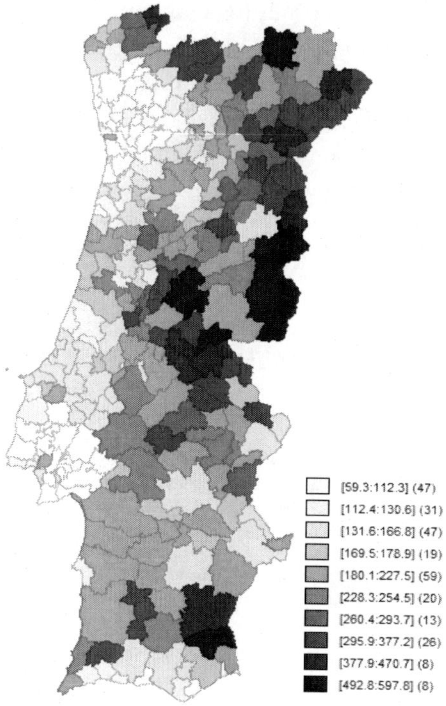

Figure 8. The aging index (2011).

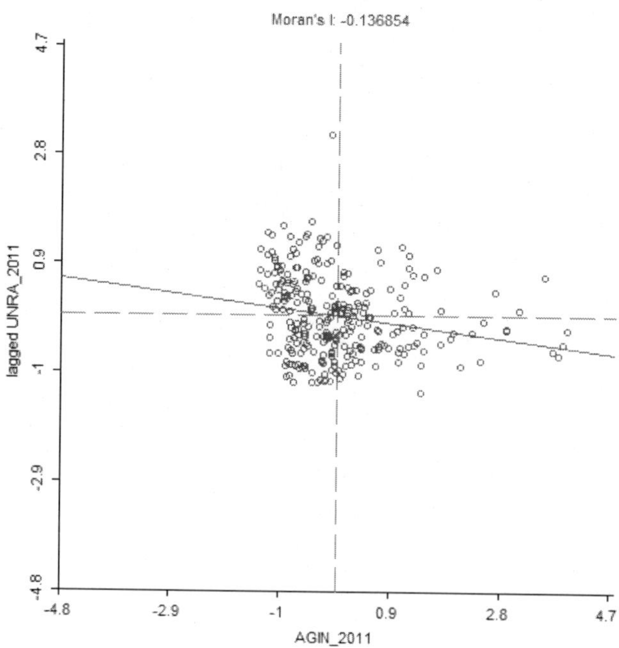

S

Figure 9. The bivariate Moran' I (aging and unemployment).

Although with some difficulty, visual analysis of figures 7 and 8 seems to indicate, as expected, the existence of a negative correlation between the unemployment rate and the aging index. This correlation is even more evident if, from the spatial point of view, the bivariate Moran's *I* is computed. The same statistic can, for easier interpretation, be determined from the graphical point of view, which represent, in standardized terms on the horizontal axis, the aging index values by municipality, and on the vertical axis, the average value of the unemployment for all neighboring municipalities.[16] See Figure 9.

Under our hypothesis, in theoretical terms, the influence of the aging index, being significant, on the election results is to be positive, in the case of centre-right parties, and, is to be negative, in the case of centre-left parties (Caleiro, 2008). This hypothesis is to be logically equivalent to that assuming that that the level of unemployment involves a higher (resp. lower) electoral cost the less (resp. more) aged is the electorate.

That being said, we will consider that spatial dependence can take two forms: spatial dependence on the explained variable, leading to a sort of spatial lags model and spatial dependence in the residuals, leading to a sort of spatial errors model. Three models were then estimated: a (OLS) non-spatial regression model, a (ML) spatial lags model and a (ML) spatial error model. The expressions corresponding to the three models are, respectively,

$$y = \beta_0 + \beta_1 x_1 + \varepsilon \qquad \text{(model 1)}$$

$$y = \beta_0 + \beta_1 x_1 + \rho W y + \varepsilon \qquad \text{(model 2)}$$

$$y = \beta_0 + \beta_1 x_1 + u, \text{ with } u = \lambda W u + \varepsilon, \qquad \text{(model 3)}$$

where y is the vector of election results, x_1 is the vector of aging index values, ε is a vector of (supposedly) i.i.d. residuals, ρ is the spatial lag autocorrelation parameter, λ is the spatial error autocorrelation parameter, and W is the so-called neighborhood matrix, i.e., a matrix of spatial weights. The results of these estimates are set out in Table 1.[17]

The first fact to note is the clear importance of the space component in the explanation of the election results of all parties, being significantly positive in all cases. Plainly, the spatial models, whether the spatial lag (2) or the spatial error (3) models outperform the non-spatial model (1). Among the spatial models, the spatial error model reveals to be the more congruent, in accordance to the AIC and BIC criteria. Due this fact, the aging index, 'loses' importance when the space component is integrated in the models, which is a statistically expected result (Franzese & Hays, 2007; Caleiro, 2008).

The third fact has to do with the confirmation of the expected sign of the coefficient measuring the influence of the aging index, as (an inverted) proxy for the unemployment rate, despite being non-significant (only) in the case of the PCP/PEV coalition. As a matter of fact, for all the (centre) left-wing coalitions/parties, the influence of aging on the election results

---

[16] It is important to highlight that these figures, as well as the Moran's *I* values and the econometric estimates, were obtained by the use of GeoDA™ 1.6.7. of Luc Anselin and associates, freely available at https://geodacenter.asu.edu/ (accessed on January 26, 2016). The use of this software requires the use of a shapefile correspondent to the Carta Administrativa Oficial de Portugal, (freely) available at http://www.dgterritorio.pt/cartografia_e_geodesia/cartografia/carta_administrativa_oficial_de_portugal__caop_/caop_em_vigor/ (accessed on January 26, 2016).

[17] See the annex for the full results.

assumes a negative value, whereas for all the (centre) right-wing coalitions/parties, the influence of aging on the election results assumes a negative value.

Table 1. The results of the econometric estimations

	β_0	β_1	ρ	λ	AIC	BIC
BE (model 1)	11.40***	-0.014***			1353.18	1360.44
BE (model 2)	3.65***	-0.008***	0.773***		1141.52	1152.40
BE (model 3)	11.41***	-0.012***		0.831***	1113.71	1120.96
PAN (model 1))	1.43***	-0.002***			366.048	373.03
PAN (model 2)	0.382***	-0.001***	0.841***		70.2185	81.1014
PAN_model (3)	1.331***	-0.002***		0.889***	51.0873	58.3425
PCP/PEV (model 1)	10.207***	-0.008*			1939.19	1946.44
PCP/PEV (model 2)	1.601***	-0.002	0.868***		1621.23	1632.12
PCP/PEV (model 3)	9.793***	-0.001		0.869***	1619.65	1626.90
PS (model 1)	30.577***	0.014***			1838.85	1846.11
PS (model 2)	8.835***	0.007**	0.050***		1720.35	1731.23
PS (model 3))	32.000***	0.008**		0.699***	1719.98	1727.3
PSD/CDS (model 1)	37.108***	0.012			2225.11	2232.36
PSD/CDS (model 2)	4.576***	0.006	0.847***		1932.96	1943.84
PSD/CDS (model 3)	35.735***	0.010**		0.032***	1929.56	1936.81

CONCLUSION

The world-wide increase in life expectancy and a decrease in fertility, which characterizes many countries, have obvious electoral consequences, since the combination of these two factors leads to greater electoral weight of the older population layer, that is to say that the probability of the voter median being older certainly increases. This, by itself, has consequences in terms of election results, with a propagation to the economic sphere but, when associated, in particular, to increase the electoral weight of pensioners, gains greater relevance.

This chapter had as main objective to introduce some of the political consequences of population aging, being reflected in the electoral costs of unemployment. Tentatively, one may conclude that the results confirm the hypothesis that the level of unemployment involves a higher (resp. lower) electoral cost the less (resp. more) aged is the electorate (Caleiro, 2007). Being those of electoral nature these costs will ultimately have reflections of an economic nature insofar as resulting in favor of more conservative parties can thus contribute to an economic policy of the incumbents that focuses more on the fight against inflation than fighting against unemployment.

Connected with that policy implication at a national level, there are also some political consequences of population aging, at a supranational level. As a matter of fact, if we admit that, in electoral terms, the political consequences of population aging will result in an added advantage of more conservative parties, then these can be extrapolated to an international level, where the economic consequences may be even more significant than those at a national level. In this respect consider, for example, the European Commission's Eurobarometers on public opinion in the European Union (European Commission, 2005a; 2005b). The fight against unemployment, as the top priority of the European Union, is mentioned more by young people, which, once again, is consistent with the theoretical and empirical results here obtained. This fact is also confirmed in European Commission (2005c), given that the fight against unemployment was considered a priority by 47% of all citizens of the European Union, and this percentage was (even) higher, 52%, for young people between 15-24 years. With regard to citizens over the age of 55 years, they tend to give more importance to fighting crime.[18]

In this chapter it was confirmed that the space component, i.e., the information corresponding to the spatial location, cannot be ignored in explanatory models of electoral results (in Portugal). Being the models, here used, quite simple they can clearly be added with other factors, namely cultural, economic, political, etc. (theoretically) considered as explaining the election results, which certainly would result in an increase of the explanatory power of these other models with regard to that considered here. This is an obvious motivation for further work. Similarly, the robustness of the results presented here may still be tested through a panel-data spatial econometrics methodology, i.e., considering other elections beyond that here considered (Franzese & Hays, 2007). In any case, it is expected that it would confirm the importance of spatial vision of electoral results (in Portugal), for which unemployment is certainly relevant (Caleiro, 2008).

ANNEX

SUMMARY OF OUTPUT: ORDINARY LEAST SQUARES ESTIMATION
Data set: nova political
Dependent Variable: BE_PERC Number of Observations: 278
Mean dependent var: 8.58208 Number of Variables: 2
S.D. dependent var: 3.08306 Degrees of Freedom: 276

R-squared: 0.210655 F-statistic: 73.657
Adjusted R-squared: 0.207795 Prob (F-statistic): 6.86229e-016
Sum squared residual: 2085.81 Log likelihood: -674.59
Sigma-square: 7.55728 Akaike info criterion: 1353.18
S.E. of regression: 2.74905 Schwarz criterion: 1360.44
Sigma-square ML: 7.50291
S.E of regression ML: 2.73914

Variable	Coefficient	Std. Error	t-Statistic	Probability
CONSTANT	11.4041	0.3678378	31.00307	0.00000
AGING_INDE	-0.01363796	0.001589068	-8.582363	0.00000

[18] Interestingly, the older population groups do not mention actually fighting inflation as the priority. In fact, as is well known, inflation levels in the EU are low enough - and substantially controlled by the European Central Bank's monetary policy - that do not represent a priority even for those population groups. In this case, apparently, some non-economic aspects, like security, are most important than the economic aspects (Blais et al., 2004). See also Howarth & Rommerskirchen (2015) for a demystification of the alleged North-South divide (of EU member-states) in what concerns inflation aversion.

REGRESSION DIAGNOSTICS
MULTICOLLINEARITY CONDITION NUMBER 4.225295
(Extreme Multicollinearity)
TEST ON NORMALITY OF ERRORS

TEST	DF	VALUE	PROB
Jarque-Bera	2	9.4708	0.00878

DIAGNOSTICS FOR HETEROSKEDASTICITY
RANDOM COEFFICIENTS

TEST	DF	VALUE	PROB
Breusch-Pagan test	1	0.6551	0.41830
Koenker-Bassett test	1	0.9161	0.33851

SPECIFICATION ROBUST TEST

TEST	DF	VALUE	PROB
White	2	21.5830	0.00002

COEFFICIENTS VARIANCE MATRIX

CONSTANT	AGING_INDE
0.135305	-0.000523
-0.000523	0.000003

SUMMARY OF OUTPUT: SPATIAL LAG MODEL - MAXIMUM LIKELIHOOD ESTIMATION

Data set: nova political
Spatial Weight: novapolitical.gal
Dependent Variable: BE_PERC Number of Observations: 278
Mean dependent var: 8.58208 Number of Variables: 3
S.D. dependent var: 3.08306 Degrees of Freedom: 275
Lag coeff. (Rho): 0.773478

R-squared: 0.689231 Log likelihood: -567.759
Sq. Correlation: - Akaike info criterion: 1141.52
Sigma-square: 2.95393 Schwarz criterion: 1152.4
S.E of regression: 1.7187

Variable	Coefficient	Std. Error	z-value	Probability
W_BE_PERC	0.773478	0.03616405	21.38804	0.00000
CONSTANT	3.652105	0.4896039	7.459305	0.00000
AGING_INDE	-0.008098127	0.001139393	-7.107407	0.00000

REGRESSION DIAGNOSTICS
DIAGNOSTICS FOR HETEROSKEDASTICITY
RANDOM COEFFICIENTS

TEST	DF	VALUE	PROB
Breusch-Pagan test	1	0.1727	0.67774

DIAGNOSTICS FOR SPATIAL DEPENDENCE
SPATIAL LAG DEPENDENCE FOR WEIGHT MATRIX: novapolitical.gal

TEST	DF	VALUE	PROB
Likelihood Ratio Test	1 213.	6628	0.00000

COEFFICIENTS VARIANCE MATRIX

CONSTANT	AGING_INDE	W_BE_PERC
0.239712	-0.000445	-0.015631
-0.000445	0.000001	0.000020
-0.015631	0.000020	0.001308

SUMMARY OF OUTPUT: SPATIAL ERROR MODEL - MAXIMUM LIKELIHOOD ESTIMATION

Data set: nova political
Spatial Weight: novapolitical.gal
Dependent Variable: BE_PERC Number of Observations: 278
Mean dependent var: 8.582079 Number of Variables: 2
S.D. dependent var: 3.083056 Degrees of Freedom: 276
Lag coeff. (Lambda): 0.831454

R-squared: 0.727329 R-squared (BUSE): -
Sq. Correlation: - Log likelihood: -554.854648
Sigma-square: 2.5918 Akaike info criterion: 1113.71
S.E of regression: 1.60991 Schwarz criterion: 1120.96

Variable	Coefficient	Std. Error	z-value	Probability
CONSTANT	11.4123	0.63112	18.08262	0.00000
AGING_INDE	-0.0122289	0.001234272 -	9.907785	0.00000
LAMBDA	0.831454	0.03485402	23.85533	0.00000

REGRESSION DIAGNOSTICS
DIAGNOSTICS FOR HETEROSKEDASTICITY
RANDOM COEFFICIENTS

TEST	DF	VALUE	PROB
Breusch-Pagan test	1	4.6566	0.03093

DIAGNOSTICS FOR SPATIAL DEPENDENCE
SPATIAL ERROR DEPENDENCE FOR WEIGHT MATRIX: novapolitical.gal

TEST	DF	VALUE	PROB

Likelihood Ratio Test	1	239.4713	0.00000

COEFFICIENTS VARIANCE MATRIX

CONSTANT	AGING_INDE	LAMBDA
0.398312	-0.000327	0.000000
-0.000327	0.000002	0.000000
0.000000	0.000000	0.001215

SUMMARY OF OUTPUT: ORDINARY LEAST SQUARES ESTIMATION
Data set: nova political
Dependent Variable: PAN_PERC Number of Observations: 278
Mean dependent var: 0.954083 Number of Variables: 2
S.D. dependent var: 0.522521 Degrees of Freedom: 276

R-squared: 0.211299 F-statistic: 73.9425
Adjusted R-squared: 0.208441 Prob (F-statistic): 6.12216e-016
Sum squared residual: 59.8639 Log likelihood: -181.024
Sigma-square: 0.216898 Akaike info criterion: 366.048
S.E. of regression: 0.465723 Schwarz criterion: 373.303
Sigma-square ML: 0.215338
S.E of regression ML: 0.464045

Variable	Coefficient	Std. Error	t-Statistic	Probability
CONSTANT	1.433094	0.06231631	22.9971	0.00000
AGING_INDE	-0.002314914	0.0002692079	-8.598983	0.00000

REGRESSION DIAGNOSTICS
MULTICOLLINEARITY CONDITION NUMBER 4.225295
TEST ON NORMALITY OF ERRORS

TEST	DF	VALUE	PROB
Jarque-Bera	2	31.1669	0.00000

DIAGNOSTICS FOR HETEROSKEDASTICITY
RANDOM COEFFICIENTS

TEST	DF	VALUE	PROB
Breusch-Pagan test	1	1.3558	0.24426
Koenker-Bassett test	1	1.2420	0.26509

COEFFICIENTS VARIANCE MATRIX

CONSTANT	AGING_INDE
0.003883	-0.000015
-0.000015	0.000000

SUMMARY OF OUTPUT: SPATIAL LAG MODEL - MAXIMUM LIKELIHOOD ESTIMATION

Data set: novapolitical
Spatial Weight: novapolitical.gal
Dependent Variable: PAN_PERC Number of Observations: 278
Mean dependent var: 0.954083 Number of Variables: 3
S.D. dependent var: 0.522521 Degrees of Freedom: 275
Lag coeff. (Rho): 0.840841

R-squared: 0.780683 Log likelihood: -32.1093
Sq. Correlation: - Akaike info criterion: 70.2185
Sigma-square: 0.0598798 Schwarz criterion: 81.1014
S.E of regression: 0.244703

Variable	Coefficient	Std. Error	z-value	Probability
W_PAN_PERC	0.8408408	0.02867307	29.32511	0.00000
CONSTANT	0.3820676	0.05520615	6.920745	0.00000
AGING_INDE	-0.00109863	0.0001620929	-6.77778	0.00000

REGRESSION DIAGNOSTICS
DIAGNOSTICS FOR HETEROSKEDASTICITY
RANDOM COEFFICIENTS

TEST	DF	VALUE	PROB
Breusch-Pagan test	1	2.6762	0.10186

DIAGNOSTICS FOR SPATIAL DEPENDENCE
SPATIAL LAG DEPENDENCE FOR WEIGHT MATRIX: novapolitical.gal

TEST	DF	VALUE	PROB
Likelihood Ratio Test	1	297.8291	0.00000

COEFFICIENTS VARIANCE MATRIX

CONSTANT	AGING_INDE	W_PAN_PERC
0.003048	-0.000008	-0.001274
-0.000008	0.000000	0.000002
-0.001274	0.000002	0.000822

SUMMARY OF OUTPUT: SPATIAL ERROR MODEL - MAXIMUM LIKELIHOOD ESTIMATION

Data set: novapolitical
Spatial Weight: novapolitical.gal
Dependent Variable: PAN_PERC Number of Observations: 278
Mean dependent var: 0.954083 Number of Variables: 2
S.D. dependent var: 0.522521 Degrees of Freedom: 276
Lag coeff. (Lambda): 0.888523

R-squared: 0.802011 R-squared (BUSE): -
Sq. Correlation: - Log likelihood: -23.543645
Sigma-square: 0.0540566 Akaike info criterion: 51.0873
S.E of regression: 0.232501 Schwarz criterion: 58.3425

Variable	Coefficient	Std. Error	z-value	Probability
CONSTANT	1.330603	0.1310833	10.15082	0.00000
AGING_INDE	-0.001592659	0.0001787439	-8.910287	0.00000
LAMBDA	0.8885228	0.0265597	33.4538	0.00000

REGRESSION DIAGNOSTICS
DIAGNOSTICS FOR HETEROSKEDASTICITY
RANDOM COEFFICIENTS

TEST	DF	VALUE	PROB
Breusch-Pagan test	1	0.4413	0.50648

DIAGNOSTICS FOR SPATIAL DEPENDENCE
SPATIAL ERROR DEPENDENCE FOR WEIGHT MATRIX: novapolitical.gal

TEST	DF	VALUE	PROB
Likelihood Ratio Test	1	314.9604	0.00000

SUMMARY OF OUTPUT: ORDINARY LEAST SQUARES ESTIMATION
Data set: novapolitical
Dependent Variable: PCP_PEV_PE Number of Observations: 278
Mean dependent var: 8.56552 Number of Variables: 2
S.D. dependent var: 7.90164 Degrees of Freedom: 276

R-squared: 0.010847 F-statistic: 3.02653
Adjusted R-squared: 0.007263 Prob(F-statistic): 0.0830281
Sum squared residual: 17168.9 Log likelihood: -967.595
Sigma-square: 62.2063 Akaike info criterion: 1939.19
S.E. of regression: 7.8871 Schwarz criterion: 1946.44
Sigma-square ML: 61.7587
S.E of regression ML: 7.85867

Variable	Coefficient	Std. Error	t-Statistic	Probability
CONSTANT	10.20671	1.055336	9.671528	0.00000
AGING_INDE	-0.007931386	0.004559076	-1.739692	0.08303

REGRESSION DIAGNOSTICS
MULTICOLLINEARITY CONDITION NUMBER 4.225295
(Extreme Multicollinearity)
TEST ON NORMALITY OF ERRORS

TEST	DF	VALUE	PROB
Jarque-Bera	2	275.2819	0.00000

DIAGNOSTICS FOR HETEROSKEDASTICITY
RANDOM COEFFICIENTS

TEST	DF	VALUE	PROB
Breusch-Pagan test	1	0.1521	0.69658
Koenker-Bassett test	1	0.0589	0.80830

COEFFICIENTS VARIANCE MATRIX

CONSTANT	AGING_INDE
1.113734	-0.004301
-0.004301	0.000021

SUMMARY OF OUTPUT: SPATIAL LAG MODEL - MAXIMUM LIKELIHOOD ESTIMATION

Data set: novapolitical
Spatial Weight: novapolitical.gal
Dependent Variable: PCP_PEV_PE Number of Observations: 278
Mean dependent var: 8.56552 Number of Variables: 3
S.D. dependent var: 7.90164 Degrees of Freedom: 275
Lag coeff. (Rho): 0.867734

R-squared: 0.751460 Log likelihood: -807.616
Sq. Correlation: - Akaike info criterion: 1621.23
Sigma-square: 15.5178 Schwarz criterion: 1632.12
S.E of regression: 3.93927

Variable	Coefficient	Std. Error	z-value	Probability
W_PCP_PEV_PE	0.8677338	0.02968612	29.23029	0.00000
CONSTANT	1.60088	0.6133369	2.610115	0.00905
AGING_INDE	-0.001602714	0.002281194	-0.7025765	0.48232

REGRESSION DIAGNOSTICS
DIAGNOSTICS FOR HETEROSKEDASTICITY
RANDOM COEFFICIENTS

TEST	DF	VALUE	PROB
Breusch-Pagan test	1	0.0365	0.84842

DIAGNOSTICS FOR SPATIAL DEPENDENCE
SPATIAL LAG DEPENDENCE FOR WEIGHT MATRIX: novapolitical.gal

TEST	DF	VALUE	PROB
Likelihood Ratio Test	1	319.9563	0.00000

COEFFICIENTS VARIANCE MATRIX

CONSTANT	AGING_INDE	W_PCP_PEV_PE
0.376182	-0.001116	-0.009310
-0.001116	0.000005	0.000004
-0.009310	0.000004	0.000881

SUMMARY OF OUTPUT: SPATIAL ERROR MODEL - MAXIMUM LIKELIHOOD ESTIMATION

Data set: novapolitical
Spatial Weight: novapolitical.gal
Dependent Variable: PCP_PEV_PE Number of Observations: 278
Mean dependent var: 8.565518 Number of Variables: 2
S.D. dependent var: 7.901644 Degrees of Freedom: 276
Lag coeff. (Lambda): 0.868939

R-squared: 0.751351 R-squared (BUSE): -
Sq. Correlation: - Log likelihood: -807.822554
Sigma-square: 15.5247 Akaike info criterion: 1619.65
S.E of regression: 3.94014 Schwarz criterion: 1626.9

Variable	Coefficient	Std. Error	z-value	Probability
CONSTANT	9.7928	1.91921	5.102517	0.00000
AGING_INDE	-0.0008553991	0.003027287	-0.282563	0.77751
LAMBDA	0.8689395	0.02955498	29.40078	0.00000

REGRESSION DIAGNOSTICS
DIAGNOSTICS FOR HETEROSKEDASTICITY
RANDOM COEFFICIENTS

TEST	DF	VALUE	PROB
Breusch-Pagan test	1	0.0120	0.91261

DIAGNOSTICS FOR SPATIAL DEPENDENCE
SPATIAL ERROR DEPENDENCE FOR WEIGHT MATRIX: novapolitical.gal

TEST	DF	VALUE	PROB
Likelihood Ratio Test	1	319.5442	0.00000

COEFFICIENTS VARIANCE MATRIX

CONSTANT	AGING_INDE	LAMBDA
3.683366	-0.001990	0.000000
-0.001990	0.000009	0.000000
0.000000	0.000000	0.000873

SUMMARY OF OUTPUT: ORDINARY LEAST SQUARES ESTIMATION
Data set: novapolitical
Dependent Variable: PS_PERC Number of Observations: 278
Mean dependent var: 33.4371 Number of Variables: 2
S.D. dependent var: 6.71595 Degrees of Freedom: 276

R-squared: 0.045589 F-statistic: 13.1835
Adjusted R-squared: 0.042131 Prob(F-statistic): 0.00033656
Sum squared residual: 11967.3 Log likelihood: -917.426
Sigma-square: 43.3597 Akaike info criterion: 1838.85
S.E. of regression: 6.58481 Schwarz criterion: 1846.11
Sigma-square ML: 43.0478
S.E of regression ML: 6.56108

Variable	Coefficient	Std. Error	t-Statistic	Probability
CONSTANT	30.57737	0.8810836	34.70428	0.00000
AGING_INDE	0.01382034	0.003806301	3.63091	0.00034

REGRESSION DIAGNOSTICS
MULTICOLLINEARITY CONDITION NUMBER 4.225295
TEST ON NORMALITY OF ERRORS

TEST	DF	VALUE	PROB
Jarque-Bera	2	9.6399	0.00807

DIAGNOSTICS FOR HETEROSKEDASTICITY
RANDOM COEFFICIENTS

TEST	DF	VALUE	PROB
Breusch-Pagan test	1	6.9063	0.00859
Koenker-Bassett test	1	5.6326	0.01763

COEFFICIENTS VARIANCE MATRIX

CONSTANT	AGING_INDE
0.776308	-0.002998
-0.002998	0.000014

SUMMARY OF OUTPUT: SPATIAL LAG MODEL - MAXIMUM LIKELIHOOD ESTIMATION

Data set: novapolitical
Spatial Weight: novapolitical.gal
Dependent Variable: PS_PERC Number of Observations: 278
Mean dependent var: 33.4371 Number of Variables: 3
S.D. dependent var: 6.71595 Degrees of Freedom: 275
Lag coeff. (Rho): 0.693179

R-squared: 0.452536 Log likelihood: -857.173
Sq. Correlation: - Akaike info criterion: 1720.35
Sigma-square: 24.6928 Schwarz criterion: 1731.23
S.E of regression: 4.96919

Variable	Coefficient	Std. Error	z-value	Probability
W_PS_PERC	0.6931788	0.05034193	13.76941	0.00000
CONSTANT	8.834797	1.717141	5.145063	0.00000
AGING_INDE	0.007272713	0.002923052	2.488055	0.01284

REGRESSION DIAGNOSTICS
DIAGNOSTICS FOR HETEROSKEDASTICITY
RANDOM COEFFICIENTS

TEST	DF	VALUE	PROB
Breusch-Pagan test	1	30.1422	0.00000

DIAGNOSTICS FOR SPATIAL DEPENDENCE
SPATIAL LAG DEPENDENCE FOR WEIGHT MATRIX: novapolitical.gal

TEST	DF	VALUE	PROB
Likelihood Ratio Test	1	120.5055	0.00000

COEFFICIENTS VARIANCE MATRIX

CONSTANT	AGING_INDE	W_PS_PERC
2.948573	-0.000850	-0.079701
-0.000850	0.000009	-0.000027
-0.079701	-0.000027	0.002534

SUMMARY OF OUTPUT: SPATIAL ERROR MODEL - MAXIMUM LIKELIHOOD ESTIMATION

Data set: novapolitical
Spatial Weight: novapolitical.gal
Dependent Variable: PS_PERC Number of Observations: 278
Mean dependent var: 33.437129 Number of Variables: 2
S.D. dependent var: 6.715954 Degrees of Freedom: 276
Lag coeff. (Lambda): 0.699395

R-squared: 0.450866 R-squared (BUSE): -
Sq. Correlation: - Log likelihood: -857.989447
Sigma-square: 24.7681 Akaike info criterion: 1719.98
S.E of regression: 4.97676 Schwarz criterion: 1727.23

Variable	Coefficient	Std. Error	z-value	Probability
CONSTANT	32.00026	1.268444	25.22797	0.00000
AGING_INDE	0.008108402	0.003749259	2.162668	0.03057
LAMBDA	0.6993955	0.05046452	13.85915	0.00000

REGRESSION DIAGNOSTICS
DIAGNOSTICS FOR HETEROSKEDASTICITY
RANDOM COEFFICIENTS

TEST	DF	VALUE	PROB
Breusch-Pagan test	1	28.5565	0.00000

DIAGNOSTICS FOR SPATIAL DEPENDENCE
SPATIAL ERROR DEPENDENCE FOR WEIGHT MATRIX: novapolitical.gal

TEST	DF	VALUE	PROB
Likelihood Ratio Test	1	118.8735	0.00000

COEFFICIENTS VARIANCE MATRIX

CONSTANT	AGING_INDE	LAMBDA
1.608949	-0.002959	0.000000
-0.002959	0.000014	0.000000
0.000000	0.000000	0.002547

SUMMARY OF OUTPUT: ORDINARY LEAST SQUARES ESTIMATION
Data set: novapolitical
Dependent Variable: PPD_PSD_C2 Number of Observations: 278
Mean dependent var: 39.6826 Number of Variables: 2
S.D. dependent var: 13.2059 Degrees of Freedom: 276

R-squared: 0.009558 F-statistic: 2.66343
Adjusted R-squared: 0.005969 Prob(F-statistic): 0.103819
Sum squared residual: 48018.5 Log likelihood: -1110.55
Sigma-square: 173.98 Akaike info criterion: 2225.11
S.E. of regression: 13.1902 Schwarz criterion: 2232.36
Sigma-square ML: 172.729
S.E of regression ML: 13.1426

Variable	Coefficient	Std. Error	t-Statistic	Probability
CONSTANT	37.10776	1.764914	21.02525	0.00000
AGING_INDE	0.01244315	0.007624469	1.632003	0.10382

REGRESSION DIAGNOSTICS
MULTICOLLINEARITY CONDITION NUMBER 4.225295
(Extreme Multicollinearity)
TEST ON NORMALITY OF ERRORS

TEST	DF	VALUE	PROB
Jarque-Bera	2	7.7600	0.02065

DIAGNOSTICS FOR HETEROSKEDASTICITY
RANDOM COEFFICIENTS

TEST	DF	VALUE	PROB
Breusch-Pagan test	1	0.0925	0.76099
Koenker-Bassett test	1	0.1564	0.69251

COEFFICIENTS VARIANCE MATRIX

CONSTANT	AGING_INDE
3.114922	-0.012029
-0.012029	0.000058

SUMMARY OF OUTPUT: SPATIAL LAG MODEL - MAXIMUM LIKELIHOOD ESTIMATION

Data set: novapolitical
Spatial Weight: novapolitical.gal
Dependent Variable: PPD_PSD_C2 Number of Observations: 278
Mean dependent var: 39.6826 Number of Variables: 3
S.D. dependent var: 13.2059 Degrees of Freedom: 275
Lag coeff. (Rho): 0.847186

R-squared: 0.722283 Log likelihood: -963.478
Sq. Correlation: - Akaike info criterion: 1932.96
Sigma-square: 48.4326 Schwarz criterion: 1943.84
S.E of regression: 6.95935

Variable	Coefficient	Std. Error	z-value	Probability
W_PPD_PSD_C2	0.8471862	0.03247527	26.08711	0.00000
CONSTANT	4.575817	1.462566	3.128622	0.00176
AGING_INDE	0.005895899	0.004053285	1.454598	0.14578

REGRESSION DIAGNOSTICS
DIAGNOSTICS FOR HETEROSKEDASTICITY
RANDOM COEFFICIENTS

TEST	DF	VALUE	PROB
Breusch-Pagan test	1	5.4665	0.01938

DIAGNOSTICS FOR SPATIAL DEPENDENCE
SPATIAL LAG DEPENDENCE FOR WEIGHT MATRIX: novapolitical.gal

TEST	DF	VALUE	PROB
Likelihood Ratio Test	1	294.1530	0.00000

COEFFICIENTS VARIANCE MATRIX

CONSTANT	AGING_INDE	W_PPD_PSD_C2
2.139100	-0.002789	-0.036626
-0.002789	0.000016	-0.000016
-0.036626	-0.000016	0.001055

SUMMARY OF OUTPUT: SPATIAL ERROR MODEL - MAXIMUM LIKELIHOOD ESTIMATION

Data set: novapolitical
Spatial Weight: novapolitical.gal
Dependent Variable: PPD_PSD_C2 Number of Observations: 278
Mean dependent var: 39.682550 Number of Variables: 2
S.D. dependent var: 13.205883 Degrees of Freedom: 276
Lag coeff. (Lambda): 0.849226

R-squared: 0.724117 R-squared (BUSE): -
Sq. Correlation: - Log likelihood: 962.779673
Sigma-square: 48.1127 Akaike info criterion: 1929.56
S.E of regression: 6.93633 Schwarz criterion: 1936.81

Variable	Coefficient	Std. Error	z-value	Probability
CONSTANT	35.73464	2.988509	11.95735	0.00000
AGING_INDE	0.0100386	0.005324167	1.885477	0.05937
LAMBDA	0.8492262	0.03240514	26.20652	0.00000

REGRESSION DIAGNOSTICS
DIAGNOSTICS FOR HETEROSKEDASTICITY
RANDOM COEFFICIENTS

TEST	DF	VALUE	PROB
Breusch-Pagan test	1	6.6281	0.01004

DIAGNOSTICS FOR SPATIAL DEPENDENCE
SPATIAL ERROR DEPENDENCE FOR WEIGHT MATRIX: novapolitical.gal

TEST	DF	VALUE	PROB
Likelihood Ratio Test	1	295.5489	0.00000

COEFFICIENTS VARIANCE MATRIX

CONSTANT	AGING_INDE	LAMBDA
8.931183	-0.006112	0.000000
-0.006112	0.000028	0.000000
0.000000	0.000000	0.001050

REFERENCES

Agnew, J. (1996). Mapping politics: how context counts in electoral geography. *Political Geography*, *15*, 129-146.

Alesina, A. (1987). Macroeconomic Policy in a Two-Party System as a Repeated Game. *The Quarterly Journal of Economics*, *CII*, August, 651-678.

Anselin, L. (1988). Spatial econometrics: methods and models. Dordrecht: Kluwer Academic.

Anselin, L. (2002). Under the hood: Issues in the specification and interpretation of spatial regression models. *Agricultural Economics*, *17*(3), 247-267.

Anselin, L. & Cho, W. (2002). Spatial effects and ecological inference. *Political Analysis*, *10*(3), 276-297.

Anselin, L. (2003). Spatial externalities, spatial multipliers and spatial econometrics. *International Regional Science Review, 26*(2), 153-166.

Auer, P. & Fortuny, M. (2000). *Ageing of the labour force in OECD countries: Economic and social consequences*. Geneva: International Labour Office.

Beck, N., Gleditsch, K. S. & Beardsley, K. (2006). Space is more than Geography: Using spatial econometrics in the study of political economy. *International Studies Quarterly*, *50*, 27-44.

Berlemann, M. (2012). Who Cares about Inflation? Empirical Evidence from the Czech Republic. *Czech Economic Review*, (3), 225-243.

Blais, A., Turgeon, M., Gidengil, E., Nevitte, N. & Nadeau, R. (2004). Which matters most? Comparing the impact of issues and the economy in American, British and Canadian elections. *British Journal of Political Science*, *34*(03), 555-563.

Caleiro, A. & Guerreiro, G. (2005). Understanding the election results in Portugal: a spatial econometrics point of view. *Portuguese Economic Journal*, *4*(3), 207-228.

Caleiro, A. (2007). Acerca das consequências políticas do envelhecimento populacional: Uma visão económica. In *Livro de Actas das VIII Jornadas do Departamento de Sociologia,* (pp. 75-85). Évora: Universidade de Évora.

Caleiro, A. (2008). Uma perspectiva demográfico-espacial dos resultados eleitorais em Portugal. In*Livro de Actas do XIV Congresso da Associação Portuguesa para o Desenvolvimento Regional,* (pp. 48-69), APDR, Outubro, Coimbra: APDR.

Caleiro, A. (2013). A Self-Organizing Map of the Elections in Portugal. *The IIOAB Journal, Special Issue (Neuroscience in Economic Decision Making)*, *4*(3), April-June, 9-14.

Darmofal, D. (2006). The political geography of macro-level turnout in American political development. *Political Geography*, *25*, 123-150.

Easterly, W. & Fischer, S. (2001). Inflation and the poor. *Journal of Money, Credit and Banking*, *33*(2), May, 159-178.

European Commission, (2005a). Standard Eurobarometer 62: Public opinion in the European Union, May.

European Commission, (2005b). Standard Eurobarometer 63: Public opinion in the European Union, September.

European Commission, (2005c). "Youth takes the floor": Young Europeans' concerns and expectations as to the development of the European Union. December.

Franzese, R. & Hays, J. (2007). Spatial Econometric Models of Cross-Sectional Interdependence in Political Science Panel and Time-Series-Cross-Section Data. *Political Analysis*, *15*(2), 140-164.

Gandelman, N. & Hernández-Murillo, R. (2009). The impact of inflation and unemployment on subjective personal and country evaluations. *Federal Reserve Bank of St. Louis Review, May/June*, *91*(3), 107-26.

Hibbs, Jr. D. A. (1977). Political Parties and Macroeconomic Policy. *The American Political Science Review*, *71*, December, 1467-1487.

Howarth, D. & Rommerskirchen, C. (2015). Inflation Aversion in the European Union: Exploring the Myth of a North-South Divide.

Jayadev, A. (2006). Differing preferences between anti-inflation and anti-unemployment policy among the rich and the poor. *Economics Letters*, *91*(1), 67-71.

Jayadev, A. (2008). The class content of preferences towards anti-inflation and anti-unemployment policies. *International Review of Applied Economics*, *22*(2), 161-172.

Jayadev, A. (2009). Income, Class and Preferences towards Anti-Inflation and Anti-Unemployment Policies. *Beyond Inflation Targeting: Assessing the Impacts and Policy Alternatives*, 71.

King, G. (1996). Why context should not count. *Political Geography, 15*, 159-164.

King, G. (1997). *A solution to the ecological inference problem: reconstructing individual behavior from aggregate data*. Princeton: Princeton University Press.

Kramer, G. (1983). The ecological fallacy revisited: aggregate- versus individual-level findings on economics and elections, and sociotropic voting. *The American Political Science Review*, *77*(1), 92-107.

Lesthaeghe, R. J. & Neidert, L. (2006). The Second Demographic Transition in the United States: Exception or Textbook Example? *Population and Development Review*, *32*(4), 669-698.

O'Loughlin, J. (2002). The electoral geography of Weimar Germany: exploratory spatial data analysis (ESDA) of protestant support for the Nazi party. *Political Analysis*, *11*(4), 217-243.

O'Loughlin, J. (2003). Spatial analysis in political geography. *A companion to political geography*, 30-46.

Ord, K. (1975). Estimation methods for models of spatial interaction. *Journal of the American Statistical Association*, *70*, 120-126.

Rubenson, D., Blais, A., Fournier, P., Gidengil, E. & Nevitte, N. (2004). Accounting for the age gap in turnout. *Acta Politica*, *39*(4), 407-421.

Sauerzopf, R. & Swanstrom, T. (1999). The urban electorate in presidential elections 1920-1996. *Urban Affairs Review*, *35*(1), 72-91.

Scheve, K. (2004). Public inflation aversion and the political economy of macroeconomic policymaking. *International Organization*, *58*(01), 1-34.

Shiller, R. J. (1997). Why do people dislike inflation? In *Reducing inflation: Motivation and strategy,* (pp. 13-70). Chicago: University of Chicago Press.

Van Lelyveld, I. (1999). Inflation or unemployment? Who cares? *European Journal of Political Economy*, *15*(3), 463-484.

Welsch, H. & Kühling, J. (2015). Macroeconomic Preferences by Income and Education Level: Evidence from Subjective Well-Being Data. *Review of Economics & Finance*, *5*, 15-32.

In: Unemployment
Editor: Tabitha Fletcher

ISBN: 978-1-63485-181-7

Chapter 7

ON THE SOCIAL ASPECTS OF UNEMPLOYMENT: THE CASE OF LIFE SATISFACTION

António Bento Caleiro*
Department of Economics, University of Évora, Portugal

ABSTRACT

Unemployment is related to economic, political and social aspects. One of the least analysed social aspects is the relationship between unemployment and the (individual) perceived levels of well-being, such as life satisfaction or happiness. This chapter complements previous work on the subject, using a panel-data econometrics methodology to analyze the relationship between unemployment and life satisfaction in a wide range of countries worldwide. The results confirm that unemployment has a negative effect, statistically significant, on life satisfaction, either for men or for women.

Keywords: economy wide countries, life satisfaction, panel data, unemployment

JEL classification: C23, E24, I31, O50

1. INTRODUCTION

Unemployment is related to economic, political and social aspects. One of the least analysed social aspects is the relationship between unemployment and the (individual) perceived levels of well-being, such as life satisfaction or happiness. It being understood that life satisfaction is not quite the same as happiness, there is, of course, a close relationship between these two concepts. As a matter of fact, being considered that happiness and life satisfaction are indistinguishable, some prefer to analyze the more comprehensive notion of

---

* caleiro@uevora.pt.

subjective wellbeing (Angner, 2010; Blanchflower, 2001;[1] Blanchflower& Oswald, 2004; Diener, 2009; Diener et al., 1993; 1995a; 1995b; 1999; Eggers et al., 2006; Fahey & Smyth, 2004; Ferrer-i-Carbonell, 2005; Helliwell, 2003; 2006; Hudson, 2006; Ingleheart, 1996; Kahneman et al., 2004; Kahneman & Krueger, 2006; Senik, 2009; and Theodossiou, 1998).

On the other hand, there are those who consider it important to draw attention to the fact that life satisfaction does not match exactly or necessarily to happiness. Generally speaking, the distinction is based upon the fact that, whereas life satisfaction refers to a cognitive assessment of the individual's life, happiness refers to the presence of positive emotions or affects and/or absence of negative ones.[2] This makes possible, for instance, not being particularly satisfied with one's life, for instance because of being unemployed, but, at the same time, being reasonably happy because the unemployment rate is low.

That being said, for our purposes it is likely to be motivating to begin by referring to the, so called, Happiness Economics viewpoint in order to proceed with the life satisfaction approach, which will be the main topic in this chapter.

Apparently, even before the economists, psychologists began to be interested by the positive emotions, including happiness, around the 1950's (Wilson, 1967; van Hoorn, 2007). At the same time, it began to exist a greater focus on the individual subjective matters (Diener et al. 1999).[3] The integration of psychological insights into economic models of behavior, due to the interest of some notable economists, notably Daniel Kahnemann, Amos Tversky or Herbert Simon, on the psychological vision of individual behavior, soon created new economics branches, such as behavioural economics or economic psychology. In this sense it is not surprising that happiness started to be analysed not only by (social) psychologists, sociologists, anthropologists but also by economists. From these different perspectives it comes out the conclusion that the level of happiness is related to economic aspects, but that there are certainly other important factors.

In general, happiness seems to depend on: (*i*) personality factors – i.e. personality matters (Steel & Ones, 2007); (*ii*) contextual and situational factors[4] – for example, the level of health,[5] as well as being married (Blanchflower & Oswald, 2004); (*iii*) demographic factors – for example, women tend to be happier than men, and the level of happiness tends to follow a u-shaped curve with age (Theodossiou, 1998); (*iv*) institutional factors – for example, the level of democracy (Radcliff, 2001), the enforcement of the rule of law, or even the level of social capital (Helliwell, 2006);[6] (*v*) environmental factors; and (*vi*) economic factors such as,

---

[1] Of importance to this chapter is the conclusion that the unemployed were found to be particularly unhappy on two well-being measures.

[2] For an interesting view on this matter, see Max Roser (2015) – 'Happiness and Life Satisfaction'. Published online at OurWorldInData.org. Retrieved on January 26, 2016 from: http://ourworldindata.org/data /economic-development-work-standard-of-living/ happiness-and-life-satisfaction/[Online Resource].

[3] Interestingly, one of the most prolific psychologists in the field, Ed Diener, is a co-autor of an economist, Daniel Kahneman - in fact, his training is also psychology - which received the Nobel Prize for Economics in 2002, specifically for his work in the area of economic psychology. See, for example, Kahneman et al. (1999).

[4] Diener et al. (1995a) show that culture itself can be important, as there are people who, by their cultural habits, more easily declare themselves to be happy.

[5] Interestingly, Ruhm (2003) presents some evidence favoring the hypothesis that economic expansions cause a decrease in health status (and therefore, in this way, can be harmful in terms of welfare).

[6] Vemuri & Constanza (2006) considered the role of human, social, built and natural capital, in determining the level of social welfare. Also Bell & Blanchflower (2007) showed that, in addition to the fact that Scots are relatively sicker and less happy than the other inhabitants of the United Kingdom, a region of Scotland (Strathclyde), where the level of capital is lower -- being true that from this point of view, the levels of capital

for example, unemployment (Blanchflower & Oswald, 2004; Caleiro, 2011; 2012; Theodossiou, 1998).

In what concerns unemployment it is to highlight that Wolfers (2003) showed that unemployment has an impact 4.7 times greater than that of inflation. Di Tella et al. (2003) argue that the costs of recessions should include, for example, the cost on happiness resulting from high levels of unemployment. Di Tella & MacCulloch (2005) used data for happiness to show that, in fact, leftist sympathizers are more dissatisfied with unemployment (vis-à-vis inflation) than those on the right. See also Clark & Oswald (2004).

Quite recently, as well as happiness, life satisfaction, while subjective measures of well-being, has earned the attention of some economic approaches. Apparently, both happiness and life satisfaction depend on many economic -- among others (for political ones, see Radcliff (2001); for a vast group see Bjørnskov et al. (2008) -- aspects (Easterlin et al., 2012) and, by means of several channels, such as aspiration, motivation, and/or expectations, are themselves important to economic performance.[7]

In what concerns life satisfaction, the literature supports the hypothesis of an inverse relationship to unemployment (Kassenboehmer & Haisken-DeNew, 2009). Considering the most recent studies on the matter, one may refer to Martella & Maass (2000) that, for Italy, concluded that unemployed indeed showed lower life satisfaction, self-esteem, and happiness than employed (or students), but both collectivism and time structure exert influence in those effects, as life satisfaction was lower among unemployed from northern Italy (where individualistic norms are more prevalent) than from southern Italy (where more collectivist norms tend to exist) and that, among unemployed, life satisfaction tended to be higher among those with good time-structure abilities.

By the use of 11 waves of German panel data, Clark et al. (2001) also concluded that life satisfaction is lower for the current unemployed (relative to the employed) but also for those that, in the past, registered higher levels of unemployment.[8] This latter result indicates that the experience of unemployment may change the baseline for life satisfaction (Lucas et al., 2004; Fujita & Diener, 2005). A test of this baseline hypothesis for life satisfaction was performed by Clark et al. (2008), that, using 20 waves of German panel data, could not reject the hypothesis of complete adaptation to several events affecting lie satisfaction, such as marriage, divorce, widowhood, birth of child and layoff, but little evidence of adaptation to unemployment for men, who are, to some extent, more affected by unemployment than are women. Besides this difference due to gender, the ethical/moral characteristics of individuals may also be relevant in the diminishment of life satisfaction. Boyce et al. (2010) concluded that, after 3 years of unemployment, individuals high in conscientiousness experience a higher decrease in life satisfaction than those at low levels.

---

in Scotland are not significantly lower than in the UK -- it is also the one that has lower levels of happiness and health.

[7] Luechinger et al. (2010) analyze the life satisfaction gap between the public and the private sector in a multi-country perspective and conclude that the sensitivity of subjective well-being to fluctuations in unemployment rates is much lower in the public sector than in the private. This suggests that increased economic insecurity constitutes an important welfare loss associated with high general unemployment. In this sense, job-satisfaction is to be related with life-satisfaction (Judge & Watanabe, 1993).

[8] Jürges (2007) shows some evidence of (past) unemployed being under-reported, particularly by individuals with diminished labor force attachment, such as women with children or individuals who are close to being retired.

Some of the previous studies were empirical but there is still an evident lack of multi-countries analysis of the eventual relationship between unemployment and life satisfaction (Bjørnskov et al., 2008; Gallie & Russell, 1998; Schyns, 2002). Hence, it is a purpose of this chapter to fill part of this gap in the literature. In doing so, we will contribute for the understanding of the vast importance of economic policies designed to reduce unemployment, given their positive influence on life satisfaction. To achieve this objective, the rest of the chapter is structured as follows: Section 2 presents the data, Section 3 applies a panel data econometrics methodology in order to disentangle the causal relationship between unemployment and life; Section 4 concludes.

2. THE DATA

The source of the data is the Organization for Economic Co-operation and Development (OECD), particularly from the 2013, 2014 and 2015 editions of the Better Life Index (http://stats.oecd.org/index.aspx?DataSetCode=BLI, accessed on February 02, 2016). The variables under consideration are the employment rate, the long term unemployment rate, as well as the life satisfaction indicator, in total terms, and by gender.[9] The countries under analysis are the following: Australia, Austria, Belgium, Canada, Czech Republic, Denmark, Finland, France, Germany, Greece, Hungary, Iceland, Ireland, Italy, Japan, Korea, Luxembourg, Mexico, Netherlands, New Zealand, Norway, Poland, Portugal, Slovak Republic, Spain, Sweden, Switzerland, Turkey, United Kingdom, United States, Brazil, Chile, Estonia, Israel, Russia, and Slovenia. This amounts to a 3-years panel data of 36 countries and 7 variables. Figures 1, 2 and 3 plot the panel data.[10]

A simple visual inspection of Figures 1, 2 and 3, indicates the existence of an inverse (resp. direct) between satisfaction in life and the unemployment rate (resp. employment rate). The statistical test of this hypothesis is to be performed in the next section by the use of a panel data econometrics methodology.

[9] The employment rate "is the number of employed persons aged 15 to 64 over the population of the same age. Employed people are those aged 15 or more who report that they have worked in gainful employment for at least one hour in the previous week, as defined by the International Labour Organization – ILO." The long term unemployment "refers to the number of persons who have been unemployed for one year or more as a percentage of the labour force (the sum of employed and unemployed persons). Unemployed persons are defined as those who are currently not working but are willing to do so and actively searching for work." The life satisfaction indicator "considers people's evaluation of their life as a whole. It is a weighted-sum of different response categories based on people's rates of their current life relative to the best and worst possible lives for them on a scale from 0 to 10, using the Cantril Ladder (known also as the "Self-Anchoring Striving Scale")."

[10] The figures for each of the three years corresponding to the relationship between life satisfaction and the unemployment rate are in the Annex.

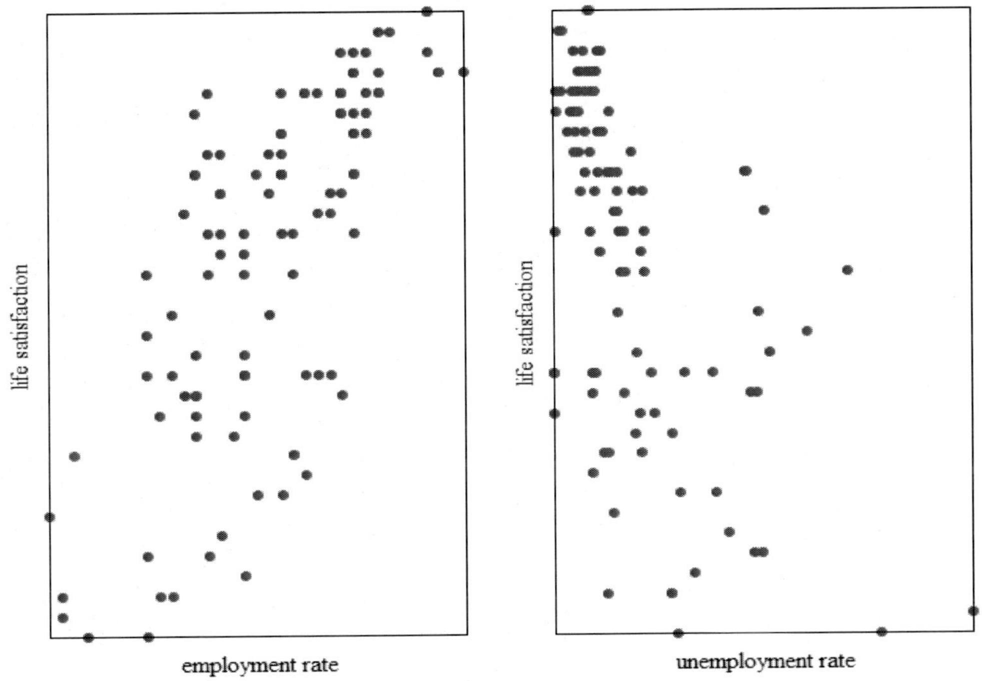

Figure 1. Life satisfaction vis-a-vis the employment and unemployment rates (total).

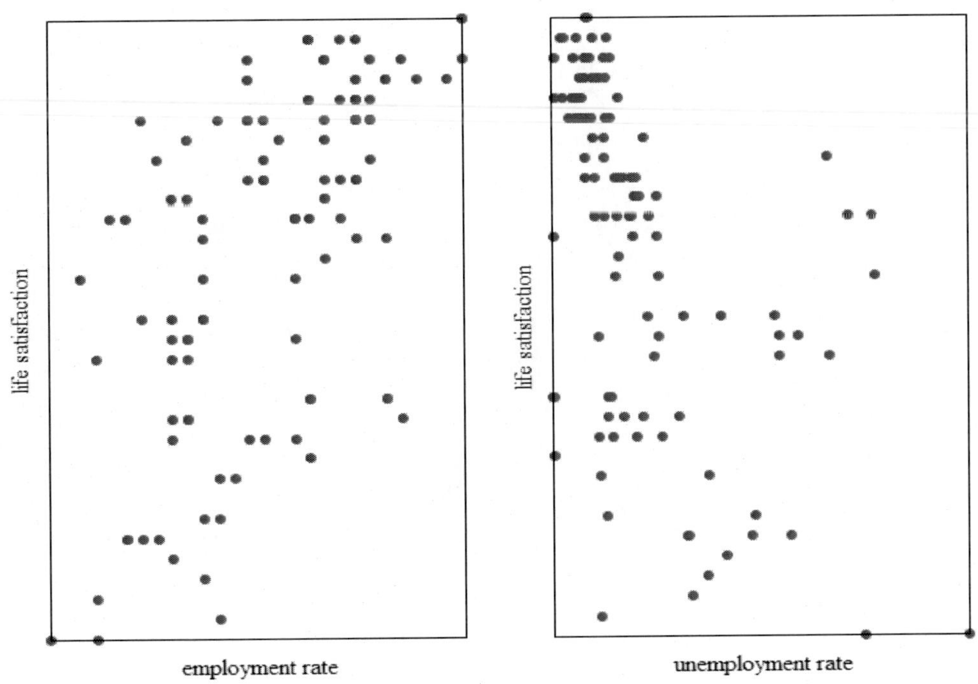

Figure 2. Life satisfaction vis-a-vis the employment and unemployment rates (men).

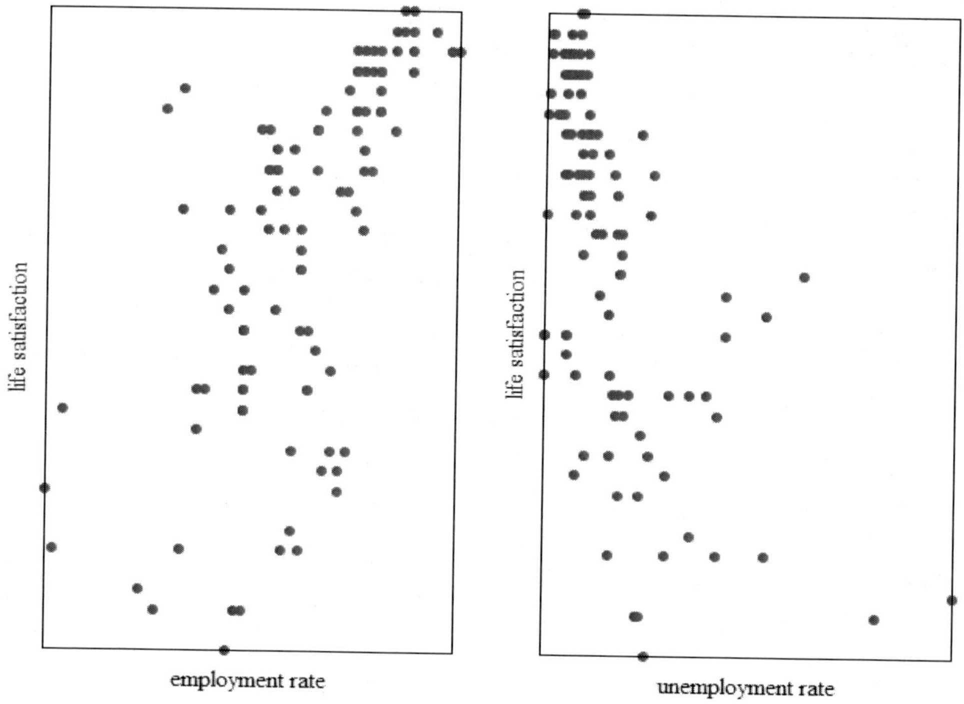

Figure 3. Life satisfaction vis-a-vis the employment and unemployment rates (women).

3. THE RESULTS

Given the nature of the data a panel data econometrics methodology is to be used in the causality analysis between life satisfaction and unemployment (and/or employment) rates. As is known, this methodology allows the control for variables that one cannot observe or measure or variables that change over time but not across entities. In simple terms, there are three methods of estimation of the model that can be used: the (pooled OLS) generalized least squares (GLS) method and the maximum likelihood method of fixed effects (FE) or random effects (RE). In order to choose the best method, a good econometric practice is to test the consistency of the GLS method against the fixed effects model by an F test and against the random effects model through a Breusch-Pagan test, eventually followed by the confrontation between the fixed effects and the random effects models through a Hausman test.[11] Following this methodology, in none of the cases, the null hypothesis that the pooled OLS model (GLS) is adequate, in favor of the fixed effects or the random effects alternatives, could not be rejected.[12]

That being said, six models were estimated, i.e. for both sexes (total), by gender (men and women) and for the unemployment and the employment rates as explanatory variables of life satisfaction. Table 1 shows the results.[13]

[11] This is precisely the methodology suggested by Gretl – freely available at http:// gretl.sourceforge.net/(accessed on February 02, 2016) – which will be used to perform the econometric computations.

[12] The results of these tests of hypothesis is available upon request.

[13] The full results can be consulted in the Annex.

Table 1. The results

	life satisfaction = f (unemployment)		life satisfaction = f (employment)	
	constant	unemployment rate	constant	employment rate
total	7.08646***	-0.146042***	1.10222***	0.0829414***
men	7.01497***	-0.135148***	0.51564	0.0833326***
women	7.12949***	-0.147694***	3.40128***	0.0538758***

As Table 1 shows, the results confirm that unemployment has a negative effect, statistically significant, on life satisfaction, for both sexes. Concomitantly, employment exerts a positive effect, statistically significant, on life satisfaction, for both sexes. In terms of gender difference, it should be noted that the effect of the unemployment rate is, in absolute value, lower for men (relative to women), and, in accordance, the higher the effect of the employment rate.

CONCLUSION

This chapter has called the attention to the importance of unemployment on life satisfaction, while a psychological variable that also reflects an economic dimension, as it was confirmed here. Considering a wide set of countries, the main contribution of this chapter was, in fact, to confirm that, *in aggregate terms,* the level of life satisfaction is (causally) related with the unemployment rate (and, naturally, with the employment rate).

The explanation, *in individual terms,* to that result would lead us to a new approach, which seems particularly promising for future work. As is known, the evaluation of individual in what concerns her life depends upon the context (or the baseline) and the prospects (of improvement or decline) in the factors that are considered as relevant for that evaluation, which indeed is inherently subjective. This means that the level of life satisfaction may, by means of taking into account the context, be sensitive to the *direction* (and not to the level) assumed by the relevant variables. In addition, the perceived level of life satisfaction is to be subjective in nature. These two features make appropriate the use of fuzzy logic in modelling the relationship between the level of life satisfaction and its explanatory factors, namely the unemployment rate.

In fact, based on incomplete information, individuals may have a certain level life satisfaction based on a vague perception of the relevant variables, such as unemployment. This means that, when taking into account, for example, the trajectory of unemployment, individuals may consider themselves more/less satisfied based on concepts rather subjective such as 'high', 'normal' and 'low' values for that variable. If this is the case, the correct approach is the fuzzy logic one (Zadeh, 1965).

Using fuzzy logic, the following reasoning: "the observed value for the unemployment rate, say 6%, can be considered 'high', 'normal' or 'low', with a certain degree of plausibility," can be modelled, which is done in accordance to the context of the values presented so far by that variable (Caleiro, 2006), from there resulting a certain level of life satisfaction. Thus, fuzzy logic can capture the fact that individuals often evaluate categories such as 'high', 'normal' or 'low' differently, given the inherent subjectivity and the different context linked with those variables. This is an approach to be taken into account in future analysis, if possible using micro-data.

ANNEX

2013 | men

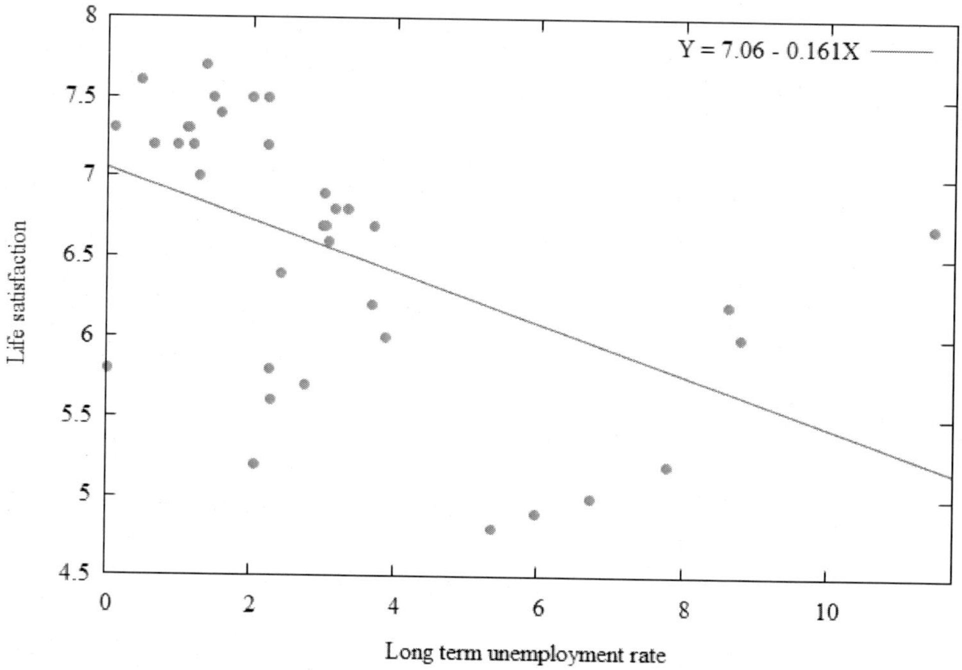

2013 | total

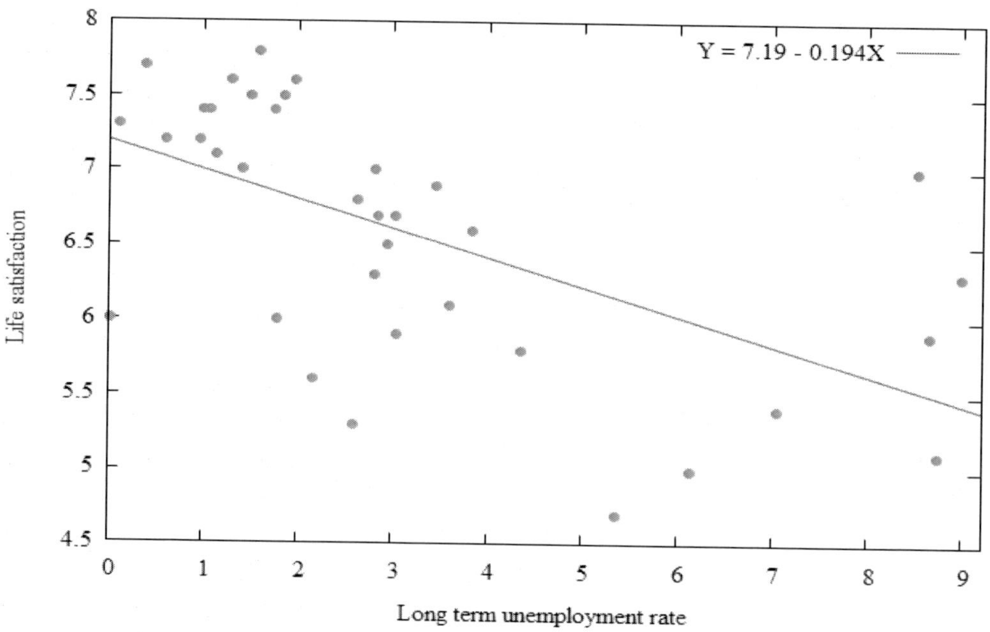

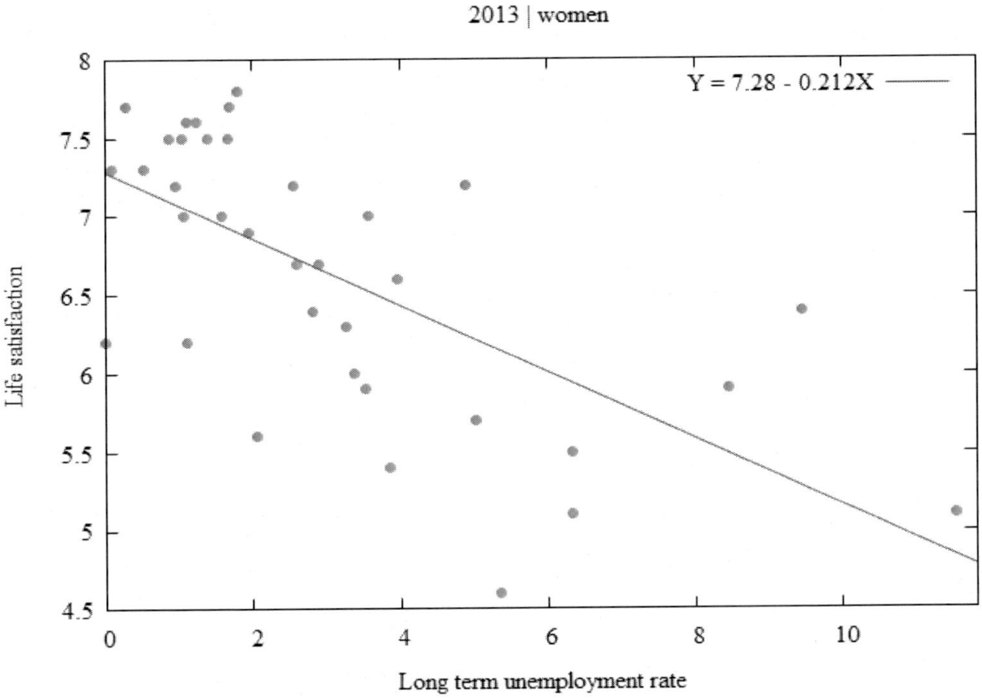
2013 | women
Y = 7.28 - 0.212X
8
7.5
7
6.5
6
5.5
5
4.5
0
2
4
6
8
10
Life satisfaction
Long term unemployment rate

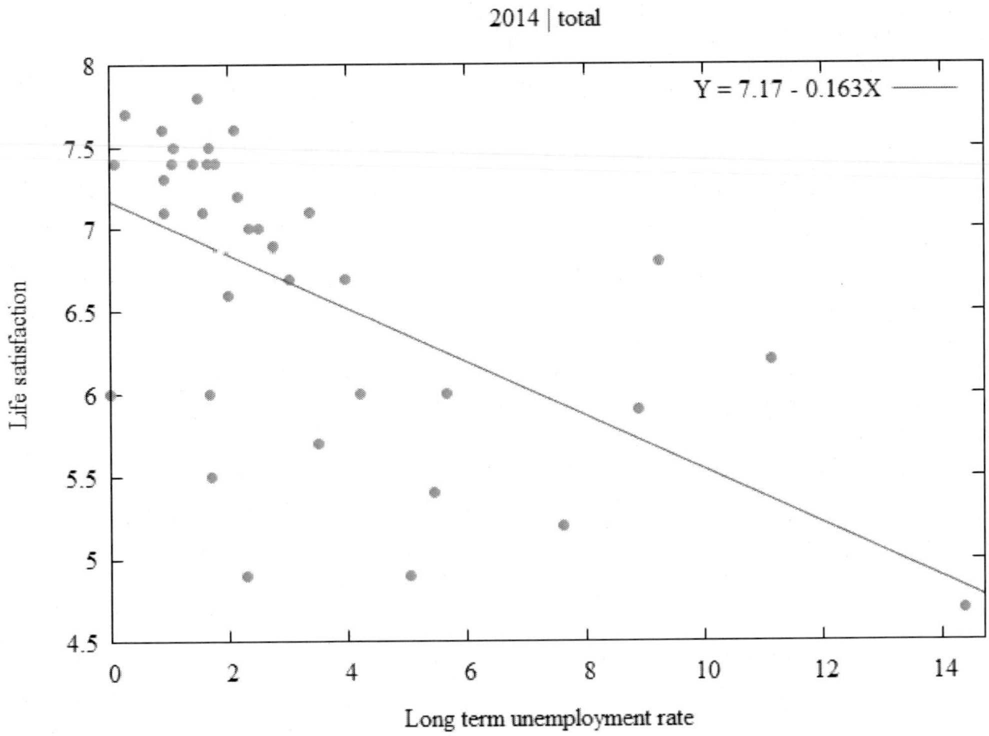
2014 | total
Y = 7.17 - 0.163X
8
7.5
7
6.5
6
5.5
5
4.5
0
2
4
6
8
10
12
14
Life satisfaction
Long term unemployment rate

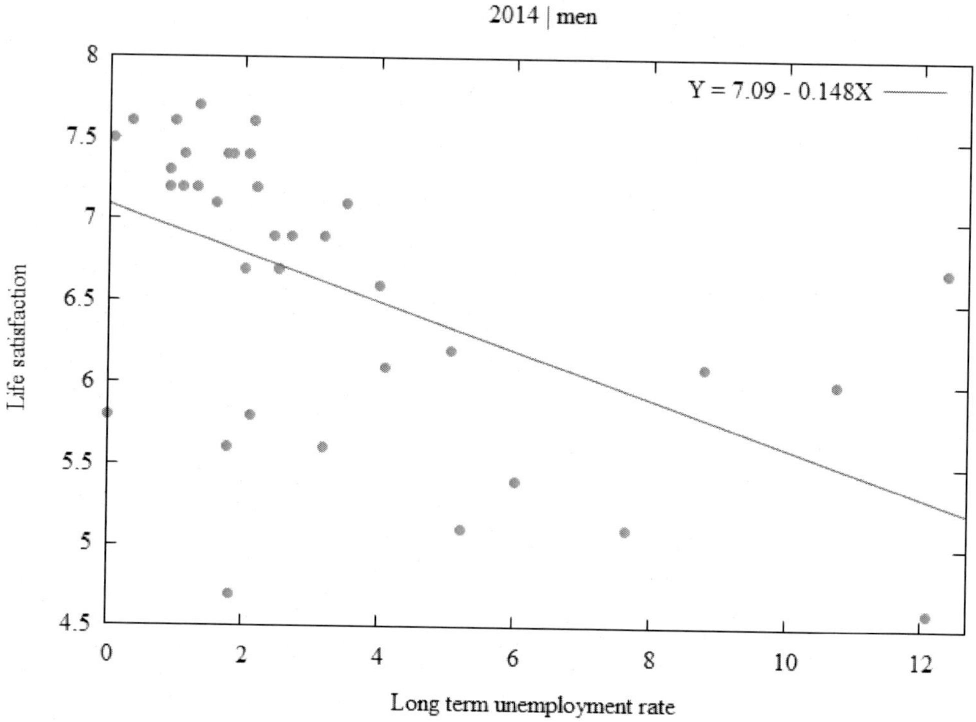
2014 | men
Y = 7.09 - 0.148X
Life satisfaction
8
7.5
7
6.5
6
5.5
5
4.5
0
2
4
6
8
10
12
Long term unemployment rate

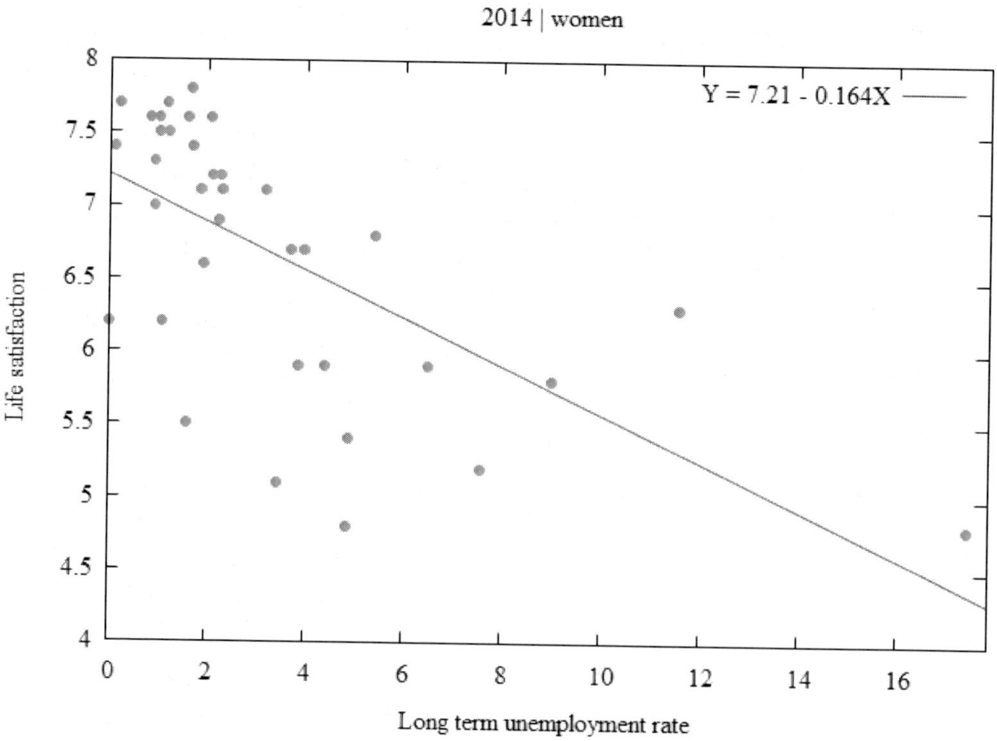
2014 | women
Y = 7.21 - 0.164X
Life satisfaction
8
7.5
7
6.5
6
5.5
5
4.5
4
0
2
4
6
8
10
12
14
16
Long term unemployment rate

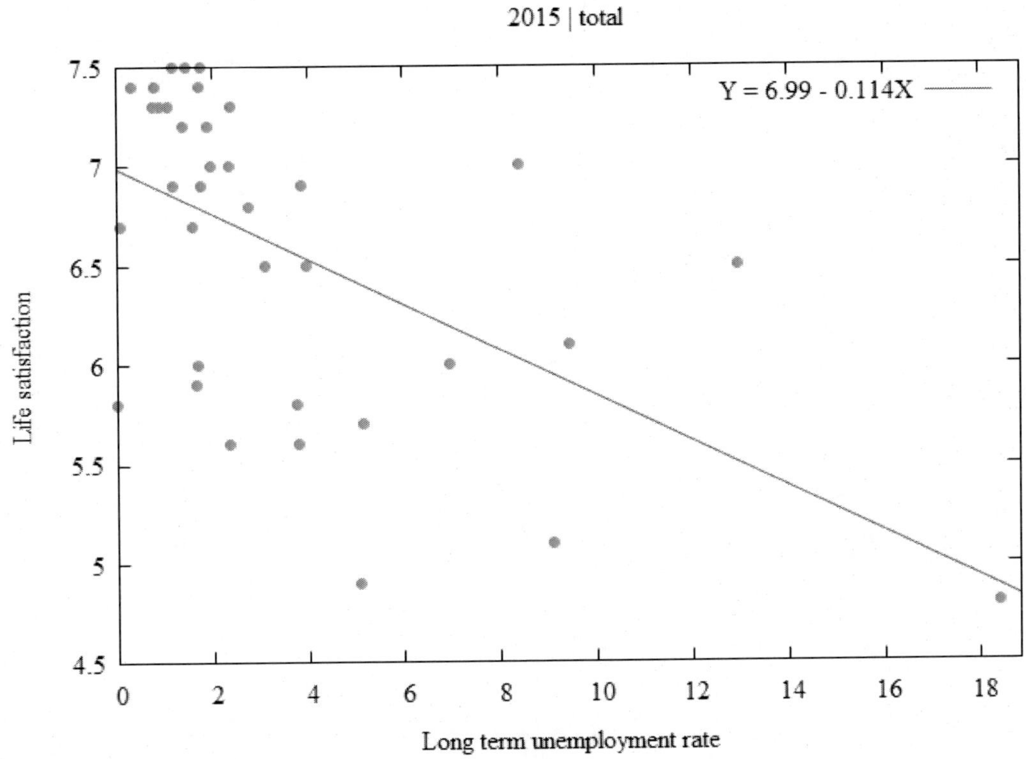
2015 | total
Y = 6.99 - 0.114X
Life satisfaction
Long term unemployment rate
7.5
7
6.5
6
5.5
5
4.5
0
2
4
6
8
10
12
14
16
18

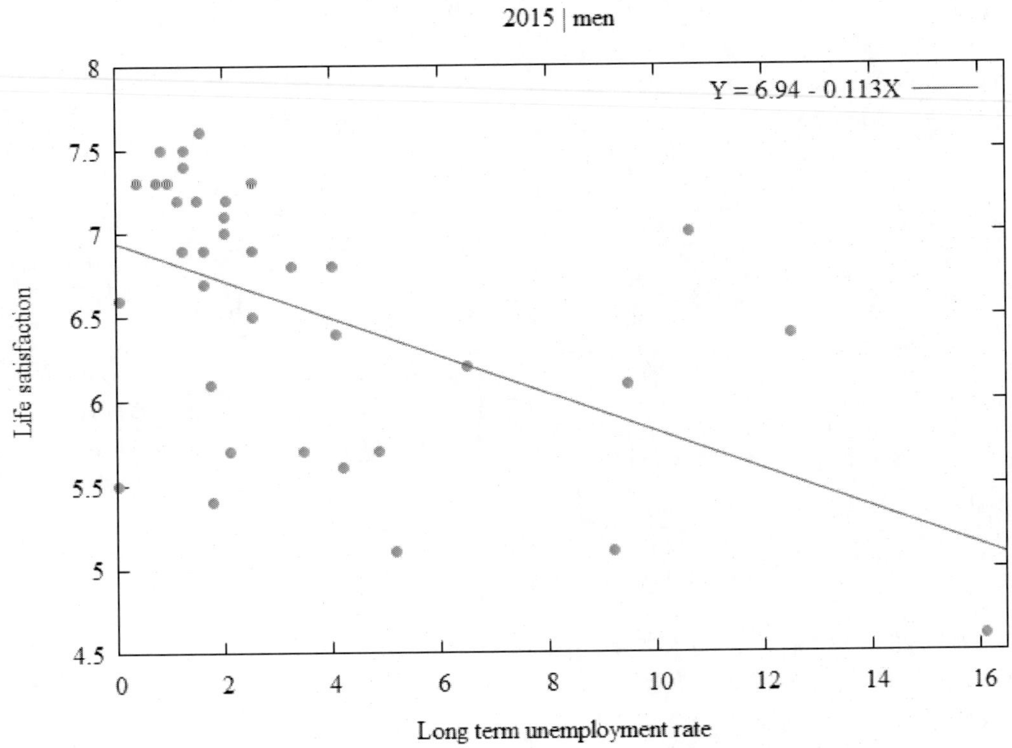
2015 | men
Y = 6.94 - 0.113X
Life satisfaction
Long term unemployment rate
8
7.5
7
6.5
6
5.5
5
4.5
0
2
4
6
8
10
12
14
16

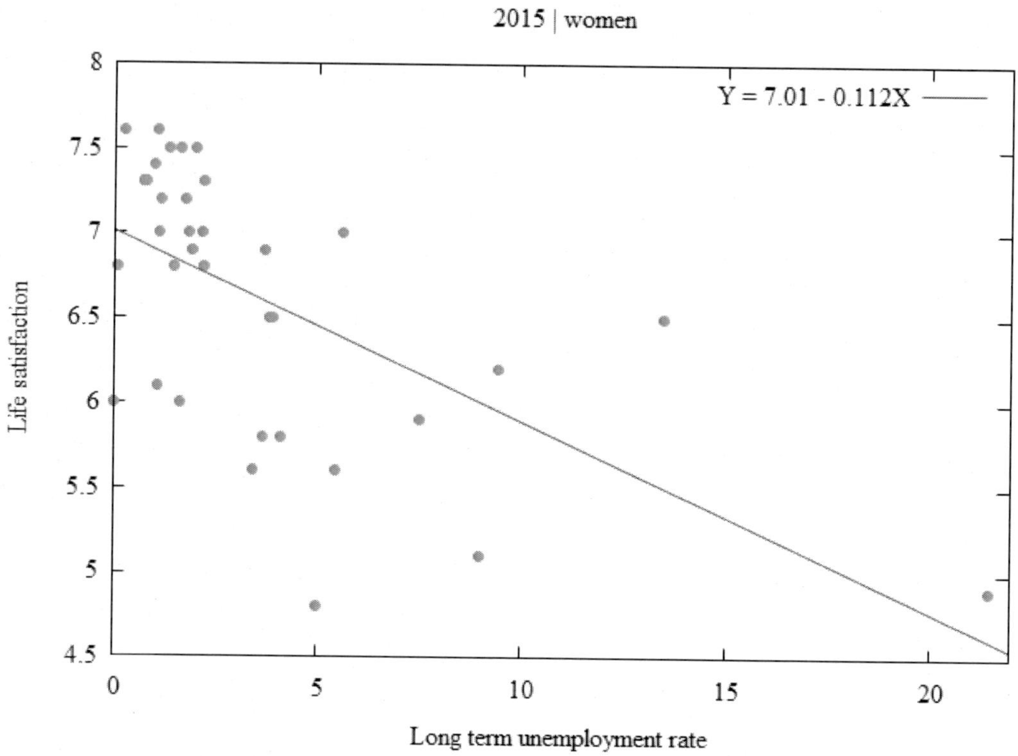

Total

Model 1: Pooled OLS, using 108 observations
Included 36 cross-sectional units
Time-series length = 3
Dependent variable: life satisfaction

	coefficient	std. error	t-ratio	p-value
const	7.08646	0.0963555	73.54	8.56e-093 ***
Unemployment rate	−0.146042	0.0207665	−7.033	2.06e-010 ***

Mean dependent var	6.600926	S.D. dependent var	0.841949
Sum squared resid	51.71911	S.E. of regression	0.698510
R-squared	0.318139	Adjusted R-squared	0.311706
F(1, 106)	49.45686	P-value(F)	2.06e-10
Log-likelihood	−113.4850	Akaike criterion	230.9699
Schwarz criterion	236.3342	Hannan-Quinn	233.1449
rho	0.903196	Durbin-Watson	0.092844

Model 2: Pooled OLS, using 108 observations
Included 36 cross-sectional units
Time-series length = 3
Dependent variable: life satisfaction

	coefficient	std. error	t-ratio	p-value
const	1.10222	0.517986	2.128	0.0357**
employment rate	0.0829414	0.00776659	10.68	1.64e-018 ***

Mean dependent var	6.600926	S.D. dependent var	0.841949
Sum squared resid	36.53812	S.E. of regression	0.587111
R-squared	0.518284	Adjusted R-squared	0.513739
F(1, 106)	114.0466	P-value(F)	1.64e-18
Log-likelihood	−94.72151	Akaike criterion	193.4430
Schwarz criterion	198.8073	Hannan-Quinn	195.6180
rho	0.883591	Durbin-Watson	0.114526

Men

Model 3: Pooled OLS, using 108 observations
Included 36 cross-sectional units
Time-series length = 3
Dependent variable: life satisfaction

	coefficient	std. error	t-ratio	p-value
const	7.01497	0.101509	69.11	5.49e-090 ***
unemployment rate	−0.135148	0.0219290	−6.163	1.31e-08 ***

Mean dependent var	6.561111	S.D. dependent var	0.842208
Sum squared resid	55.87519	S.E. of regression	0.726033
R-squared	0.263799	Adjusted R-squared	0.256854
F(1, 106)	37.98244	P-value(F)	1.31e-08
Log-likelihood	−117.6588	Akaike criterion	239.3176
Schwarz criterion	244.6818	Hannan-Quinn	241.4926
rho	0.902631	Durbin-Watson	0.092218

Model 4: Pooled OLS, using 108 observations
Included 36 cross-sectional units
Time-series length = 3
Dependent variable: life satisfaction

	coefficient	std. error	t-ratio	p-value
const	0.515638	0.755742	0.6823	0.4965
employment rate	0.0833326	0.0103797	8.028	1.44e-012 ***

Mean dependent var	6.561111	S.D. dependent var	0.842208
Sum squared resid	47.19737	S.E. of regression	0.667277
R-squared	0.378136	Adjusted R-squared	0.372270
F(1, 106)	64.45539	P-value(F)	1.44e-12
Log-likelihood	−108.5445	Akaike criterion	221.0891
Schwarz criterion	226.4533	Hannan-Quinn	223.2641
rho	0.899956	Durbin-Watson	0.102454

Women

Model 5: Pooled OLS, using 108 observations
Included 36 cross-sectional units
Time-series length = 3
Dependent variable: life satisfaction

	coefficient	std. error	t-ratio	p-value
const	7.12949	0.0896397	79.54	2.46e-096 ***
unemployment rate	−0.147694	0.0186012	−7.940	2.26e-012 ***

Mean dependent var	6.639815	S.D. dependent var	0.849732
Sum squared resid	48.44558	S.E. of regression	0.676043
R-squared	0.372944	Adjusted R-squared	0.367029
F(1, 106)	63.04396	P-value(F)	2.26e-12
Log-likelihood	−109.9541	Akaike criterion	223.9082
Schwarz criterion	229.2724	Hannan-Quinn	226.0832
rho	0.903683	Durbin-Watson	0.105438

Model 6: Pooled OLS, using 108 observations
Included 36 cross-sectional units
Time-series length = 3
Dependent variable: life satisfaction

	coefficient	std. error	t-ratio	p-value
const	3.40128	0.381129	8.924	1.47e-014 ***
employment rate	0.0538758	0.00625318	8.616	7.20e-014 ***

Mean dependent var	6.639815	S.D. dependent var	0.849732
Sum squared resid	45.43856	S.E. of regression	0.654726
R-squared	0.411866	Adjusted R-squared	0.406317
F(1, 106)	74.23088	P-value(F)	7.20e-14
Log-likelihood	−106.4938	Akaike criterion	216.9876
Schwarz criterion	222.3518	Hannan-Quinn	219.1626
rho	0.893193	Durbin-Watson	0.091886

References

Angner, E. (2010). Subjective well-being. *The Journal of Socio-Economics*, *39*(3), 361-368.

Bell, D., & Blanchflower, D.G. (2007). The Scots may be brave but they are neither healthy nor happy. *Scottish Journal of Political Economy*, *54*, 166-194.

Boyce, C.J., Wood, A.M., & Brown, G.D. (2010). The dark side of conscientiousness: Conscientious people experience greater drops in life satisfaction following unemployment. *Journal of Research in Personality*, *44*(4), 535-539.

Bjørnskov, C., Dreher, A., & Fischer, J.A. (2008). Cross-country determinants of life satisfaction: Exploring different determinants across groups in society. *Social Choice and Welfare*, *30*(1), 119-173.

Blanchflower, D.G. (2001). Unemployment, well-being, and wage curves in Eastern and Central Europe. *Journal of the Japanese and International Economies*, *15*(4), 364-402.

Blanchflower, D.G., & Oswald, A.J. (2004). Well-being over time in Britain and the USA. *Journal of Public Economics*, *88*(7), 1359-1386.

Caleiro, A. (2006). How is Confidence related to Unemployment in Portugal. *Applied Economics Letters, 13*, 887-890.

Caleiro, A. (2011). Poverty, takes strong nobler wealth: The point of view of Economics of Happiness ", IN II Proceedings of the International Congress: Interfaces Psychology - Quality of Life ... Quality Lives, University of Évora, Évora, 14-15 November 2011, Centre for Research in Education and Psychology.

Caleiro, A. (2012). "Unemployment versus Happiness in Portugal", IN Bento-Gonçalves, A.; Vieira, A. (eds.), Portugal: Economic, Political and Social Issues, pp. 113-123, Nova Science Publishers, New York, (ISBN: 978-1-62257-474-2).

Clark, A.E., & Oswald, A.J. (1994). Unhappiness and unemployment. *Economic Journal*, *104*, 648-659.

Clark, A., Georgellis, Y., & Sanfey, P. (2001). Scarring: The psychological impact of past unemployment. *Economica*, *68*(270), 221-241.

Clark, A. E., Diener, E., Georgellis, Y., & Lucas, R.E. (2008). Lags and leads in life satisfaction: a test of the baseline hypothesis. *The Economic Journal*, *118*(529), F222-F243.

Diener, E. (2009). Subjective well-being. In The science of well-being (pp. 11-58). Springer Netherlands.

Diener, E., Sandvik, E., Seidlitz L, & Diener M. (1993). The relationship between income and subjective wellbeing – relative or absolute, *Social Indicators Research*, *28*, 195-223.

Diener, E., Suh, E.M., Smith, H., & Shao, L. (1995a). National differences in reported subjective wellbeing – Why do they occur?. *Social Indicators Research*, *34*, 7-32.

Diener, E., Diener, M., & Diener, C. (1995b). Factors predicting the subjective wellbeing of nations. *Journal of Personality and Social Psychology, 69*, 851-864.

Diener, E., Suh, E.M., Lucas, R.E., & Smith, H.L. (1999). Subjective wellbeing: Three decades of progress. *Psychological Bulletin*, *125*(2), 276-302.

Di Tella, R., MacCulloch, R.J., & Oswald, A.J. (2001). Preferences over inflation and unemployment: Evidence from surveys of happiness. *American Economic Review*, 335-341.

Di Tella, R., MacCulloch, R.J., & Oswald, A.J. (2003). The macroeconomics of happiness. *Review of Economics and Statistics*, *85*(4), 809-827.

Di Tella, R., & MacCulloch, R. (2005). Partisan Social Happiness. *Review of Economic Studies*, *72*, 367-933.

Easterlin, R.A., Morgan, R., Switek, M., & Wang, F. (2012). China's life satisfaction, 1990–2010. *Proceedings of the National Academy of Sciences*, *109*(25), 9775-9780.

Eggers, A., Gaddy, C., & Graham, C. (2006). Well-being and unemployment in Russia in the 1990s: Can society's suffering be individuals' solace? *The Journal of Socio-Economics*, *35*, 209-242.

Fahey T., & Smyth E. (2004). Do subjective indicators measure welfare? Evidence from 33 European societies. *European Societies*, *6*, 5-27.

Ferrer-i-Carbonell, A. (2005). Income and wellbeing: An empirical analysis of the comparison income effect. *Journal of Public Economics*, *89*, 997-1019.

Fujita, F., & Diener, E. (2005). Life satisfaction set point: stability and change. *Journal of personality and social psychology*, *88*(1), 158.

Gallie, D., & Russell, H. (1998). Unemployment and life satisfaction: A cross-cultural comparison. *European Journal of Sociology*, *39*(02), 248-280.

Helliwell, J. (2003). How's life? Combining individual and national variables to explain subjective wellbeing. *Economic Modelling,* 20, 331-360.

Helliwell, J. (2006). Wellbeing, social capital and public policy: What's new? *Economic Journal*, *116*, C34-C45.

Hudson, J. (2006). Institutional trust and subjective wellbeing across the EU. *Kyklos*, *59*, 43-62.

Inglehart, R. (1996). The diminishing utility of economic growth: From maximizing security toward maximizing subjective wellbeing. *Critical Review*, 10, 509-531.

Judge, T.A., & Watanabe, S. (1993). Another look at the job satisfaction-life satisfaction relationship. *Journal of Applied Psychology*, *78*(6), 939.

Jürges, H. (2007). Unemployment, life satisfaction and retrospective error. *Journal of the Royal Statistical Society: Series A (Statistics in Society)*, *170*(1), 43-61.

Kahneman, D., Diener, E., & Schwarz, N. (eds.) (1999). *Well-being: Foundations of hedonic psychology*. New York: Russell Sage Foundation Press.

Kahneman D., Krueger A.B., Schkade D., Schwarz N., & Stone, A. (2004). Toward national wellbeing accounts. *American Economic Review*, *94*, 429-434.

Kahneman D., & Krueger A.B. (2006). Developments in the measurement of subjective wellbeing. *Journal of Economic Perspectives*, *20*(1), 3-24.

Kassenboehmer, S.C., & Haisken-DeNew, J.P. (2009). You're fired! The causal negative effect of entry unemployment on life satisfaction. *The Economic Journal*, *119*(536), 448-462.

Lucas, R.E., Clark, A. E., Georgellis, Y., & Diener, E. (2004). Unemployment alters the set point for life satisfaction. *Psychological Science*, *15*(1), 8-13.

Luechinger, S., Meier, S., & Stutzer, A. (2010). Why does unemployment hurt the employed? Evidence from the life satisfaction gap between the public and the private sector. *Journal of Human Resources*, *45*(4), 998-1045.

Martella, D., & Maass, A. (2000). Unemployment and Life Satisfaction: The Moderating Role of Time Structure and Collectivism. *Journal of Applied Social Psychology*, *30*(5), 1095-1108.

Radcliff, B. (2001). Politics, markets, and life satisfaction: The political economy of human happiness. *American Political Science Review*, 95, 939-952.

Ruhm, C.J. (2003). Good times make you sick. *Journal of Health Economics*, *22*, 637-658.

Senik C. (2009). When information dominates comparison – Learning from Russian subjective panel data. *Journal of Public Economics*, *88*, 2099-2123.

Schyns, P. (2002). Wealth of nations, individual income and life satisfaction in 42 countries: A multilevel approach. *Social Indicators Research*, 60, 5-40.

Steel, P., & Ones, D.S. (2002). Personality and happiness: A national-level analysis. *Journal of Personality and Social Psychology*, *83*, 767-781.

Theodossiou I. (1998). The effects of low-pay and unemployment on psychological wellbeing: A logistic regression approach. *Journal of Health Economics*, 17, 85-104.

van Hoorn, A. (2007). “A Short Introduction to Subjective Well-Being: Its measurement, correlates and policy uses”, Is happiness measurable and what do those measures mean for policy?, Conference organized by Bank of Italy, Centre for Economic & International Studies (CEIS), Joint Research Centre of the European Commission, and OECD, 2-3 April 2007, (University of Rome ‘Tor Vergata’, Italy).

Vemuri, A.W., & Constanza, R. (2006). The role of human, social, built, and natural capital in explaining life satisfaction at the country level: Toward a National Well-being Index (NWI). *Ecological Economics*, *58*, 119-133.

Wilson, W. (1967). Correlates of avowed happiness. *Psychological Bulletin*, *67*, 294-306.

Wolfers, J. (2003). Is Business Cycle Volatility Costly? Evidence from Surveys of Subjective Well-Being. *International Finance*, *6*, 1-31.

Zadeh, L.A. (1965). Fuzzy Sets. *Information and Control, 8*, 338-353.

In: Unemployment
Editor: Tabitha Fletcher

ISBN: 978-1-63485-181-7

Chapter 8

EFFECT OF HOMELESSNESS IN JOBLESS PERSONS: SURVIVAL ANALYSIS FROM A RETROSPECTIVE COHORT STUDY IN POLAND

Pawel Zagozdzon*
Department of Hygiene and Epidemiology,
Medical University of Gdansk,
Gdansk, Poland

ABSTRACT

Objective: Homelessness is associated with increased risks of mortality but it's relationship to unemployment has not been investigated in the context of economic transition in East European countries. The aim of this study was to assess the association between homelessness and survival in a population of unemployed individuals in one region of northern Poland.

Methods: To analyze the association between the homelessness and mortality we collected survival data on a cohort of 47 247 subjects registered as unemployed ones at the Office of Employment in Gdansk for the period of 1999 and 2004. Causes of death were analyzed based on the data from deaths certificates. Data on mortality from matched local general population was selected for comparison with homeless group. Cox proportional hazard method was used to analyze the association between homelessness and survival. Sex and age were included into multivariate analysis. Over 6 years of observation, 2.8% (23/816) of the homeless persons and 2% (952/46 431) of the non-homeless unemployed population died. After adjustment for age and sex homeless status was associated with 70% increase in risk of death compared to non-homeless unemployed people: hazard ratio 1.69, 95 % confidence interval 1.11 - 2.55. Homeless people experienced more than threefold increase in overall mortality compared to matched general population. External causes and alcohol-related causes explain the excess mortality among homeless unemployed individuals.

* Phone: +48 58 349 1820. Fax: +48 58 349 1928.

Conclusion: Homelessness is a risk factor for mortality among unemployed individuals. Specific preventive programs might be most effectively targeted at the homeless people with unemployed status.

Keywords: homelessness, unemployment, survival, retrospective study, Poland

RESEARCH HIGHLIGHTS

- Homelessness is associated with increased risk of mortality.
- It was not known whether the higher risk of death among homeless people, typically associated with socioeconomic deprivation, could be explained by unemployment status or the homelessness increases the risk observed among unemployed individuals.
- After adjustment for age and sex homelessness among unemployed population was associated with 70% increased mortality hazard compared to non-homeless individuals and 3.4 times greater mortality rates than age-matched local general population.
- Homelessness associated with unemployment carries the greater risk than being non-homeless unemployed and more active public health initiatives should target such populations.

INTRODUCTION

The relationship between homelessness and health and access to employment is complex. There is a great deal of evidence that the homeless have poor health outcomes in terms of both physical and mental health problems (Bines, 1994). Data indicates also high rates of alcohol and drug dependence, with half of the rough sleepers alcohol dependent, and one-quarter drug dependent (Gill et al., 1996). Evidence from more recent cross-sectional surveys also indicates that among homeless individuals the most common mental disorders were alcohol dependence and drug dependence (Fazel et al., 2014). For psychotic illness, the prevalence in the same meta-analysis was smaller, up to 40%, with similar findings for major depression. Hospitalizations for psychiatric disorders and infectious diseases such as tuberculosis and HIV represent larger proportions of inpatient admissions among the homeless compared with non-homeless patients in western countries.

The definitions of homelessness vary across different authors. It can include people living in marginal accommodation, as well as roofless people. Others definitions include only those sleeping in designated shelters or public spaces. It should recognize also those who are without appropriate housing or suffer from the social marginalization (Fazel et al., 2014). Homeless state is usually part of a process - people may be transiently, episodically, or chronically homeless. It could be the consequence of immigration or the social cost that *accompany* persistent unemployment preceded by financial hardship and *poverty or simply the* choice of the individual. In the latter case it may be due to pre-existing mental illness – the phenomenon responsible for potential selection bias in the analysis of the association

between homelessness and mortality. The number of homeless people in Poland evaluated in 2000 was ranging between 24 000 and 45 000 (Przymenski, 2001). Difficult labour market situation and unemployment during economic transition in Poland contributed to the homelessness problem.

Similarly the psychosocial condition of unemployment appears also have an effect on health outcomes. Consistent with this, job insecurity and the anticipation of job loss have been found to be associated with poorer health outcomes (Laszlo et al., 2010; van der Noordt et al., 2014). Individuals with health problems are predisposed to experiencing job insecurity and in consequence in some cases homelessness (Bender and Theodossiou, 2015; Jusot et al., 2008). Poor health can be caused, triggered or aggravated by unemployment or housing that does not meet a certain standard of adequacy, affordability and suitability (Adams et al., 2007; Clemens et al., 2015; Garcy and Vagero, 2012; Roelfs et al., 2011; Zagozdzon et al., 2014). The largest meta-analysis showed that unemployment was associated with 60% increased mortality risk (Roelfs et al., 2011). Several large cohort studies showed increased mortality among homeless people (Babidge et al., 2001; Barrow et al., 1999; Hibbs et al., 1994; Hwang, 2000; Hwang et al., 1997; Morrison, 2009; Nielsen et al., 2011; Nordentoft and Wandall-Holm, 2003; Roy et al., 2004).

Number of studies have unequivocally demonstrated a strong relationship between unemployment and health (Jin et al., 1995). This occurs for some specific causes of death (such as cirrhosis, suicides) as well as for a number of specific chronic illnesses like lung cancer and coronary heart disease (Zagozdzon et al., 2009). Unemployment has been shown to be associated with certain forms of mental illness, such as depression and adjustment disorders (Leinonen et al., 2014; van der Noordt et al., 2014).

Homelessness is associated with increased risks of mortality but it's relationship to unemployment has not been investigated yet. The aim of this study was to assess the effect of homelessness on mortality among a cohort of unemployed adults in Northern Poland in the context of economic transition.

METHODS

Ethics Approval

Ethics approval for this study was provided by the Ethics Committee of the [Details omitted for double-blind reviewing]. Informed consent was not needed and was therefore not requested from participants, as this is a register-based study where participants were not contacted and analyses involved anonymised data.

Design

This cohort study was performed in Gdansk City and Gdansk County in Northern Poland, with about 550 000 inhabitants. The study was based on the registry data from the Gdansk City and Gdansk County Branch of the Labour Office for the period between January 1, 1999 and December 31, 2004. Labour Office is a state institution that finances unemployment benefits and provide health insurance for registered unemployed individuals. Study period 1999-2004 has been chosen in order to assure the reliability and validity of unemployment registrations and to *minimize loss to follow-up* after accession of Poland to the European Union in May 2004. The implementation from 1999 of the 1997 General Health Insurance Act encouraged people working in the 'grey economy' to register with labour offices in order to obtain health insurance coverage. Year 2004 could be considered as a symbolic termination of the transition period and after May 2004 a massive migration to western countries had started.

Unemployment Benefits Regulations

Labour Offices collects data on people eligible for unemployment compensation and covers the cost of health insurance for those unemployed who fulfilled criteria of unemployment. At the time of data collection the right to unemployment benefit was granted to a person registered as unemployed, able and ready to take up employment on a full time basis, according to the working time rate applied in a given occupation or service, who has reached the age of 18 years and has not reached the retirement age (60 years for women and 65 years for men). Persons applying for unemployment benefits may not be owners or possessors of an agricultural estate, with arable land exceeding the area of 2 hectares taken for the purposes of calculation nor have monthly income in the amount exceeding half the minimum pay. They should not be the recipients of permanent compensatory allowance, guaranteed periodic allowance or social pension, on the basis of the social assistance legislation. Additional eligibility criterion for unemployment compensation is a history of at least 1 year of employment within the last 18 months before registration.

Study Population

Study population consists of subjects registered by Labour Office as unemployed in Gdansk City and Gdansk County between January 1, 1999 and December 31, 2004. We analyzed the data for all 47 247 subjects registered by Labour Office as unemployed in Gdansk City and Gdansk County during a 6-year period between 1999 and 2004. Therefore, the study population included all individuals who have been registered at least ones as unemployed. All the subjects were 20 years of age or older. The date of the first registration was considered the date of subject's entry into the study. Mortality data and death causes coded according to ICD-10 (*International Classification of Diseases*, Tenth Revision) were obtained from the Death Registry as of December 31, 2004. In addition, deaths from alcohol-related causes (ICD-10 codes C01–C06, C09, C10, C12–C15, C22, C32, F10, K70) were analysed.

Statistical Analysis

The Student's t-test for independent samples was used for continuous variables with normal distribution. Differences between categorical variables were tested with the chi-square test. To assess the effect of homelessness on survival in unemployed subjects we calculated sex and age-adjusted hazard ratio and 95% confidence intervals by conducting Cox proportional hazards analyses. Incidence rates for death with 95% confidence intervals were calculated, cumulatively for 1999-2004 period. Two groups of unemployed were considered: homeless individuals and persons with identified place of residence. Moreover, the respective incidence rate for death in geographically-matched population from Pomeranian voivodeship and corresponding incidence rate ratio were calculated. Proportional mortality ratios were calculated for both homeless and non-homeless group. All analyses were carried out using STATA version 12.0.

RESULTS

The 47,247 participants accrued 129,570 person-years of follow-up (mean follow-up: 33.4 months). The mean age at the time of first registration was 46 years. There were 51% men in analyzed unemployed population. A detailed report on overall and cause specific mortality in that population was published elsewhere (Zagozdzon et al., 2009).

Characteristics of the homeless and non-homeless unemployed individuals are presented in Table 1. The groups of homeless (N = 816) were slightly older and included higher proportion of men than the group of (N = 46,431).

Table 1. Baseline characteristics of study participants

	Homeless	Non-Homeless	p
N	816	46 431	
Age (mean ± SD)	45.9 ± 7.0	45.5 ± 7.5	0.12
Male sex	69.6 %	50.7 %	<0.001
Deaths (%)	23 (2.8)	952 (2.0)	<0.001
Person-years	1 777	143 370	
Incidence rate (per 1000 person-years)	12.94	6.64	0.004

Table 2. Hazard ratios for death of unemployed individuals with regard to homelessness

	Hazard ratio	p	95% Confidence intervals
Non-Homeless	1	-	-
Homeless	2.01	0.001	1.33 – 3.04
Homeless*	1.69	0.01	1.11 – 2.55
Homeless in men#	1.62	0.03	1.04 – 2.54
Homeless in women#	2.11	0.198	0.67 – 6.62
Age (years)	1.06	<0.001	1.05 – 1.07
Male sex	3.31	<0.001	2.82 – 3.87

*Age and sex adjusted, #age adjusted.

The proportion of unemployed people who died during the analyzed period was 2.8% for homeless and 2% for non-homeless individuals. The unadjusted and adjusted hazard ratios for death in relation to homelessness are shown in Table 2. The homelessness was associated with 70% increased risk of death compared to non-homeless unemployed people: hazard ratio 1.69, 95% confidence interval 1.11 – 2.55. The excess of death risk was bigger in women compared to men, although it did not reach statistical significance.

Incidence Rate Ratio for death regarding homeless unemployed group compared to matched general population was 3.42, 95% confidence interval 2.16 – 5.13.

Table 3. Causes of death in homeless unemployed group and unemployed population

	Homeless	Non-Homeless	p
Infections	-	1% (14)	
Neoplasms	26% (6)	31% (300)	0.6
Endocrine and metabolic dis.	-	1% (10)	
Psychiatric diseases	-	1% (6)	
Nervous system	-	1% (10)	
Cardiovascular diseases	30% (7)	22% (215)	0.37
Digestive system	4% (1)	7% (68)	0.6
Symptoms not elsewhere classified	4% (1)	8% (82)	0.6
External causes	17% (4)	22% (213)	0.6
Suicides	4% (1)	6% (63)	0.6
Alcohol-related causes	17% (4)	7% (72)	0.08
Total	100% (23)	100% (957)	

Table 4. Causes of death among homeless individuals

C15.9 Malignant neoplasm of esophagus, unspecified
C16.9 Malignant neoplasm of stomach, unspecified
C21.0 Malignant neoplasm of anus, unspecified
C34.9 Malignant neoplasm of unspecified part of bronchus or lung
C48.0 Malignant neoplasm of retroperitoneum
C80.0 Malignant neoplasm, without specification of site
I21.9 Acute myocardial infarction, unspecified
I25.1 Atherosclerotic heart disease of native coronary artery
I26.9 Pulmonary embolism without acute cor pulmonale
I40.9 Acute myocarditis, unspecified
I49.9 Cardiac arrhythmia, unspecified
I64.0 *Stroke, not specified as haemorrhage or infarction*
I69.1 Sequelae of nontraumatic intracerebral hemorrhage
K74.6 Other and unspecified cirrhosis of liver
R99.0 Other ill defined and unspecified causes of mortality
V03.1 Pedestrian injured in collision with car, pick up truck or van in traffic accident
X78.8 Intentional self harm by sharp object
X31.0 Exposure to excessive natural cold
X45.0 Accidental poisoning by and exposure to alcohol

There were no statistically significant differences between homeless group and the rest of unemployed population in proportional mortality ratios (Table 3). The most prevalent causes of death were cardiovascular diseases. There were more alcohol-related causes among homeless people compared to non-homeless (17% vs. 7%). External causes were related to injury after collision with car, intentional self-harm, exposure to cold and poisoning by alcohol (Table 4).

DISCUSSION

Our results provide evidence on increased mortality in homeless individuals in Poland. The risk of death could be related not only to economic deprivation due to unemployment but also to effect of homelessness. The 70% increased risk associated with homelessness is in accordance with other study where the control group was selected from local non-homeless population and homeless had a mortality hazard 1.6 times greater (Morrison, 2009). Also more than threefold increased risk of death compared to general population was in accordance with standardized mortality rations calculated in other studies (Barrow et al., 1999; Nordentoft and Wandall-Holm, 2003). Recent Danish study found higher estimates of death risk in homeless population: standardized mortality ratio for homeless men was 5.6 and 6.7 for women (Nielsen et al., 2011). The higher risk of death associated with homelessness in women compared to men was also found in our study. External causes, suicides and alcohol-related causes explain the excess mortality among homeless unemployed individuals.

The health hazard of homelessness have been reported before, but this study adds different perspectives. First, homelessness was analyzed in the context of unemployment and compared to non-homeless unemployed population. It has been shown that effect of homelessness went beyond unemployment related poverty. Second, study was conducted during dynamic unemployment changes in the context of economic transition in Poland. The whole cohort and matched local general population experienced similar economic adversities. The sample includes all unemployed individuals interested in having health insurance. The implementation from 1999 of the 1997 General Health Insurance Act encouraged people working in the 'grey economy' to register with labour offices in order to obtain health insurance coverage. The new health reform resulted in registering of not actively seeking jobs non-working individuals, including those affected by homelessness, as unemployed in order to secure them health insurance (Tymowska, 2001). The potential for selection bias was *minimized through choosing year 1999 as the beginning of the study period.* Our unemployed cohort was large although number of homeless people within this cohort was moderate.

There are *many limitations* in *our study*. The major study limitation is related to lack of data on baseline morbidity. We were unable to control the effect of homelessness neither for the education nor the lifestyle factors. Homeless people are more likely to have alcohol dependence and the prevalence of psychotic disorders are higher (Fazel et al., 2014; Geddes and Fazel, 2011; Nielsen et al., 2011). Therefore the direction of the relationship between health and homelessness, and particularly mental health is unclear. It is very likely that the health problems of participants predates their homelessness. There was no reliable data when homelessness began. The start of follow-up in our study was determined by date of registration with labour office and the homeless status came from registry of unemployed individuals as there was the requirement to provide a registration document for permanent residence.

There are some evidence on effective health interventions among the unemployed (Audhoe et al., 2010; Brouwer et al., 2015; Wanberg et al., 2005). Evidence on such interventions among the homeless are limited (Fitzpatrick-Lewis et al., 2011; Hwang and Burns, 2014). Preventive programmes might be most effectively targeted at the homeless experiencing non-employment. Housing policies should aim to provide affordable housing of acceptable standard.

Further research is *required* to *establish whether* the interventions to mitigate homelessness in persons after job loss are helpful in reducing excess mortality we observed.

REFERENCES

Adams, J., R. Rosenheck, L. Gee, C. L. Seibyl, and M. Kushel, 2007, Hospitalized younger: A comparison of a national sample of homeless and housed inpatient veterans: *Journal of Health Care for the Poor and Underserved,* v. 18, p. 173-184.

Audhoe, S. S., J. L. Hoving, J. K. Sluiter, and M. H. W. Frings-Dresen, 2010, Vocational Interventions for Unemployed: Effects on Work Participation and Mental Distress. *A Systematic Review*: *Journal of Occupational Rehabilitation,* v. 20, p. 1-13.

Babidge, N. C., N. Buhrich, and T. Butler, 2001, *Mortality among homeless people with schizophrenia in Sydney,* Australia: a 10-year follow-up: Acta Psychiatrica Scandinavica, v. 103, p. 105-110.

Barrow, S. M., D. B. Herman, P. Cordova, and E. L. Struening, 1999, Mortality among homeless shelter residents in New York City: American *Journal of Public Health, v.* 89, p. 529-534.

Bender, K. A., and I. Theodossiou, 2015, A reappraisal of the unemployment-mortality relationship: Transitory and permanent effects: Journal of Public Health Policy, v. 36, p. 81-94.

Brouwer, S., R. H. Bakker, and J. M. H. Schellekens, 2015, Predictors for re-employment success in newly unemployed: A prospective cohort study: *Journal of Vocational Behavior*, v. 89, p. 32-38.

Clemens, T., F. Popham, and P. Boyle, 2015, What is the effect of unemployment on all-cause mortality? A cohort study using propensity score matching: *European Journal of Public Health*, v. 25, p. 115-121.

Fazel, S., J. R. Geddes, and M. Kushel, 2014, The health of homeless people in high-income countries: descriptive epidemiology, health consequences, and clinical and policy recommendations: *Lancet*, v. 384, p. 1529-1540.

Fitzpatrick-Lewis, D., R. Ganann, S. Krishnaratne, D. Ciliska, F. Kouyoumdjian, and S. W. Hwang, 2011, Effectiveness of interventions to improve the health and housing status of homeless people: a rapid systematic review: *Bmc Public Health*, v. 11.

Garcy, A. M., and D. Vagero, 2012, The length of unemployment predicts mortality, differently in men and women, and by cause of death: A six year mortality follow-up of the Swedish 1992-1996 recession: *Social Science & Medicine*, v. 74, p. 1911-1920.

Geddes, J. R., and S. Fazel, 2011, Extreme health inequalities: mortality in homeless people: *Lancet*, v. 377, p. 2156-2157.

Hibbs, J. R., L. Benner, L. Klugman, R. Spencer, I. Macchia, A. K. Mellinger, and D. Fife, 1994, Mortality in a Cohort of Homeless Adults In Philadelphia: *New England Journal of Medicine*, v. 331, p. 304-309.

Hwang, S. W., 2000, Mortality among men using homeless shelters in Toronto, *Ontario: Jama-Journal of the American Medical Association*, v. 283, p. 2152-2157.

Hwang, S. W., and T. Burns, 2014, Health interventions for people who are homeless: *Lancet*, v. 384, p. 1541-1547.

Hwang, S. W., E. J. Orav, J. J. Oconnell, J. M. Lebow, and T. A. Brennan, 1997, Causes of death in homeless adults in Boston: *Annals of Internal Medicine*, v. 126, p. 625-628.

Jin, R. L., C. P. Shah, and T. J. Svoboda, 1995, The Impact of Unemployment on Health - A Review of the Evidence: *Canadian Medical Association Journal*, v. 153, p. 529-540.

Jusot, F., M. Khlat, T. Rochereau, and C. Sermet, 2008, Job loss from poor health, smoking and obesity: a national prospective survey in France: *Journal of Epidemiology and Community Health*, v. 62, p. 332-337.

Laszlo, K. D., H. Pikhart, M. S. Kopp, M. Bobak, A. Pajak, S. Malyutina, G. Salavecz, and M. Marmot, 2010, Job insecurity and health: A study of 16 European countries: *Social Science & Medicine*, v. 70, p. 867-874.

Leinonen, T., P. Martikainen, M. Laaksonen, and E. Lahelma, 2014, Excess mortality after disability retirement due to mental disorders: variations by socio-demographic factors and causes of death: *Social Psychiatry and Psychiatric Epidemiology*, v. 49, p. 639-649.

Morrison, D. S., 2009, Homelessness as an independent risk factor for mortality: results from a retrospective cohort study: *International Journal of Epidemiology*, v. 38, p. 877-883.

Nielsen, S. F., C. R. Hjorthoj, A. Erlangsen, and M. Nordentoft, 2011, Psychiatric disorders and mortality among people in homeless shelters in Denmark: a nationwide register-based cohort study: *Lancet*, v. 377, p. 2205-2214.

Nordentoft, M., and N. Wandall-Holm, 2003, 10 year follow up study of mortality among users of hostels for homeless people in Copenhagen: *British Medical Journal*, v. 327, p. 81 83.

Roelfs, D. J., E. Shor, K. W. Davidson, and J. E. Schwartz, 2011, Losing life and livelihood: A systematic review and meta-analysis of unemployment and all-cause mortality: *Social Science & Medicine*, v. 72, p. 840-854.

Roy, E., N. Haley, P. Leclerc, B. Sochanski, J. F. Boudreau, and J. F. Boivin, 2004, Mortality in a cohort of street youth in Montreal: *Jama-Journal of the American Medical Association*, v. 292, p. 569-574.

van der Noordt, M., H. Ijzelenberg, M. Droomers, and K. I. Proper, 2014, Health effects of employment: a systematic review of prospective studies: *Occupational and Environmental Medicine*, v. 71, p. 730-736.

Wanberg, C. R., T. M. Glomb, Z. L. Song, and S. Sorenson, 2005, Job-search persistence during unemployment: A 10-wave longitudinal study: *Journal of Applied Psychology*, v. 90, p. 411-430.

Zagozdzon, P., J. Parszuto, M. Wrotkowska, and D. Dydjow-Bendek, 2014, Effect of unemployment on cardiovascular risk factors and mental health: *Occupational Medicine-Oxford*, v. 64, p. 436-441.

Zagozdzon, P., L. Zaborski, and J. Ejsmont, 2009, Survival and cause-specific mortality among unemployed individuals in Poland during economic transition: *Journal of Public Health*, v. 31, p. 138-146.

In: Unemployment
Editor: Tabitha Fletcher

ISBN: 978-1-63485-181-7

Chapter 9

UNEMPLOYMENT AND VOCATIONAL TRAINING IN THE GREEK LABOUR MARKET: A THREE-LEVEL EVALUATION

Stavros Rodokanakis*

Department of Social and Policy Sciences,
University of Bath, England

ABSTRACT

The basic aim of this research is to study the impact that educational level and vocational training programmes (mainly funded by the European Community Support Frameworks) had on the labour market of semi-peripheral EU countries, using Greece as a case study. In particular, the paper focuses on the Greek regions of Attica and Central Macedonia, as well as Greece as a whole, during the period 1988-2000. It investigates econometrically whether the training courses in these two regions were compatible with the skill needs and thus, helped the trainees to increase their chances of finding a job, as well as to what extent there were skill mismatches between education-training programmes and the labour market. Attica and Central Macedonia were chosen because they are the largest regions in Greece in terms of population, and the two biggest urban centres in the country (Athens and Thessaloniki) are situated in the regions under study. So, in effect, the analysis investigates half of the Greek population and compares it econometrically with the rest of Greece. This investigation was undertaken using Labour Force Survey (LFS) micro-level data. As all training actions in the country are co-financed by EU funds, the research also probes the outcomes of these funds during the period of the Community Support Framework - CSF-1 (1989-93) and CSF-2 (1994-99) in the domain of training.

My analysis at the micro-level indicates that this training "revolution" was not accompanied by any real improvement in matching supply with demand or increasing people's chances of finding a job. The study moves beyond the micro-level and embeds the empirical findings within the institutional/organizational environment of Greek vocational training (meso-level) and the broader political economy of Greece and its position in the EU political economy (macro-level) to provide a comprehensive

* E-mail: srodokanakis@hotmail.com

explanation of what empirically is identified as the minimal impact of these policies. That is, the study goes further than the often narrow micro-economic explanations of the impact of training upon labour markets in that it explores the wider politico-economic context of these policies and assesses its impact on their effectiveness. Consequently, the findings are of relevance beyond the Greek case as they are also useful for comparative research pertaining to European regions or countries. Moreover, the study outcomes will be valuable to those who are interested in designing and implementing training programmes for structural change, as a number of key failings that have occurred in the Greek case are identified. The results of my research challenge the usefulness of the active labour market policies (ALMPs) alone. Training mechanisms, concrete political economy, inadequate public administration and the clientelistic system were the main obstacles to the matching process. This does not mean that training and ALMPs are not needed in Greece, but they can only function effectively in the presence of a suitable institutional framework, which has yet to become a reality.

1. Introduction

Given the current tendency towards continuous globalisation of market economies and the rapidly changing scientific and technological knowledge, investment in human capital has become as important as that in capital for competitiveness and economic development. Consequently, evaluation of the impacts from this type of investment is crucial for future labour market planning. In Europe, investment in human capital and especially the salience of vocational training has grown substantially since the early 1990s, in terms of both the funds allocated and the number of participants on training programmes. This growth represented a 'policy paradigm' shift from the so-called 'passive' to active labour market policies (ALMPs). It placed strong emphasis on skills and life-long learning to maintain employability [1] in increasingly more 'flexible' labour markets under conditions of global competition. Indeed, from the early 1990s onwards, the EU's strategic policy documents (e.g., the White Paper on Education and Training [CEC, 1996], and the Lisbon agenda) highlighted the priority of training and skills in employment policy, promoting it as a universal principle applicable to all EU economies and labour markets.

However, the evidence regarding the success of such policies is inconclusive, at least for the economies of Southern European member states, thus casting doubt on their impact on the labour market prospects of those participating on training courses. Part of the explanation is the lack (and difficulty, due to data restrictions) of systematic evaluation of these policies that connects the micro-level practices of individuals with the macro-level characteristics of the labour markets in their respective societies. There is much evidence that Southern European member states' labour markets and production regimes are considerably different to those of the core EU member states. Against this background, with its focus on Greece, this research serves as a case study on the effectiveness of EU training policy within the context of a Southern European economy at the periphery of the EU.

Indeed, in the case of Greece the role of the EU was pivotal in changing the extent and nature of practice of training in the country. This is evident from the amounts spent on

[1] It should be emphasized here that employability is not the same as gaining a job, but rather, implies something about the capacity of a person (skills, understandings and personal attributes) to function in a job and be able to move between jobs, thus remaining employable throughout life.

training activities from the end of the 1980s onwards through the structural funds and the European Social Fund (ESF) in particular, the numerous training agencies which have been established in order to be involved in the training process and the increasing numbers of trainees on the various training courses. However, it is questionable whether this training "revolution" was accompanied by any real improvement in matching supply with demand or increasing people's chances of finding a job. It is not asserted categorically here that the mismatch between supply and demand for labour was due to training mismatch alone, but it is contended that this should be seriously considered as one of the reasons for the unemployment problem in Greece, at least for the period prior to the current crisis.

Training activities in Greece have been jointly financed by the EU, the government and private providers, but despite the EU having been the biggest contributor, it has not at any time evaluated the impact of training on employment or taken steps to ensure that the types of training courses funded in that country were compatible with the needs of its economy. Consequently, behavioural models (micro-level), institutions and investment in relation to training (meso-level) in Greece have yet to be considered along with the macro-context of its political economy, thereby allowing for robust evaluation of its effectiveness. The EU, through the European Employment Strategy (EES), expected that national systems would be reformed into supply-side oriented systems (Seferiades, 2006), but was never explicit about the manner in which this should be achieved. The conditions for making the employment and growth model functional as happens in Northern European countries, have been absent in the Greek context.

2. The Rationale Underpinning the Research and the Research Questions

This research is not only based on the econometric analysis of the Labour Force Survey (LFS) micro-data, namely, at the level of individuals (micro-level), but also focuses on what happened at the level of vocational training institutions and employment offices (meso-level), as well as at the level of the wider political and economic dynamics in Greece and the EU (macro-level of analysis). To this end, a comprehensive analysis is undertaken in an attempt to link all three levels (micro, meso, macro). To the best of this researcher's knowledge, such an approach on training evaluation has not been undertaken for Greece, to date, or for that matter, any other EU member state.

In particular, I test the human capital theory (Becker, 1964 and 1975; Ben-Porath, 1967; Mincer, 1974), which underpins many of the important developments in modern economics (Berman et al., 1994; Machin and van Reenen, 1998; Le et al., 2003; Jones and Chiripanhura, 2010), especially whether the more educated and the more trained a person is, the higher the probability of him or her finding a job, as well as the matching theory (van Smoorenburg and van der Velden, 2000). In my opinion, what has become clear is that the EU approach to vocational training has been very much influenced by the human capital theory. For the policy makers in the EU the key aim has been to improve job matching within a (market driven) European economy, where private investment will generate a demand for high skills in national labour markets. High-skilled economies presuppose more and better jobs and for them more and better training is necessary.

The matching theory is also considered, because in contrast to the human capital view under this perspective too much education leads to a lack of training and consequently, an over-educated often unemployable workforce, which appears to be the case in Greece and other Southern European countries.

Prior to discussing the research questions, it is necessary to offer a clarification of terminology. The term micro-level refers to behavioural models, behaviours and characteristics of individuals, with special emphasis on education. These are classical micro-economic models (incentive structures, disincentives, models examining the individual and his/her characteristics). Meso-level analysis essentially pertains to institutions and policies. Specifically, in this work the meso-level refers to the role of regional and national institutions and investment on training, how training is organised, whether and if so how, the institutional framework at this level leads to productive choices of individuals at the micro-level. The macro-level aspect of the study covers both the national and supra-national dimensions. This includes analysis on how a national political economy functions, as well as how it is affected by supranational policy frameworks and agendas, such as the EES. The Greek national institutions and policies function at both the meso and macro levels, specifically at the meso-level national institutions and policies impacted downwards to the regional level, which in turn impacted on the micro outcomes. Moreover, at the macro-level the Greek policy makers were tasked with interpreting how EU policies would be rolled out in the Greek context. Clearly, all these levels are inter-related and investigation into their impact will allow for a comprehensive understanding of the labour market dynamics during the last decade of the last millennium.

Against this background the key research questions of the chapter are as follows:

a) What was the impact of EU funded vocational training on the Greek labour market and individual job seekers who undertook this training from 1988 to 2000?
b) How can this impact be explained?

To address these questions my research is organized along three inter-related levels of analysis (micro, meso and macro) that correspond to the following research sub-questions:

1) What was the impact of the training programmes at the participant level? (micro-level);
2) Was the training system, i.e., the institutions, in Greece, both regionally and nationally, effective in helping people to find jobs and if not, why? (meso-level); and
3) To what extent did the ALMPs in Greece, in particular the policies of vocational training, integrate EU-funded training in their skills strategy? To what extent was any (in) effectiveness of ALMPs related to the characteristics of the Greek political economy? (macro-level).

3. Justifying the Choice of Greece and the Time Period for the Study. Structure of the Chapter

One of the key issues I identify is that the attempt to provide universal applicability of abstract and de-contextualised micro-level theories of skills mismatch, such as human capital theory, is problematic in some contexts. Indeed, Greece is an interesting testing case, precisely because high unemployment has traditionally coincided with phenomena like over-education and high demand for low skill jobs by employers. In addition, administration of vocational training in Greece has been highly problematic. All these factors lead to an initial hypothesis that the training programmes have not had any impact on the Greek labour market. The application of ALMPs alone did not ensure that people would find a job more easily than before. In fact, it would appear that training programme participation was mainly engaged in as the benefits accruing were higher than those provided for being unemployed. As such, the Greek government was able to give the public the impression that they were helping the unemployed back into work through substitution of unemployment benefit with training grants. Greece entered the euro under these conditions and dynamics and their non-resolution contributed, to an extent, to the country's current economic and social bottlenecks.

The reference time period for my study will be 1988-2000 (with some data and analyses often covering up to the mid 2000s). The reasons are as follows:

1) The year 1988 was the last year before the start of CSF-1 and in this research I explore the time period between the first two CSFs.
2) From the early 1990s, there was a change in the philosophy of labour market policies (e.g., of the Manpower Employment Organization - OAED) with emphasis being placed on the increased role of ALMPs in the economy, and the availability of more resources for training. This has to do with two shifts: one external (a 'policy paradigm shift' in EU towards employability and ALMPs), and one internal (a shift in the economy from mainly agriculture and weak industry to predominantly services during the 1980s and 1990s).
3) The 1990s was the decade in which Greece entered the procedure of accession to the new common currency, thus involving its participation in a large array of institutional developments towards the 'Europeanization' of employment policies (see EES, Lisbon Strategy, and Open Method of Co-ordination (OMC)).

Sections 2, 3 and 4 set the background to the study and the research questions by discussing the increasing role of training in Europe. Section 5 is the methodology chapter. The analysis will follow three steps. First, sections 6 and 7 will focus on the micro-level of analysis. In section 6, the relevant literature on the meaning and importance of skills shortages, the training mismatch, as well as the labour market theories in relation to education and training is reviewed. Also, the role of education and training in addressing unemployment, as well as the problem of over-education which is crucial for Greece are covered.

Section 7 comprises the original econometric work of the research (it answers the first main research question, namely "What was the impact of EU funded vocational training on the Greek labour market and individual job seekers who undertook this training from 1988 to 2000?", and also the first research sub-question, namely "What was the impact of the training programmes at the participant level?", which involves a logistic regression for the two NUTS-2 regions and the rest of Greece based on micro-data of the Greek LFS for the years 1992, 1994 and 2000.

Sections 8 and 9 address the second main research question, namely, "How can this impact be explained?". Section 8 covers the second step and the meso-level of analysis, and answers the second sub-question, namely, "Was the training system, i.e., the institutions, in Greece, both regionally and nationally, effective in helping people to find jobs and if not, why?".

Section 9 covers the third step and contains the macro-level analysis. This chapter answers the third sub-question, namely, "To what extent did the ALMPs in Greece, in particular the policies of vocational training, integrate EU-funded training in their skills strategy? To what extent was any (in)effectiveness of ALMPs related to the characteristics of the Greek political economy?".

Section 10 is the last section of the research and concludes on the policy implications in the field of training in Greece, and more specifically the impact of the EU intervention and the effect of training on unemployment in Central Macedonia, Attica and the whole of Greece, and a discussion follows from micro to meso and macro-level of analysis.

4. The EU Involvement with the VET Systems of the Member States

Regarding the Southern European nations, like Italy, Greece and Spain, despite ALMPs not being fully developed, they grew in significance during the period under investigation. There were two reasons for this: firstly, attention being directed to supply-side policies owing to the restrictions on macroeconomic policy; and, secondly, new active policies being funded by the structural funds (Rubery et al., 2008). However, the key area where the impact of EU funding was most obviously manifested was in the changes and expansion in training policies (Zartaloudis, 2014).

For decades prior to this development, vocational education and training (VET) policy was an autonomous domain of EU member states, thus leaving little room for a common EU policy. However, the 2000s witnessed substantial transformation. While in the 1960s and early 1970s, education and vocational training were considered as appropriate measures for the reduction of income inequalities, by the early 1990s corresponding measures aimed at the provision of vocational training in the European economies seemed to have been adopted for other reasons (Green et al., 1998). The term Europeanization in the field of training refers to the impact of European developments, particularly the EU, on institutional change in vocational training regimes (Heyes, 2007). In fact, the EES began to encourage social dialogue connected to training (see Goetschy, 1999; Seferiades, 2003), with the ability of European firms being competitive in the long-run and the 'modernization' of work organizations being the discourses they promoted regarding the role of training at the time. In particular, technological change and globalization were believed by those promoting the EES to have led to a growing necessity to change and reform the labour market. Hence, adaptability and flexibility were therefore seen as achievable mainly by means of organizations' use of training. In addition, it was the ability to enhance social inclusion by dealing with the unemployed and disadvantaged sections of the population that led to training to be viewed as an instrument of ALMPs. Consequently, gaining skills as the route to improvement of a person's 'employability' status was emphasized. Employees, also, were thought to gain through this process as well as the unemployed, since by gaining skills their job security and perspectives of finding a job in the long-run were improved in a labour market that supposedly involved them in more risks than in previous years (Heyes, 2007).

The role of EU moneys was to act as a "carrot" for administration and VET reform in the member states. In other words, the purpose of the funding was not simply to re-skill individuals, but also to promote indirectly different administration and policy (Zartaloudis, 2014). However, despite some of the EU funding being earmarked for reforms in terms of administration and policies, in Greece there was little of this.

5. METHODOLOGY

This section presents the methodology of the research. Given the main aim is to investigate why the training programmes in Greece during the period 1988-2000 were unsuccessful in helping those with the greatest need to find work, the purpose here is to explain and justify the approach adopted for carrying out the research. I begin by discussing the relationship between the micro, meso and macro levels (section 5.1), which sheds light on why I have researched all of these three. In section 5.2 there is a discussion of the challenges faced regarding the collection of data and limitations in terms of the nature and coverage of these. This is followed in section 5.3 with an explanation of the econometric analysis involving the application of the logit model to the LFS data.

5.1. The Three Levels (Micro-Meso-Macro) of Analysis and How They Are Related

The aim of this research is to explore the impact of EU funded training in Greece. The key point is to make explicit how we can evaluate success or failure of EU funded training programmes. Underpinning this work is the notion that we need to take also into account other institutional factors apart from individual trainee characteristics. However, ultimately it is the micro-level results that show if they had any impact on the labour market (hence the importance of the micro-level analysis). I propose an analytical strategy that brings together three levels of analysis that demonstrates that they relate to each other. I argue that the micro-meso interaction is not independent from the meso-macro.

So far, the existing research on the impact of training on the Greek labour market has been only qualitative, based on interviews which covered only specific NUTS-2 or NUTS-3 areas and not the entire country nor do they cover both of the two first CSFs.[2] This analysis comprises three steps in accordance with the three identified levels. For all three levels, first, I discuss the relevant literature and this is followed by consideration of the empirical evidence. At the micro-level (sections 6 and 7), I examine whether there was a lack of effective

[2] Kassimati et al. (1984), University of Piraeus (1990), KODE (1991), URDP (1992), ANA.V.EL. (RDA of Northern Greece Ltd) - (1993), Panteion University-PLA.NE.T. A.E. (1993), Chasapis (1994), EKOM Business Consulting Services (1994), Getimis et al. (1994a), Getimis et al. (1994b), Getimis and Gravaris (1994), KOE (1994), T.Q.M. Hellas Ltd (1994), University of Macedonia (1994), University of Patra (1994), University of Piraeus Research Centre (1994), Dedoussopoulos et al. (1995), Goumenakis and Michaelides (1995), Kafkalas et al. (1995), Chasapis (1996), Dimoulas and Michalopoulou (2008), Zartaloudis (2014).

information networks for the prospective trainees, especially for the unemployed, and whether the vocational training courses increased the chances of finding a job at the participant level. The chapters on the micro-level include a literature review on micro-theories followed by an econometrics chapter. This part of the research will determine whether or not the programmes did help the unemployed to get any work and addresses the first sub-question, namely "What was the impact of the training programmes at the participant level?". This question was operationalized by empirically testing the following sub-questions:

- Did the social and demographic characteristics of an individual in Greece affect the probability of finding employment during the period under investigation?
- Did the introduction of training courses funded by the EU have a statistically significant effect on the probability of finding employment?
- Did university graduates in Greece face greater difficulties in finding a job compared to those less educated (as relevant literature and aggregate statistics have suggested - see Meghir et al., 1989; OECD, 1990; Eurostat: Education and Employment Prospects, 1995; Iliades, 1995; IN.E./GSEE-ADEDY, 1999; Katsikas, 2005)?

At the meso-level (section 8), I probe whether there were legal regulations concerning the teachers of vocational training courses in Greece, and if there was any serious evaluation of the training programmes in terms of participant monitoring after training and the effects of vocational training courses on employment. Also, I explore whether there was a mechanism to estimate the real needs regarding continuing vocational training (CVT), if the function of employment offices was helpful for the matching between supply and demand for labour, and if there was an involvement of social partners in determining the needs regarding education and training. I also identify any parameters that were not working effectively in Greece and how these impacted on the matching mechanisms in the Greek labour market. This addresses the second sub-question "Was the training system, i.e., the institutions, in Greece, both regionally and nationally, effective in helping people to find jobs and if not, why?". It is at this point where the meso meets the macro and vice versa: the institutional/ meso level operationalises the ALMPs. This analysis of the meso-level helps in identifying which institutional factors affected the implementation of ALMPs and how far the institutional structure and capacity of the Greek state played a role in facilitating or not the effective and efficient implementation of policies.

For the research at the meso-level, given the paucity of statistical data, I had to rely on previously compiled data and secondary documentary evidence. Collecting data for this level of analysis involved an extensive literature review of policy documents and academic research published in English as well as in Greek. In sum, this literature was drawn upon to help explain the findings in section 7, thereby helping to build the bigger picture involving the three levels. The aim of section 8 is to describe the VET structure and to investigate why the Greek organisational structure could not provide adequate skills-matching, through the use of secondary data (other studies).

Lastly, the macro-level of analysis is presented in section 9, with the aim being to contextualize the focal phenomenon of EU training and job outcomes in Greece, during the period of interest, the political system is examined by international comparison across the EU. Specifically, I investigate the features of labour markets and ALMPs as well as different VoC characteristics. This is so as to provide understanding of the particular aspects of the Greek political economy that resulted in an institutional framework that was incapable of delivering an effective training policy. Moreover, the impact of ALMPs on labour markets in certain EU countries is examined as well as the wider macroeconomic policy. As with the meso-level of analysis, the discussion is constructed by drawing on academic scholarship from across the EU. In addition, there is detailed analysis of the structure of unemployment during the focal period. This final level of analysis completes the three level approach aimed at providing a comprehensive response to the research questions, which could be not achieved by omitting either of the meso and macro levels from the analysis. In sum, it is contended that it is essential to consider all three levels if the goal is to obtain deep understanding of the phenomenon of interest, namely, the function of EU training programmes in Greece between 1988 and 2000.

5.2. Challenges with Data Collection and Limitations

The questionnaire of the Greek LFS was greatly modified in 1992 and 1998. In this research, the individual anonymised records (micro-data) of the 1992, 1994 and 2000 LFS for both employed and unemployed (1.5% of the total population of each area) are examined. The reason I chose these years is because 1992 was the first year in the Greek LFS questionnaire with detailed questions on training, 1994 was the first year after the end of the CSF-1, whereas 2000 was one year after the end of the CSF-2. In Greece, the LFS is still the most reliable and widely used source of labour market data. Carried out annually until 1997 with a sample of about 150,000 records for the whole country, it provided information about long-term changes, but being always conducted in the second quarter of every year, it provided no information about seasonal movements. Since 1998, it has been conducted four times a year with a sample of about 80,000 records in each of the four quarters with one sixth of the sample rotating (being replaced) every quarter (ESYE). The system of codification excluded any linkage of data for the same household in successive years, as was true in other countries.

Also, the Greek LFS has no information on wages. Another limitation of the research is that the data available are cross-sectional rather than longitudinal and therefore, it has not been feasible to study any population changes across time. In sum, having considered all the available sources the only way to achieve the desired results of the current research was to use the LFS micro-data, which are survey data based on probability sampling (random sample). For, the European Community Household Panel Survey (ECHPS) and Survey on Income and Living Conditions (SILC) data have been designed for the countries as a whole and so cannot be analyzed at the regional level. Equally, individual census records do not exist for Greece, unlike in some EU countries, so the LFS was deemed the only option to achieve the research goals.

5.3. The Econometric Analysis: The Logit Model for Applying the Micro-Data of the Greek LFS

The basic aim of the econometric analysis was to test the impact that training programmes (apprenticeship, intra-firm training, CVT and popular training) and educational level had on people's job prospects in the regions of Central Macedonia and Attica, as well as in the rest of the country, during the implementation of the CSF-1 (1989-93) and the CSF-2 (1994-99), accounting for demographic characteristics, such as age, gender, marital status, area of residence and immigrant status. The term "popular training" (*laiki epimorphosi* in Greek) refers to training courses intended mainly for elderly people independent of their educational level, the curricula for which mainly cover courses of general knowledge; however, there are some people who do rely on this type of training in order to get a job.

I used a logistic regression model for studying differences between those that did participate in training programmes and those that did not. Moreover, regression models allow for group comparisons by adjusting for demographic and socioeconomic variables. I merged all three years together in order to take advantage of the time-series features of the data (three time-sets of observations in 1992, 1994 and 2000) and used dummies for the years instead. I have generated one model with all the main effects, all variables of interest, plus all the control variables and have run it in a pooled format. Namely, I have pooled together all the available data into one database. Also, I have aggregated some of the categorical variables with few observations (types of training) in order to increase the observations within each cell, so as to avoid exceptionally large coefficients and confidence intervals.

In the logit model, the dependent variable takes two possible values (employed versus unemployed). The nine explanatory variables are the participation in training courses with five categories, including the four types of training completed (as mentioned above) all together as one variable in order to increase the number of training records and non-participation in training courses as the reference category. In addition, there are six levels of education, gender, four categories of age group, marital status, location (Athens or Thessaloniki, the remaining urban areas, semi-urban areas and rural areas), geographical area at the NUTS-2 level and above (Central Macedonia, Attica and rest of Greece), the time (1992, 1994 and 2000), and immigrant status according to citizenship. The estimated coefficient of b is very high in the case of the variable "registered in OAED" and so this variable has been left out from the analysis.

The effect of demographic variables, such as age, gender, marital status, location, as well as educational level and participation in training programmes on the employment status, is investigated with a logistic regression model due to the categorical nature of the dependent variable.

The explanatory variables I used in the model are among the most important ones generally acknowledged as affecting access to labour markets notwithstanding the fact that the Greek LFS lacks some important information recommended as salient variables in other studies. The base (or reference) categories are those with which the rest of the corresponding variables are compared. The reference categories are chosen so as to match the needs of the research.[3] In the next section, the literature review pertaining to the micro-level on training and labour market mismatch is discussed.

[3] The working age population is between 14-65 years old. However, SPSS would not accept these age limits, defaulting to 13 and 66 years old, so I included people from 15 to 64 years of age, which the programme was able to compute.

6. MICRO-LEVEL OF ANALYSIS I: THEORETICAL APPROACHES

When considering micro-level interactions in the labour market, this covers behavioural models, examining behaviours and the characteristics of individuals, with a special emphasis on training. Behavioural models are classical micro-economic models (incentive structures, disincentives, models examining the individual and his/her characteristics etc.) and the key interest here is to assess whether it can shed light on why job matching is effective or not in the labour market.

6.1. The Human Capital Approach and Human Capital Theory

The role of education in explaining how the labour market operates represents one of the main areas of disagreement amongst labour market theorists. During the late 1950s and early 1960s, the neoclassical theory of the labour market emerged with the development of human capital theory. Becker (1964 and 1975) published a book with the title "Human Capital," which developed a theory of human capital formation and analysed the rate of return on investment in education and training. Whilst the human capital literature has highlighted several productivity-related characteristics, theorists traditionally put most emphasis on the importance of education and training as the main component of productivity (Blaug, 1975). Education, it was suggested, provides the basic skills of reading and writing, cognitive skills, and the ability to learn, which will increase an individual's productivity in all jobs (general human capital). Whilst vocational education, on the other hand, will increase an individual's productivity in a narrower range of jobs by providing more specific skills (specific human capital). Becker (1962) distinguished general and specific human capital of workers as well as dividing the latter into employer- and employee-financed on-the-job training. More broadly, the theory of specific human capital predicts that where the fixed costs of employment due to on-the-job training are greatest then unemployment is lowest (Rees, 1973, pp.118-20). Unlike human capital theory, Iversen and Soskice (2001) rather than classifying skills as being general or specific, termed them portable or not portable, respectively. For them, the portability of general skills resides not in their market situation, but rather, in their intrinsic nature as assets, with their being substantively broad, i.e., unspecialised and requiring a high academic education level. Specific skills, by contrast, are non-portable and narrow, in the sense of being specialised as well as low level in that they require little academic training (Streeck, 2012).

In keeping with the traditional theory of human capital (Becker, 1964; Ben-Porath, 1967; Mincer, 1974), which pertains to its economic role, particularly with regards to education achievement, there has been a considerable amount of empirical research on the closely related topics of education and skills, including Prais (1995) and Murray and Steedman (1998). Moreover, closely related to the current research is study on the increasing role of skilled labour in the economy (Berman et al., 1994; Machin, 1996; Machin and van Reenen, 1998). Human capital can be measured in three main ways according to Le et al. (2003): the cost-based approach, the income-based approach, and the educational-stock-based or indicators approach. This distinction also appears in the work of Liu and Greaker (2009), Gu and Wong (2010), Li et al. (2010), and Jones and Chiripanhura (2010). Below, the role of training as human capital as found in the literature is examined in more detail, because the theories associated with it have been informing policies on training for a number of decades.

6.2. Training as Human Capital and the Matching Theory

To examine what constitutes training, it is necessary to divide it into its two significant forms. Firstly, it is possible to view it as an investment in human capital, perhaps adding to the skills gained during compulsory education. Secondly, it can represent a replacement of general schooling by specific company training owing to there being a mismatch between skills the employee has and those needed. Theoretically, these different types come under two main theoretical viewpoints, the: human capital theory and matching theory. At a first glance, these perspectives appear to be similar as they both support the notion of investing to train in order to add to skills. However, as becomes apparent below, the two theories are based on diverse approaches to training (van Smoorenburg and van der Velden, 2000).

Proponents of human capital theory hold that it is the type of training input that largely determines the amount of increase in job tenure and this will be greater if it is particularly connected to the company, than if it is general (in the classroom). Moreover, under such circumstances it is less likely the worker will leave and employers are not inclined to let workers go when they have paid for them to learn particular skills. By contrast, when training is general, there is nothing to tie the worker to his existing job, since his skills might be of use in all companies. If these assumptions are true, it is reasonable to assume that classroom training is more transferable for the unemployed and training at work leads to greater job tenure (Cockx et al., 1998). On the whole, employers need skilled workers, who have a record of work experience as well as training, so classroom training is not sufficient on its own.

However, the theory of human capital has been criticized for not being able to explain comprehensively the functions of vocational training, for it merely considers it as an investment (Papakonstantinou, 1998). Nonetheless, it has provided the spearhead for the spread of programmes of intensive continuous training and the mass participation of young people in them, regardless of their impact on the improvement of labour skills of the trainees and the possibility of finding work. This is due not only to the restriction of indirect cost (namely, the opportunity cost, that of the loss of wages) owing the recession and the accompanying unemployment, but also to the fact that this type of training is subsidised. In other words, it creates incomes for the trainees, who are motivated to take part regardless of whether they believe that their participation will help them in their vocational reinstatement or to obtain their first job (Dedoussopoulos, 1995).

By contrast, the advocates of matching theory claim that under-education will result in an increased necessity for more training. However, it is not yet clear whether training can make up for inadequacies in formal education (substitution) or if it can just add to variations in human capital (complementarity) that are already present. It could be the case that it is only the features of the job (level and kind of job) in which the substitution aspects of training are to be found, and that it is only in those aspects of formal education (level and breadth) that the complementarity nature of training is obvious (van Smoorenburg and van der Velden, 2000).

Regardless of their different approaches to training and their contributions in understanding the incentives and behaviours of employers, employees and job seekers, it is questionable if micro-level theories can be universally applicable across different political economies for explaining persistent unemployment of trained or well educated job seekers. Indeed, one can seriously question to what extent, for example, human capital theory is applicable to political economies that are not high-skilled ones, with no well developed vocational training structures, as is the case for Greece and to some extent, other Southern European economies. To investigate this matter further, in the next two subsections relevant academic work and policy documents from the period under investigation as well as later, where appropriate, are discussed.

6.3. Mismatch and Skills Shortages

What is meant by a skills shortage is still a matter for debate and to some extent surrounded by a large amount of confusion. A classic old definition from the British Government's Training Agency, defined the existence of a "skills shortage" as being "when there are not enough people available with the skills needed to do the jobs which need to be done" (Training Agency, 1990, p.29). That is, under this lens a skills shortage refers to the situation where it is hard to find workers with appropriate skills. However, it could also mean that a company's existing staff lack the skills necessary to do their job properly. In general, what employers understand by a skills shortage may be different and indeed, earlier research had conflicting views about the meaning of skills and also how a shortage could be defined (Green et al., 1998). Frequently, the skills referred to by employers are basically technical ones, defined as the capability to carry out certain jobs or to learn some techniques, of either a manual or cognitive nature. It has been noted by Oliver and Turton (1982), however, that when employers talk about skills (in terms of skills shortages) they also refer to a number of qualities like reliability, not being dependent on supervision and permanence of employment. Extant research generally concurs that qualities related to conduct as well as technical abilities are part of the package of skills that employers are searching for (Bosworth et al., 1992).

Problems regarding the filling of vacancies have invariably been used to define shortages in empirical studies, both implicitly and explicitly. As a consequence, Green et al. (1998) pointed out that difficulties with existing company employees' skills or their abilities have not been included in skills shortages assessment in any of these studies. In this regard, Haskel and Martin (1993a) considered the CBI (Confederation of British Industry) skills shortage indicator to be a proxy for the mean length of time of skilled labour vacancies, and Stevens (1994) made use of the same indicator as a proxy for the relatively insignificant cost of hiring skilled labour. Jones and Goss (1991), Bosworth (1993), and Haskel and Martin (1993b) counted skills shortages explicitly as vacancies that are difficult to fill in various ways.

6.4. Mismatch and Over-Education

It is Freeman's contention in the original work on over-education in 1976, that over-education is a temporary condition resulting from competition in the labour market, however, UK evidence challenges this (Chevalier and Lindley, 2007). Despite a great deal of American and European empirical evidence now being available on the subject of over-education, it has been argued that "a solid relation [regarding the over-education / under-education literature] with a formal theory of the labour market is lacking" (Hartog, 1997). A further difficulty is the confusion between the term 'over-education' specifically, and very different notions like 'qualification inflation' or 'credentialism' (Green et al., 1999). According to Chevalier and Lindley (2007), over-education can be defined as not being in a graduate job when a person has a degree, thus resulting in skill mismatching.

Nevertheless, when Hartog (1997) extensively surveyed the literature he found signs that over-education has grown in frequency over the years in Europe, i.e., especially since the 1970s, whilst there has been a lesser occurrence of under-education. In general, the vast majority of studies during the period 1990-2000 have indicated greater prevalence of over-education rather than under-education (Green et al., 1999).

According to human capital theory, over-education is not a permanent occurrence and is the result of a poor match between employer and employee. This appears to go against the empirical evidence, which suggests there is always a large percentage of the labour force that is over-educated (Green et al., 1999). It is possible that there is always over-education in the labour market generally, but for each individual it is short lived. However, it could also be the case that an individual chooses to be over-educated for a position, temporarily, so as to remain in touch with the labour market in order to find a better job in the future. From this point of view, over-education could be thought of as being a sort of human capital investment (Green et al., 1999).

A different interpretation of over-education is offered by matching theory. Under this lens, there might be a poor match between employer and employee causing over-education, often resulting in the worker looking for a better match elsewhere. The fact that both over- and under-education are to be found lends credence to the opinion that they are both indications of the occurrence of poor matching in the labour market. In this instance, or if the substitution hypothesis (by which employment is not actually greater) is right, over-education would be just short lived for the worker concerned (Green *et al.*, 1999). It is necessary to discover whether over-education is temporary or not, for it does not constitute a social problem if it is. That is, it is an instability condition related to age, mobility and/or training. However, when persistent over-education occurs, according to Patrinos (1997), the focus needs to be shifted away from the individual and his/her characteristics towards institutions and policies regarding employment and vocational training across the focal society and its political economy.

Given newer graduates are probably of less 'value' than those in work for a significant time and increased instability in the labour market, the percentage of over-educated graduates has risen enormously and their situation has worsened (Chevalier and Lindley, 2006).

The next section presents the micro-econometric work of the research. It is an established methodology and involves one logit model for all three areas under examination (Central Macedonia, Attica and the rest of Greece) based on micro-data from the Greek LFS for the years 1992, 1994 and 2000.

7. Micro-Level of Analysis II: Econometric Analysis for Greece

The *Table 1* presents the results, namely, the estimated coefficients (B), the standard errors (S.E.) and the p values for each explanatory variable in the logistic regression for unemployment in Greece for 1992, 1994 and 2000, pooling together all the available data into one database. *Table 1* presents the main effects. Column "Sig." (level of statistical significance or p value) provides the coefficients for the variables and those above 0.05 are not statistically significant. In *Table 1*, b_k is the log of the odds, whereas Exp (b_k) is the odds ratio.

If exp(B) > 1 ⇒ more likely for someone to be unemployed.

If exp(B) ≈ 1 ⇒ same probabilities for someone to be unemployed or not to be unemployed.

If exp(B) < 1 ⇒ less likely for someone to be unemployed.

The descriptive statistics of the logit model are summarised in *Table 2*. After taking into account missing records, restricting the sample by age (15-64 years old) and removing the non-active population, *Table 3* shows the numbers of records eligible for analysis in the LFS samples (covering the spring and early summer, namely, from the 14th to 26th week of the year) of both NUTS-2 regions under examination, and the rest of Greece as well, for 1992, 1994 and 2000 together.

Females, non-married individuals, people in the age group 15-24 years old, people who lived either in the Athens or Thessaloniki areas, the other urban areas or semi-urban areas were more likely to be unemployed than males, married people, people aged between 25 to 64 and those in rural areas. University graduates had more chances of finding a job compared to all other educational categories apart from MSc or PhD holders (these differences were not found significant). These results are in contrast to some studies which have asserted the opposite. The variable "immigrant status" was found to be statistically non-significant.

Most importantly, the participation in vocational training programmes did not seem to reduce the odds of unemployment, that is, training was found to be statistically non-significant during the first and the second CSFs. This means that the results of training variables are not compatible with the human capital theory. In other words, the more trained a person was did not affect his chances of finding a job, in Greece, during the time period of CSFs 1 and 2. The same results on training were found for other Greek regions and the entire country as well (see Livanos, 2007 and 2009a; Rodokanakis, 2009; Rodokanakis and Tryfonidis, 2009; Rodokanakis, 2010a, 2010b and 2011; Rodokanakis and Vlachos, 2013a and 2013b). The exceptions are the findings for the region of Eastern Macedonia and Thrace in 2000 concerning the training variables "apprenticeship" and "CVT" (less likely to be unemployed than the non-trainees - see Rodokanakis and Vlachos, 2012).

Whether or not someone lived in Central Macedonia in 1992, 1994 or 2000 was statistically non-significant. By contrast, people who lived in the region of Attica were more likely to be unemployed than those living in the rest of Greece. Both of the years 1994 and 2000 were found to be statistically non-significant, i.e., the variable "time" did not influence the probability of being unemployed.

Table 1. Results (main effects) for Greece, 1992, 1994 and 2000 (parameter estimates b_k, standard errors (s.e.), p-values, exponent of b_k)

Variables	b_k	S.E.	Sig.	Exp (b_k)
Gender	0 .915	0 .019	0.000	2.497
Marital status	-0.398	0.039	0.000	0.671
Aged 15-24	ref.	ref.	ref.	ref.
Aged 25-34	-1.023	0.024	0.000	0.359
Aged 35-44	-1.706	0.029	0.000	0.182
Aged 45-64	-1.977	0.031	0.000	0.139
University graduates	ref.	ref.	ref.	ref.
MSc or PhD holders	0.110	0.183	0.546	1.116
TEI graduates	0.371	0.046	0.000	1.449
12 years of schooling	0.601	0.038	0.000	1.824
9 years compulsory education	0.550	0.044	0.000	1.734
Primary school graduates and below	0.518	0.040	0.000	1.679
Rest of Greece	ref.	ref.	ref.	ref.
Attica	0.083	0.041	0.046	1.086
Central Macedonia	-0.075	0.041	0.064	0.927
Rural areas	ref.	ref.	ref.	ref.
Athens area	0.738	0.050	0.000	2.091
Thessaloniki area	0.787	0.054	0.000	2.196
Rest of urban areas	0.899	0.030	0.000	2.457
Semi-urban areas	0.518	0.037	0.000	1.679
Non-participation in training course(s)	ref.	ref.	ref.	ref.
Training	-0.013	0.052	0.808	0.987
Citizenship	0.077	0.058	0.179	1.080
Year 1992	ref.	ref.	ref.	ref.
Year 1994	0.025	0.022	0.266	1.025
Year 2000	0.055	0.033	0.096	1.056
Constant	-2.262	0.062	0.000	0.104

Table 2. Descriptive statistics of the logit model

The reference or base categories are in bold

Variables/Area/Year	**Frequencies**	**Percent**
Employed	138,405	90,4%
Unemployed	14,628	9,6%
Males	94,943	62,0%
Females	58,090	38,0%
Non-married	10,339	6,8%
Married or divorced or widows	142,694	93,2%

Variables/Area/Year	Frequencies	Percent
Aged 15-24	19,395	12,7%
Aged 25-34	39,975	26,1%
Aged 35-44	39,708	25,9%
Aged 45-64	53,955	35,3%
Training	4,208	2,7%
Non-participation in training	148,825	97,3%
Greek Citizenship	149,881	97,9%
Foreigner Ctizenship	3,152	2,1%
Athens area	45,994	30,1%
Thessaloniki area	12,662	8,3%
Rest of urban areas	36,433	23,8%
Semi-urban areas	18,989	12,4%
Rural areas	38,955	25,5%
MSc or PhD holders	554	0,4%
University graduates	15,048	9,8%
TEI graduates	11,358	7,4%
Twelve years of schooling	40,762	27,8%
Nine years compulsory education	14,532	9,9%
Primary school graduates and below	64,561	44,0%
Central Macedonia	24,398	15,9%
Attica	53,773	35,1%
Rest of Greece	74,862	48,9%
Year 1992	53,297	34,8%
Year 1994	65,858	43,0%
Year 2000	33,878	22,1%

Table 3. Numbers of records eligible for analysis in the LFS samples

Year	**Geographical level**	**No. of records**
1992	Greece	53,297
	Rest of Greece	23,706
	Central Macedonia	9,290
	Attica	20,301
1994	Greece	65,858
	Rest of Greece	33,916
	Central Macedonia	9,543
	Attica	22,399
2000	Greece	33,878
	Rest of Greece	17,240
	Central Macedonia	5,565
	Attica	11,073

In the main, my econometric results for Greece confirm the human capital theory concerning education, namely, university graduates had higher probabilities of finding a job than people from lower educational categories. However, this was not the case in the field of training, since this variable was found to be statistically non-significant. Thus, it would appear that matching theory has better explanatory power than human capital theory in the Greek context. This is because the former perspective holds that those with more education need less training and in Greece there are many over-educated people.

The micro-level individual characteristics analysis has addressed the question “what was the impact of the training programmes at the participant level?” and links to next level, namely the organisation of VET system to facilitate skills formation and skills matching. In the next section, I examine the training system and research the situation in the field of vocational training during the implementation of the first three CSFs. Also, I follow a critique of skill mismatches between education, training and the labour market in that country.

8. Meso-Level Analysis

The aim here is to describe the VET structure and investigate how adequate or not was the Greek organisational structure to do skills-matching, through secondary data (other studies). The meso-level organisational structure analysis addresses the question “Was the training system, i.e., the institutions, in Greece, both regionally and nationally, effective in helping people to find jobs and if not, why?”. The next section focuses on the characteristics of the vocational training system in Greece during the time period of the study.

8.1. The Greek VET and CVT Systems

To date, there has never been a single, official, institutionalised system of CVT in Greece, even though the term itself was introduced in the late 1980s. Vocational training in Greece developed fast and in an un-coordinated manner under the influence of funding from the ESF. This process was characterised by an intense lack of co-ordination and delays in relation to meeting the social and economic needs of the country. Initial activities of a CVT form started developing in the middle of the 1950s in the country, being organised by state agencies and organisations, but mainly by large private industrial enterprises. However, the absence of an organised and efficient public system of initial vocational training until the beginning of the 1960s and the lack of a specialised workforce to meet imperative needs emerging in the labour market due to the fast and heterogeneous economic growth at that time, led to most of such training activities becoming poor substitutes for initial vocational training (Chasapis, 1994). As a result of this development there was a conceptual ambiguity in Greece concerning the distinction between activities of initial and continuing vocational training. Activities of CVT in the real sense of the word had, therefore, remained essentially marginal, both in terms of their extent and in terms of their role until the end of the 1980s (Chasapis, 1994). Since then, and especially during the period 1990-2010, there was an impressive development of CVT activities, mainly as a result of fast restructuring of manufacturing processes, due to the rapid introduction of new technologies to Greek industry and the service sector.

In this context, as the 1st CSF did not require any ratification or recognition by the state (Chasapis, 1994), the market of CVT was open and characterised by a multitude of heterogeneous agencies providing training to both working and unemployed persons with the state assuming an assisting role. This network was developed irrespective of the official vocational training system, while most major companies in Greece developed and implemented systematic training courses for their personnel (Linardos-Rylmon, 1995). Although CVT was generally privatised it was supported by the Greek state in the last decade of the twentieth century and in the 2000s. According to Prokou (2011), the increasing reliance on the private sector for training was because public initiatives against unemployment were increasingly being called into question.

There were problems which created obstacles and made it difficult for the CVT programme to reach its recipients, even when it was specially designed for them. This was the result of a lack of preparatory and reinforcing efforts as well as the absence of an adequate and effective information networks (Dedoussopoulos, 1996). In Greece, the meaning of the term vocational training teacher had not been defined. There were no relevant legal regulations which defined the scope of a a professional template or procedures that would determine the individuals who would have the right to be teachers on training programmes. There were no figures relating to the whole picture for the number of people who were working on CVT programmes (Iliades, 1995). Moreover, the programmes that were funded were selected using criteria that did not allow for the evaluation of their effects on production and employment. The prevailing criteria referred to typical specifications relating to the management of the programmes, and not to the content of the training. Owing to the impossibility of collecting the relevant information regarding the skills that were being selected and the content of the education, Centres for Vocational Training (KEK) programmes could not be evaluated (Linardos-Rylmon, 1998). Also, Brussels did not (and until now does not) evaluate the impact of vocational training programmes funded by the EU on the Greek labour market, focusing only on ensuring that bureaucratic and financial controls were in place.

The lack of a general institutional framework in relation to CVT resulted in, apart from other things, the weakness of the planning and application of a training policy, in connection with the development of specific geographical regions and branches of the economy (Iliades, 1995). The education-training policy could not, by itself, constitute the solution to unemployment, because unemployment was not exclusively due to the lack of educational qualifications and skills, but to the absence of a particular model of economic development (Chletsos, 1998).

8.2. Vocational Training in Greece during the First Three CSFS (1989-2006)

Even during the CSF-2 an issue of fundamental importance in the field of CVT was that there was no certification or recognition of skills and competences acquired by trainees. No system of examinations was in place and the structure and content of curricula was not controlled, which came under the responsibility and jurisdiction of the KEK. Thus, ordinary certificates of course attendance issued to participants had no value whatsoever in the labour market, as they reflected no recognised qualifications (IN.E./GSEE-ADEDY, 2000). As a result, a system similar to that of initial training was established for CVT, the main features of which were as follows:

- The majority of training course contents were neither job-specific nor firm-specific, but rather subject-specific (annual reports by the National Employment Observatory)[4].
- The prevalence of a casual attitude to the preparation of curricula and the selection of teaching means, teaching methods and teaching staff[5].
- The absence of any systematic evaluation of the activities of various agencies and the skills and knowledge acquired by the trainees upon completion of the course, which often led to the preparation of programmes only minimally corresponding to the objectives and principles of the implementation framework (IN.E./GSEE-ADEDY, 2000).

Furthermore, the implementation of CSF-2 was characterised by:

- Serious inability of state mechanisms in handling issues of planning and implementation (incapacity to deal with complex problem-solving, insufficient planning and shortcomings of effective implementation).
- Difficulties in implementing actions, especially the more innovative ones.
- Insufficient preparation for the implementation of interventions, which lacked necessary measures and pilot applications, while in many cases planning was undertaken *a posteriori*.
- Lack of data with clear information on the funds spent on different programmes, e.g., comparing programme participants and their educational characteristics (IN.E./GSEE-ADEDY, 2000).

It should be noted that in designing a global system for evaluating and monitoring the operational results of training interventions in the human resources, the aim should be to ensure the greatest possible active participation of training institutions in a framework of self-evaluation procedures, whose reliability, adequacy and effectiveness should be continually monitored and evaluated by outside auditors. This, however, had never happened in Greece, with either of the first two CSFs, apart from there being bureaucratic controls (Balourdos and Chryssakis, 1998). The 2000-06 Operational Programme (OP) of CVT and Promotion of Employment was one of the most important policies for the development of human potential in the country. It was consistently supported by hard data with clear, well-focused and prioritised goals. It was anticipated that 2000-06 OP planning would underline the creation of mechanisms that would allow for the tackling of various problems. Furthermore, it was to be the first time that a framework for the implementation of employment policies that was capable of evaluating the efficacy of its interventions would be established and hence, implement corrective actions (IN.E./GSEE-ADEDY, 2000). One of the main points discovered by the Ministry of Labour and Social Security about the above OP (Regional Development Plan 2000-06) was that it did not provide for nor implement in good time ways of studying the impact of training (IN.E./GSEE-ADEDY, 2000).

---

4 GSEE Memorandum to the National Employment Observatory, June 1999.

5 KEPE-REMACO (1998), Initial approach to the interim evaluation of CSF-2, ch. 2 (Athens: Ministry of National Economy, unpublished study), pp. 21-3.

The programme was characterised by contradictions in the preparation of policies responding to recognised needs for the development of the human potential in Greece, also being limited to generalities. Furthermore, there was a complete lack of co-ordination of policies and actions to resolve the employment issue, which were not fully processed and, therefore, the programme could not guarantee their timely, reliable and effective implementation. Finally, all the vocational training policies, whether they were initial, continuing or training for the unemployed, did not apply a complete system of evaluation and observation of their results that allowed permanent re-providing and readjustment. Instead, they functioned as closed systems where the determining factor for the planning and materialization of policies was the supply and not the demand of the relative vocations and specializations (INE/GSEE-ADEDY, 2007).

In contrast to the institutional agreements and relevant laws, collective bargaining did not give high priority to matters of vocational training (European Industrial Relations Observatory [EIRO] – Karakioulafi, 2006). Developments in vocational training were ignored except for some instances of discussion on lifelong learning, such as, for example, in the banking sector (European Industrial Relations Observatory, 2007). The next section of this chapter examines whether there was matching between supply and demand for labour in the Greek labour market in the 1990s.

8.3. Skills Mismatching in Greece during the Reference Time Period

8.3.1. Matching Mechanisms in Greece

In Greece, the matching of labour supply and demand remained the exclusive responsibility of the state during the reference time period of the study, and legally the only institution competent to supply such services was OAED. Efforts to rationalise the distribution of personnel and the staffing of employment bureaus - both territorially and administratively - made during the 1980s came to nothing. It should be noted, meanwhile, that the staff of the organisation had been significantly reduced over the period 1987-1997, while at the same time there had been a considerable increase in the volume of work (unemployment subsidies and active interventions) (Dedoussopoulos et al., 1998). Subsequently, several international institutions (OECD, EU) viewed reforming the OAED as essential, if Greek employment policy were to be improved. In line with this, successive laws were passed during the late 1990s and 2000s, which represented a substantial break from the historical legacy of immobility and stagnation (Zartaloudis, 2014).

Findings acquired from an interviewed sample of policymakers (see Zartaloudis, 2014), demonstrated that the EES impact was limited to two out of the five policy stages of Greek employment policy (see *Table 4*). The reason for this has been attributed to their overlooking the strategy as it was not on their agenda and hence, did not feature in their proposed reforms of the OAED. By contrast, ESF conditionality appears to have an impact on the attention paid to the third and fourth policy stages (decision making and policy-implementation, respectively). Moreover, the nature of EES-induced change was indirect, whereby the Greek employment policy introduced new programmes through Centres of Employment Promotion (KPA) and KPA2, aimed at providing individualized support to the unemployed in the form of consultation, training and employment subsidies. Nevertheless, the EES did not succeed in heading off the original aims of the Greek employment policy, KPA and KPA2, because they did not replace the OAED as its main institution. Indeed, despite the change of the Greek employment policy's content, it remained and Europeanization was outsourced to small independent agencies tasked with delivering the new EES-induced policy. Consequently, it becomes apparent that the EES did not bring about a paradigm shift (third-order change or transformation) in the Greek employment policy. That is, Greece merely adjusted its existing processes, policies and institutions without altering their basic features or the underlying collective meanings attributed to them. In particular, although there was pressing the need to provide robust data on ESF programme performance, the Greek employment policy did not manage to achieve this. As a result, there was little produced at the policy evaluation level and there was no change at the domestic level, largely because the EES drivers failed to take hold.

Table 4. EES impact on Greek public employment services

Policy stages	Degree of EES-induced change
Agenda-setting (problem recognition)	Inertia (no change)
Policy-formulation (proposal of solution)	Inertia (no change)
Decision-making (choice of solution)	Upgrading (second-order change)
Policy-implementation (putting solution into effect)	Upgrading (second-order change)
Policy-evaluation (monitoring results)	Inertia (no change)

Source: Zartaloudis, 2014.

8.3.2. Matching Educational System and Labour Market Needs in Greece

The existing literature has not given enough importance to the high level of graduate unemployment, despite it being one of the major features of the Greek labour market. Using the micro-data from the Greek LFS that is obtainable, Livanos (2009b) examined the variations in the employment status of university degree holders up to 35 years old in relation to their discipline of study. The results indicated that graduates of technical universities and having studied subjects like computer science that were associated with high levels of employment in private companies, were more likely to be in a superior position in the Greek labour market. Graduates in fields that were normally connected to the requirements of the public sector, however, such as sociology and the humanities, had lower probabilities of being employed in the private sector.

According to Tsakloglou and Cholezas (2005), between 1988 and 1999 the percentage of the labour force with tertiary education qualifications rose from 14.1% to 22.2%. Furthermore, between 1994 and 2001 Greece had one of the highest over-education rates of all the EU countries examined, according to Dolton and Marcenaro-Gutierrez (2009), using comparable ECHPS data. It would therefore seem to be true that a high proportion of the large investment of Greeks in human capital had gone into professions that were not compatible with the needs of the labour market (Livanos and Pouliakas, 2009).

During the reference time period of the study, the state was not equipped with the mechanisms and the flexibility required to change the curricula and follow the evolution of science and technology and local labour market conditions (Kanellopoulos, 1996). At the same time, procedures for education, training and entry into the labour market were not anticipated for the vast numbers of young people who did not succeed in obtaining tertiary education places (Iliades, 1995). Later studies by Greek researchers shed more light upon the reasons for high unemployment rates among graduates in Greece and their problems moving into work from education. According to Kanellopoulos et al. (2003), these transition problems arose because higher education was geared towards public sector needs and thus failed to meet the needs of the business sector. However, Liagouras et al. (2003), Karamessini (2008, 2010) and Thomaidou et al. (2009) claimed that the most important reason was the discrepancy between the outflows from higher education and the domestic demand for well educated staff.

I now proceed to discuss some macro-economic data on the Greek economy and labour force from secondary sources, as well as discuss the literature on the comparative political economy (CPE) of VET systems to situate the Greek case. Then, I will explore how well does Greece fit the Southern European model using secondary data. Also, I will consider the employment policies in Greece, the EES and reform capacity for that nation.

9. Macro-Level Analysis

Having presented the findings at the micro and meso levels regarding the Greek labour market for the focal period, 1988 to 2000, obtained through my empirical calculations as well as secondary data analysis, as explained previously, it is important to contextualize these by considering macro-level labour market policy. That is, it is considered beneficial to outline the wider macro-economic and labour market context of Greece as a part of the EU during this period. I aim to demonstrate that although EU funded training policy in Greece has been taking place since 1988, there has been and still is, little or no impact on the matching between the supply and demand for labour. The following macro-level policy and macro-economic conditions analysis addresses the questions "To what extent did the ALMPs in Greece, in particular the policies of vocational training, integrate EU-funded training in their skills strategy? To what extent was any (in)effectiveness of ALMPs related to the characteristics of the Greek political economy?". I also consider whether approaching Greece as typical case of the Southern European political economy can help us understand this low-skills equilibrium. First, I discuss the macro-economic data for Greece, as well as the role of ALMPs in Greece. Then, a discussion on the Greek political economy and that nation's reform capacity follows. Finally, I follow a critique of the EU's model for financing vocational training in the Greek context and link my research to the present economic situation in Greece. The next section and the subsequent sub-section provide information about the macro-economic data of Greece from secondary sources.

9.1. Macro-Economic Data for Greece and the Two NUTS-2 Regions

According to the 1991 census, the Greek population was approximately 10.26 million (10.81 million according to the 2001 census). In 1988, the nation's GDP was equal to 58% of the EU-12 average, whereas by 1996 it had improved its position to 68% of the EU-15 mean (OECD, 1998). Moreover, by 2008 the Greek GDP (PPP) per capita was 80% of the EU-15 (World Economic Outlook Database, April 2009, IMF). Also, according to the UN classification of human development index released in December 2008, covering the period up to 2006 - Greece was ranked 18th in the world and 11th in the EU. Central Greece, Southern Aegean and Attica were the richest regions since 1991 in per capita GDP [ESYE (www.statistics.gr)]. Greece (from 2000 onwards) and Ireland (from the early 1990s onwards) had the highest GDP growth rates in the EU-15 (Eurostat) until the current economic and financial crisis. During the period under investigation, the expansion of the service sector and the reduction of agricultural sector continued and by 2008, roughly 66% of the workforce in Greece was involved in the service sector, 23% in industry, and 11% in agriculture (ESYE, various years).

The region of Attica is geographically situated in Central Greece. According to the 1991 census its population size was approximately 3.5 million, in other words, three out of 10 Greeks lived there (about the same in the 2001 census). The capital of the region is the city of Athens, which is by far the most important Greek city in economic, administrative and political terms. In 1988, Attica's GDP was equal to 61% of the EU-12 average (58% for Greece as a whole), whereas in 1996 the region improved its position to 77% of the EU-15 mean (68% for the country as a whole), which rose to 86% of the EU-25 mean in 2003 (80.9% for Greece as a whole). The region produced 37.4% of the country's GDP, entailing 2.7% of the country's agricultural produce, 35.5% of manufacturing and 42% of services (2001) - www.ypes.gr/attiki and (ESYE [www.statistics.gr]).

Central Macedonia is the largest region of Greece (19,147 km^2 - 14.5% of the country's surface), it is situated in the centre of Northern Greece and is the second largest Greek region in terms of population (about 1.7 million inhabitants according to the 1991 census, and 1.88 million according to 2001 census). The major urban centre and capital of Central Macedonia is Thessaloniki, which is the second most important Greek city. The main industries were textiles, plastic-chemicals, food-beverages and clothing. In 2003, the region's per capita GDP (PPS) was 17,110 euros (83% of the EU-25 average), with Thessaloniki and Chalkidiki being the richest NUTS-3 areas having a GDP per head equal to 90.3% and 89.5%, correspondingly, of the EU-25 mean. In 2003, the region produced 17.6% of the country's GDP (the second largest contributor after Attica), 18% of the national agricultural produce (first in the country), 20% of the manufacturing production (second in the country) and 18% of services (second in the country).

9.1.1. Unemployment in Greece during the Period 1988-2002

The unemployment rate[6] climbed from 7.7% in 1988 to 11.5% in 1998[7] (LFS). Unemployment in Greece was, and remained, a structural phenomenon from the mid-1990s onwards of considerable dimensions and with a particular dynamic. According to Eurostat data, the unemployment rate in the EU-15 increased from 8.2% in 1991 to 10.9% in 1996 (Eurostat, Unemployment in the EU, 1997). The rate in Greece rose above the EU average for the first time in 1998 and continued increasing, and the gap was widening, since the EU average was falling (IN.E./GSEE-ADEDY, 2000). Despite a reduction in 2001 in the rate of unemployment for the second year running, it stayed the highest in the EU-15 at 10.5% apart

[6] The percentage of unemployment is characterized by an augmentative tendency from 1988 to 1998 with the exception of the two year period 1989-1990, during which it shows a temporary decrease.

[7] On the basis of Eurostat figures, unemployment in 1998 was 10.8% (1997=9.6%). However, on the basis of the definitions used up until 1997, the unemployment rate in 1998 was 11.5%.

from Spain (10.6%) and was the fourth highest in the OECD, lower only than Slovakia (18.8%) and Poland (16.1%) (Seferiades, 2006).

Gender and age group seem to have been and remain significant determining factors affecting the probability of someone becoming unemployed. It was common knowledge that females and the young were much more vulnerable to unemployment than older persons. The meagre payments for the unemployed could hardly be considered as providing incentives for someone to remain so (Bouzas and Ketsetzopoulou, 1998; Papadopoulos, 2006). It is reasonable to accept that the problematic matching of the unemployed with jobs made it more difficult for the young unemployed to find work, as they were inexperienced and therefore, had to try longer before they could find a job (Petrinioti, 1999).

Table 5 indicates that despite years of EU funding of training, Greece had the highest unemployment rate for both the EU and Euro area averages in 2002. The picture alters when unemployment is broken down according to gender. The unemployment rates of Greek females were higher than the respective EU averages during the introduction year of the euro (2002), but the opposite was the case for the Greek males.

Table 5. Unemployment rates by gender and age

Gender/geographical area - year/age		2002	
		Aged 15-24	Total
Total	European Union	18.0	8.9
	Euro area	16.0	8.4
	Greece	26.8	10.3
Males	European Union	17.9	8.3
	Euro area	15.3	7.5
	Greece	19.9	6.8
Females	European Union	18.1	9.7
	Euro area	17.0	9.7
	Greece	35.3	15.7

Source: Eurostat (http://epp.eurostat.ec.europa.eu/portal/page/portal/statistics/ search_ database).

9.2. ALMPs in Greece

Before proceeding, it is important to clarify what is meant by ALMPs. Here, the OECD's standard typology of ALMPs into five categories is adopted (OECD, 1993):

- temporary job creation;
- training;
- help with job-hunting;
- wage subsidies for regular employment; and
- aid for people beginning their own businesses.

In Greece, the ALMPs developed systematically at the beginning of the 1980s with ESF backing and were placed originally in the micro-economic intervention measures. From the beginning of their application, ALMPs in Greece were placed in a framework of the reinforcement of the labour supply, functioning as a substitute for the policies for the protection of the unemployed. The absence of a systematic evaluation of the results of ALMPs was the reality, despite the fact that these had been functioning for at least 20 years continuously, starting from the late 1980s. In the cases, moreover, where evaluation studies were carried out, following a demand by the EU, their basic financial backer, they showed the results of ALMPs in Greece were not particularly encouraging, but these were never published (INE/GSEE, 2008).

In the Greek case, the effectiveness of ALMPs was undermined by serious deficiencies in the policy implementation measures. According to Dedoussopoulos and Karamessini (1998), despite national differences, very widely used ALMPs, such as wage subsidies and vocational (re)training, had a small and diffuse impact on employment creation. The ALMPs did not function "therapeutically" by promoting the employment of the unemployed who were exhibiting increased social and professional needs, but rather, they actually appear to have financed even more the employment of those unemployed who had comparative advantages in the labour market (Balourdos and Chryssakis, 1998). Dedoussopoulos and Karamessini (1998) pointed out that the reasons for the low effectiveness of ALMPs in Greece differed from programme to programme and did not exclusively relate to the policy implementation measures in place, i.e., to national particularities in relation to other EU countries. Regarding the policy formation and implementation aspects, the common factors that led to poor outcomes and diversion of all the relevant programmes in Greece from their expected goals were:

a. Insufficient monitoring of labour market changes and trends.
b. Problems in the design of the programmes and insufficient control against mismanagement.
c. Lack of an integrated approach to the treatment of the unemployed, in particular, failure to combine participation in ALMPs with guidance and assistance for job search.

9.3. Comparative Political Economy, Skills Formation and Southern Europe

There has been a plethora of literature on CPE or varieties of capitalism (VoC) over the last twenty five years. At first, the discussion centred on the bipolar relation of Anglo-Saxon vs. Rhineland/Nippon capitalism. Hall and Soskice have been criticised for their contention (see Morgan et al., 2005) that Southern European countries are 'ambiguous' cases belonging to neither of the two ideal types, thus excluding France, Italy, Spain, Portugal and Greece from either of their models (2001:21). They have pointed to the historical and institutional characteristics of Southern European political economies to justify their position. Specifically, these nations followed a different path to industrialisation, had a markedly long historical experience of authoritarianism and hence, late political democratisation. Moreover, they developed hybrid forms of welfare state arrangements where fragmented systems of social insurance, of Bismarckian inspiration, were supportive of the prominent welfare agent, the family (and in catholic Southern European countries, the Church). These aspects were difficult to integrate in the original VoC framework and hence, other authors attempted to expand it considerably.

Molina and Rhodes (2005) put forward a different model for the Mediterranean countries, that while based on that of Hall and Soskice, adds the concept of mixed market economies (MMEs). Despite employers and unions having tougher organisational structures in MMEs than in LMEs (like the U.S. and UK) they are less cohesive and find it more difficult to clarify their interests than in co-ordinated market economies (CMEs). In particular, they have a problem maintaining autonomous co-ordination in collective bargaining and in delivering collective goods. Nevertheless, they succeed in rejecting reform, in fact, the political system is remarkable for its inability to deal with reform pressures. Furthermore, MMEs are hybrid systems: countries in Southern Europe that are characterised by high employment protection and low social protection. Hall and Soskice (2001), however, viewed the model differently, considering production and welfare to be two complementary institutions where the efficiency of one was greater because of the existence of the other (see Amable, 2003:6; Featherstone, 2008). Molina and Rhodes (2005), by contrast, believed hybrid of MMEs could perhaps be more capable of compromise and adaptation.

The debate about whether the Southern European nations' welfare states represent a distinct entity goes back to the early 1990s (Leibfried, 1992; Castles and Ferrera, 1996; Ferrera, 1996; Petmesidou, 1996; Gough et al., 1997; Rhodes, 1997; Esping-Andersen, 1999; Andreotti et al., 2001; Katrougalos and Lazaridou, 2003; Vasconcelos and Figueiredo, 2005), which has since been extended to include family models and care regimes (Jurado and Naldini, 1997; Trifiletti, 1999; Saraceno, 2000; Bettio and Plantenga, 2004). Research comparing gender inequality in the labour market, the family and the welfare state in Spain, Portugal, Italy and Greece, although finding similarities in relation to changes in the 'gender order' in the latter part of the last century (Gonzalez et al., 2000), has failed to provide sufficient evidence of the Southern European 'gender regime.'

Whether Italy, Greece, Spain and Portugal represent a "fourth world of welfare capitalism" (Karamessini, 2007) or simply a subset of the welfare states of Continental Europe is contested. The latter have social security systems based on employment tenure and type of occupation, such that those without work receive mimimum state benfefits. Moreover, they lack strong labour market regulation and strong familialism. The latter refers to the family as care-giver as well as welfare provider, with a male bread-winner being the focu of welfare protection (Esping-Andersen, 1999). Katrougalos and Lazaridou (2003) also consider the Southern European countries as a variant of the conservative welfare regime, but they stress that the main reason these differ from their Continental European counterparts, is because of their immaturity and relative inefficiency of their social protection system. At the other extreme, Leibfried (1992), Ferrera (1996) and Petmesidou (1996) have argued in favour of there being a distinct Southern European model of social protection and welfare, although each of these authors claims this on different grounds.

Gallie and Paugam (2000) having studied unemployment for different welfare regimes, subsequently classified Greece, Italy, Spain and Portugal as being of the familialist type. This was concluded through assessing different combinations of responsibility taken by the welfare state and the family aimed at providing for the unemployed. Much of the literature on the Southern European nations has pointed to familial actions common to these societies, including: pooling incomes, mobilising clientelism to obtain social benefits as well as public sector jobs, transferring home ownership amongst other things, geared towards supporting unemployed family members (Castles and Ferrera, 1996; Ferrera, 1996; Petmesidou, 1996). Further, family and family policy models as well as those relating to care regimes have provided support for the notion that Southern European welfare regimes are a distinct entity (Jurado and Naldini, 1997; Trifiletti, 1999; Saraceno, 2000; Bettio and Plantenga, 2004).

Mingione (2002) highlighted these nations' labour market similarities in terms of the common political, social and economic features that they have evolved. Specifically, he pointed out that these are late industrialising countries in which the state has promoted the role of small and family enterprises by protecting the internal market and tolerating tax avoidance.

Amable (2003) classifies a wider range of national capitalisms, identifying five types:

- market-based (similar to an LME for Hall and Soskice, 2001);
- social democratic;
- continental;
- Mediterranean;
- Asian.

Table 6 offers a summary of Amable's Mediterranean type.

Table 6. The Southern European variety of capitalism according to Amable (2003)

Institutional Area	South European capitalism
Product-market competition	Price - rather than quality - based competition, involvement of the state, little'non-price' co-ordination, moderate protection against foreign trade or investment, importance of small firms
Wage–labour nexus	High employment protection (large firms) but dualism: a 'flexible' fringe of employment in temporary and part-time work, possible conflicts in industrial relations, no active employment policy, centralization of wage bargaining
Financial sector	Low protection of external shareholders, high ownership concentration, bank-based corporate governance, no active market for corporate control (takeovers, mergers and acquisitions), low sophistication of financial markets, limited development of venture capital, high banking concentration
Social Protection	Moderate level of social protection, expenditures structure oriented towards poverty alleviation and pensions, high involvement of the State
Education	Low public expenditures, low enrolment rates in tertiary education, weak higher education system, weak vocational training, no lifelong learning, emphasis on general skills

Sources: Amable et al. (1997); Amable (2000).

Social protection against unemployment improved throughout Southern Europe in the 1970s and 1980s, in particular in Spain and Portugal, but the benefits remained the lowest for the former EU-15 (Karamessini, 2007).

Various actions to upskill in Southern Europe have been taken. In particular, tertiary education has been made available to rapidly increasing numbers of students, except for Italy with much slower growth. Notably, both, Italy and Greece have grown the numbers of youths completing upper secondary education. In Spain and Portugal, during the 2000s major institutional reforms in continuing training and accreditation of training skills and qualifications were made (Karamessini, 2007). As regards labour market structures of the four Southern European countries mentioned here, their similarities and some differences have been identified by numerous comparative socio-economic studies as mentioned above in this section. From the debate summarised irrespective of whether there is a distinctive 'Southern European social model' the following similarities in the pattern of social reproduction in Southern European countries can be discerned:

- Much higher self-employment rates than the EU average;
- Low female employment rates in all countries except Portugal;
- Low part-time rates and widespread informal work;
- High unemployment rates among youth and women, but low among prime age men and older workers;
- Pronounced labour market segmentation along different divisions (public/private sector, large/small firms, formal/underground economy, age, gender and ethnicity);
- The family is the primary locus of solidarity whose role is both social (provision of care and support) and productive (creation of family businesses);
- The unemployment compensation and vocational training systems are underdeveloped;
- Jobs in the public sector or cash benefits are selectively distributed through clientelism and patronage networks;
- Welfare-state institutions are highly inefficient (Karamessini, 2007).

What we need to take from the VoC literature is that skills regimes and associated vocational training are embedded in particular institutional configurations and national political economies where institutions act complementary with each other. However, processes such as Europeanisation also need to be considered, as they had and continue to impact upon the direction of policy reforms. This is where EU funding and priorities is associated with processes of national adaptation to EU policy objectives which may or may not be compatible with the characteristics of the national VoC. This, in turn, can provide an explanation as to why, despite all the training that have taken place (mainly EU funded), the link between training, skills and the Greek labour market was so weak during the period under investigation. The next section discusses the labour market policies in Greece and the rest of the EU member states.

9.4. Greek Political Economy, the EES and Reform Capacity in Greece

The tradition of state-driven development in Southern Europe is central to Greece's economic history (Tsoukalas, 1993:62; Diamandouros, 1993, 1994:11) and its antipathy to decentralization goes back a long way. Since the Greek political system is based on centralism, this has significantly affected economic advancement and the way society works, as the central state is fundamentally weak (Tsoukalis, 1997). The limited capacity of the Hellenic state to fulfil its regulatory function can be observed in the fact that the state has been incapable of managing the changes needed to modernize a series of sectors (Spanou, 1996). The fragmentation of interest representation and decision-making resulting from the clientelist tradition and perpetuated by the deficiencies in the political/administrative system, has undermined the chances of success of any rationalization policy. Pagoulatos has identified Greece in the post-war period as a weak and incomplete "developmental state," based on a "state-driven policy pattern" with a protected market (2003:47). By means of extensive regulation, protectionist measures, transfers and subsidies the state exerted undue influence on the economy. Furthermore, it was characterized by 'rent-seeking' conduct, whereby particular sectors and interests were able to gain greater benefits from the government than others, in particular, owing to corrupt practice (Sotiropoulos, 2004). Moreover, it was a semi-peripheral type of capitalism, mainly financed by foreign sources rather than income generated domestically (Giner, 1982:176; Mouzelis, 1993; Diamandouros, 1994:23). These capital funds were used for enterprises in the banking, commerce and shipping sectors, instead of manufacturing (Mouzelis, 1993).

Greece has had a poor record when it comes to adopting reforms in accordance, for example, with the Lisbon Agenda (2000), in spite of the desire to implement them being voiced by successive governments. This was largely because the notion of an economic or social 'model' for Greece was absent in those responsible for policy making (Featherstone, 2008).

As mentioned previously, a very small number of big firms and a very large number of small and medium size businesses made up the structure of the economy and this affected the role of the state in terms of mediation between the interest groups. Amable (2003) termed the conditions that applied in this instance as those of high governmental rules and low level of competition. Although protection of employment was powerful, labour was comparatively cheap and inflexibility was widespread (e.g., obligatory overtime). Moreover, through the underground economy state regulation could be avoided by business enterprises. As the CPE approach to Southern European states anticipates, in Greece distorted welfare and heavy regulation have gone hand in hand. The Greek state's ability to provide public goods was also weakened by its relatively low competence and capability. The OECD reported additional reasons for the weakness of competition policy in Greece, namely the absence of a competition culture combined with the well-established and widespread state regulation and price controls (OECD, 2001).

Zartaloudis (2014) pointed out that the Greek ministerial elites saw the EES goals as being inappropriate for the Greek context and consequently, it was largely ignored. That is, policymakers were not prepared to engage in policy learning from other countries in terms of drawing up National Action Plan (NAP)/ National Reform Programme (NRP), viewing it as an excessive bureaucratic burden. Consequently, no centralized body covering the EES was established. Up to that point in time, EES ideas, goals, reports, country-specific proposals and benchmarking failed to deliver any noticeable impact on Greek employment policy, regardless of their being reproduced in numerous official documents (Zartaloudis, 2014). On the basis of the extensive review of labour market characteristics, vocational institutional structures, welfare policies and nature of the Greek political economy, it is concluded that the rolling out of EU money for training and its training policie were not effective.

9.5. Critique of the EU's Model for Financing Vocational Training in the Greek Context

In what follows, I discuss the obstacles to the effective implementation of the EU funded vocational training programmes in Greece. The EU did not, and still does not, impose or recommend the type of vocational training courses to Greece that may be appropriate to the demands of its labour market and the Greek economy, more generally. The Greek agencies decided which programmes to run, whilst the EU simply provided the financial resources and only audited whether were spent appropriately, not if they met any objectives regarding labour market outcomes. Another major criticism, is that consecutive Greek administrations failed to ensure the training programmes were run in a manner that took into account the needs of the Greek labour market.

Human capital theory is not applicable to all countries' economies. The EU's approach regarding vocational training is based on this theory, but the policy generated from it had no impact in the Greek context. In reality, the EU's policy paradigm with respect to vocational training, whilst being logical, presupposed better organization of the Greek labour market than was the case. The Greek institutional framework for skills/ VET/ matching supply and demand was inefficient/ineffective and perhaps totally incompatible with EU funded vocational training programmes. The key point here is that the OAED did not play an effective role, as employers were not obliged to record their needs in terms of skills and shortages. Moreover, there was also no obligation for employers to take people from the register of the unemployed compiled by the OAED. The latter was thus peripheral in the functioning of the labour market even prior to the EU money being made available. As a consequence of this situation, the money that came from Europe and the exposure to Europeanization did not work as a push factor for any serious reorganisation (Zartaloudis, 2014). In sum, the conditions that led to vocational training being effective in some Northern European countries were not present in the Greek labour market.

In Brussels, the perspective was that so as to combat unemployment the supply-side of the economy needed to be reinforced and the demand-side was viewed as being the responsibility of the private sector (banks, entrepreneurs). In addition, institutional reforms in public administration as well as the labour market needed to be carried out by the countries themselves. That is, it was the EU's view that the European countries had, and still have to, put in place the necessary macro-economic conditions for the skilled or high-skilled to be able find employment. The Greek labour market did not produce high-skill jobs despite many Greek people being highly educated.

9.6. Linking This Research to the Present Economic Situation in Greece

Although it is beyond the period under investigation, it is worth discussing some evidence from the impact of the current crisis on the Greek labour market which magnified dramatically the structural problems identified earlier. Despite the unemployment rate in Greece decreasing to the euro area average before the crisis (OECD, 2011), in international terms structural and long-term unemployment remained high in Greece. Moreover, the employment rates for the young, females and the elderly were low. Employment in Greece was seriously affected by the crisis, raising the estimated structural unemployment and the

LTU even further (OECD, 2011). High structural unemployment probably reflected policies that caused the labour market to function less strongly, including quite rigorous employment protection legislation, according to OECD surveys (OECD, 2009). Obstacles, like restrictions on investment, have also been noted by business surveys (World Bank, 2010). It appears that cyclical unemployment has become structural in Greece, which means that it is more difficult to return people to employment after the recession (OECD, 2010; Guichard and Rusticelli, 2010).

During the ten years of vigorous expansion (mid 1990s to mid 2000s) leading up to the crisis, a large number of structural problems persisted in spite of the noticeable improvement in actual labour market outcomes. Subsequent to this, the Greek economy experienced severe recession, with it registering a negative growth rate for the first time since 1993 in 2008, the year of the global financial crisis. In the past, the weaknesses of budget deficits, increasing public debt and a growing external trade deficit, had been partly offset by EU Funds and policies. However, by 2009 the Greek economy was in an extremely bad way. In 2010, the government put forward a "rescue" plan (Memorandum I in April 2010), which has continuously been modified and extended (notably, in July 2011 and in the February 2012 Memorandum II) (Dedoussopoulos et al., 2013), culminating in Memorandum III being set up in the summer 2015. These memoranda chiefly pertained to wage bargaining processes, with the goals of increasing labour market flexibility and productivity. Specifically, these changes included such as: reducing the minimum wage to help the young into the labour market, lowering firing costs, reducing the overtime premium, cutting the salaries paid, prolonging temporary employment, making it easier to sack staff, reducing the severance pay for white collar workers and shortening the notice period for dismissal (Bakas and Papapetrou, 2014).

Since 2008, the GDP has fallen by over 25% (Antonopoulou et al., 2014) and the events that caused this have been subject to heated debate. There are still unresolved questions regarding the extent of the problem, its management by the then Government and the rationale for the policy advocated (Dedoussopoulos et al., 2013). Parallel to this steep fall in GDP, not experienced by any other Western economy, unemployment has continued to increase at an alarming rate. Regarding which, 75% of the job losses happened during the time when Greek policy has been subject to EC-ECB-IMF (Troika) control (2010-13). In terms of figures, the unemployment rate rose from 7.7% in 2008, with the onset of recession, to over 27.8% in October 2013. In absolute terms, 1,000,000 more people became unemployed, making a total of 1,387,520 per (ELSTAT, LFS, January 2014), of whom, 71% have been out of work for over a year (ELSTAT) (Antonopoulou et al., 2014). These statistics are the worst for any Western economy since the Second World War and even the 1929–34 U.S. Great Depression levels have now been overtaken by Greece in terms of depth and duration (Papadimitriou et al., 2013).

The extant structure of unemployment suggests that the likelihood of a large section of the out of work labour force getting a job is very low. Consequently, the Greek economy is going to have to deal with a large permanently poor section of society (more than 20% of the total population), which will not be capable of meeting pension requirements. The increase in social security demand will drive pensions down with significant new resources being allocated to pension funds (Dedoussopoulos et al., 2013). In particular, the rates of youth unemployment are among the highest in the EU and unlike other countries, a substantial proportion is graduates from tertiary education (Mitrakos et al., 2010). Both being unemployed and its duration have been found to be detrimental to employment and career trajectories. Moreover, a brain drain by the educational elite to Northern Europe has impacted badly on the quality of the labour force, although there are no solid numbers regarding this. This could prove to be serious barrier to any re-orientation of the Greek economy involving higher level skills (Dedoussopoulos et al., 2013).

Concerning now the linking of past and present in Greece comparing the meso and macro levels, I can only think of one way in which we can do this. What my research found empirically is that:

a. there was no effect of training for the period under investigation (micro-level). I then, further, contextualised this finding with reference to secondary analysis of evidence and available academic research. I found that:
b. this 'non-effect' took place in (and can be seen as a by-product of) a particular context of vocational training 'system' that had specific characteristics (meso-level);
c. this 'non-effect' and the 'inedequate"/limited vocational training 'system' are outcomes and institutions of a type of political economy that produces and sustains a labour market with a low-skills equilibrium (macro-level).

So, logically, one can expect that if (b) and (c) continue to be unreformed in the second period under investigation (post crisis Greece) then (a) will also remain the same. From my preliminary extra work it does not seem to be any serious changes in the political economy, or reforms in the VET system, to indicate that any change in the outcomes is to be expected. Of course, this is an empirical question that we can only be expected to investigate as part of future research. But all indications are that even 10-15 years later the combination of political economy and the character of Greek VET system will produce similar 'non-effects' - especially now in crisis where unemployment is 'sky-high.' The EU seems to continue to promote/fund ALMPs/training inspired by the same paradigm - which does not seem to work for Greece. Current reforms in Greece seem only to drive the labour costs even lower without any increase in demand for high skills. The solution for many well educated Greeks is now to migrate.

The recent financial crisis that started in the U.S. impacted badly on Ireland and Southern Europe, but Greece was the hardest hit (Antonopoulou et al., 2014). After the 2010 debt crisis, unemployment became a serious matter for Eurozone countries. In Spain, by October 2012 it had reached 26.2%, an unprecedented level. Whilst in Greece and Portugal the rates in September 2012 rose to 26% and 16.2%, respectively, levels not seen for over half a century (Cheng et al., 2014).

The next section is the concluding section of this chapter.

CONCLUSION

The econometric results for Greece (main effects) support the human capital theory with regards to education, i.e., university graduates had a higher probability of finding employment than people with lower education levels. Hence, my findings support the main policy lessons of human capital theory in the field of education. However, this was not so in the case of training, as this variable emerged as being statistically non-significant. That is, the results of the logistic regression confirm the conclusions of the various studies that there was very limited impact of training on the labour market in terms of helping people to find long-term employment (see the critique of the vocational training policies in Greece in section 8 and that on ALMPs in section 9). Also, the output of the logistic regression contrasts with some studies in that they found a positive impact of apprenticeship on the labour market (see below).

The results support matching theory better than human capital theory, because the former supports the perspective that more education leads to less training and Greece has many over-educated people. This supports even more my stance that the human capital theory could (and still can) not provide an explanation for the training configuration found in Greece. The econometric findings on training are in line with those of Livanos (2007 and 2009a) and to the best of my knowledge, our studies are the only econometric studies for Greece on this topic based on LFS micro-data. My results, in general, verify the conclusions of the studies carried out by other authors discussed in section 8 based on qualitative research concerning the impact of training courses on the Greek labour market (meso-level). However, the econometric findings contrast with a number of studies that set out to evaluate the apprenticeship system in Greece as a whole and found a positive influence (Kassimati et al., 1984; University of Macedonia, 1994; University of Patra, 1994). But they are consistent with the more pessimistic perspective that the training was not ‘fit for purpose’ as determined in other studies (University of Piraeus, 1990; University of Piraeus Research Centre, 1994 - as found in Dedoussopoulos et al., 1998), and even by the OAED itself. My econometric results are compatible with those of studies exploring the basic characteristics of the Mediterranean and the MME type models analysed in section 9 (macro-level). In sum, micro-econometric analyses for European countries invariably confirm that training has had “mixed” results, but most of the time they have found a statistically insignificant impact on the participants’ prospects of employment.

With regards to the meso-level analysis, my research was guided by the following sub-question: “Was the training system, i.e., the institutions, in Greece, both regionally and nationally, effective in helping people to find jobs and if not, why?”. My secondary analysis of evidence referring to the period under investigation revealed numerous weaknesses in Greece’s vocational training policy. These mainly stemmed from the fact that it was put together in a piecemeal fashion, and that its objectives were undefined. The system of CVT did not function complementarily nor in co-ordination with initial VET and was often aimed at curing the weaknesses of the system of the latter. The field of continuing training was not clearly defined, whilst the division between initial and continuing vocational training was also obscure. Many organizations of CVT offered, in reality, initial-basic vocational training; for instance, many of their programmes provided general knowledge aimed at flexibilisation and adaptability, an objective which should be the target of basic training. My findings support the arguments of Iliades (1995) that the lack of a holistically organized system of basic and continuing training resulted in more young people becoming involved in the labour market without any form of training.

Funding for CVT was earmarked for on-the-job training programmes and CVT programmes for the unemployed. In both cases, the selection criteria for the programmes focused on formal specifications regarding the way in which they were conducted rather than on the content, and they did not allow for evaluation from the point of view of their impact on production and employment. The general characteristic of vocational training policies was their lack of any link, co-ordinated or otherwise, with unemployment policies. The problems in the processes of ratification and the absence of impact evaluation during the implementation of vocational training programmes within the first and second CSFs, resulting in significant negative consequences with long-lasting impact, were also due to the lack of a cohesive developmental programme for the country and the absence of a suitable institutional framework. Even during the third CSF (2000-2006) there were no evaluation procedures evaluated by outside auditors, apart from bureaucratic controls, that is, there was only external economic audit. In general, there was a failure in planning a global system for appraising and following the functional outcomes of training intervention.

Reskilling as a strategy to improving employability did not seem to work. My research indicates that the main cause of the OAED's limited intervention in the matching process was due to institutional matters (poor institutional frameworks, absence of motivation to announce job vacancies), and a second cause relates to functional matters (inadequate network of employment offices, failure to define their responsibilities exactly, absence of specialization of their personnel, insufficient formation of schemes to provide the unemployed with information, etc). Given that OAED was the main organisation tasked with helping the unemployed find work and its inability to implement the above necessary systems, it is not surprising that it failed to find solutions to unemployment.

In spite of the absence of systematic evaluation of the results of active employment policies, the results of the rather limited studies that were in fact carried out were not particularly encouraging. These findings go hand in hand with the results of similar studies targeting the evaluation of the results of ALMPs mainly in the developed countries of the EU. ALMPs in Greece functioned as labour supply reinforcement policies in order to manage unemployment, but more often than not, they were used to, temporarily, serve the needs of the unemployed in relation to social protection. At the same time, although ALMPs contributed to the management of the unemployed, especially of the young and females, this did not lead to tangible results in relation to their placement in employment or even more to the reduction of the total levels of unemployment.

Overall, during the period under investigation, the more 'proactive' employment policy in Greece - which expanded mainly due to ESF financing - was apparently not integrated into a broader developmental model. That is, it was focused on targeted funding for very small businesses and those unemployed with reasonable access to employment, anyway. In sum ALMPs did not function "therapeutically" in promoting the employment of those unemployed facing increased social and professional restrictions, but rather, they appeared to fund those unemployed who had comparative advantages over them.

The third (macro) level of my analysis involved addressing the following sub-questions: 'To what extent did the ALMPs in Greece, in particular the policies of vocational training, integrate EU-funded training in their skills strategy? To what extent was any (in)effectiveness of ALMPs related to the characteristics of the Greek political economy?".

My secondary analysis of evidence and academic research at the meso and macro levels referring to the period under investigation complements the work of Economou (1997), who contended that the first Greek CSF (1989-1993) turned out to be a failure. The problems of today had already been identified in the late 1980s, but apparently little has been done to rectify them. Of course the current crisis has not been magnified in Greece because of the ineffectiveness and inefficiency of these training programmes, but has to do with the structural problems already existing in the economy and the labour market well before the crisis. The country entered the euro under these conditions and dynamics and their non-resolution contributed, to an extent, to the country's current economic and social bottlenecks.

The overall conclusion for the period under investigation from sections 8 and 9 concerning training delivery in Greece, is that the findings of the econometric analysis go hand-in-hand with the analysis I have made at the meso and macro-levels concerning the structural deficiencies of the Greek labour market, the ALMPs and the Greek state in general. On the basis of the extensive review of the interactions between a wide array of labour market structures and characteristics, vocational institutional characteristics and attributes of the Greek political economy, it is concluded that the cascading of EU money for training and the EU training policies, were not effective in the case of Greece. Training could be ineffective even in Northern European countries, but the reasons underlying this were not be the same as those in Greece. One key particularity of that nation's circumstance is the very high levels of unemployment amongst the skilled labour force.

The problems in the way the various feedback mechanisms interlinked/interacted, which still exist today, was the result of negative domestic factors and the nature of the EU training financing. Regarding the latter, the EU body providing the funding restricted itself to auditing that the money was being spent on skills training and totally disregarded labour market outcomes. Although the EU approach to vocational training is very much influenced by the human capital theory, the Greek VET system was, and remains, incompatible with this EU perspective. In the field of education and vocational training there was no integrated system of recording the skill needs and shortages in the Greek economy, which seriously damaged the prospects of matching between supply and demand for labour. Despite this, the EU continues to finance training activities that will most likely continue to fail in Greece, as long as it remains a low-skilled economy in terms of the specialities demanded. In other words, the human capital theory on training does not appear to be applicable in the Greek context. Still, for the period under investigation, the high-skilled labour force could not be absorbed in Greece. It appears that a strategic plan to create demand for training was absent. Intentionally or not, and without wanting to sound too cynical, the evidence suggests that EU funded training was utilized more for 'parking' the unemployed and less as part of a well articulated national economic strategy.

By the time of the focal period of this research EES ideas, goals, reports, country-specific proposals and benchmarking had failed to have any significant impact on Greek employment policy, despite their featuring in numerous official documents. Based on the review of labour market characteristics, vocational institutional structures, welfare policies and nature of the Greek political economy, it would appear that the EU money earmarked for training produced non effects. Following the VoC literature, whereby the nature of skills and vocational training in a country is determined by the particular institutional configuration and national political economy, I illustrated how the non-effects of training at the micro and meso levels described for Greece can be attributed to the nature of the labour market and its political economy, i.e., the macro-level. Clearly, the macro-level institutions both internal and external to Greece failed to address the structural problems that were causing high levels of unemployment, as well as the predominantly low skills base.

REFERENCES

Amable B. (2000), Institutional complementarity and diversity of social systems of innovation and production, *Review of International Political Economy,* 7(4), pp. 645-87.

Amable B. (2003), The diversity of modern capitalism, Oxford: Oxford University Press.

Amable B., Barré R. and Boyer R. (1997), Les systèmes d' innovation à l'ère de la globalisation, Paris: Economica.

ANA.V.EL. (RDA of Northern Greece Ltd) - (1993), Sample survey for the evaluation of the 1992 ESF Training Programmes in the Region of Central Macedonia, Thessaloniki (in Greek).

Andreotti A., García S., Gomez A., Hespanha P., Kazerov Y. and Mingione E. (2001), Does a Southern European model exist?, *Journal of European Area Studies,* vol. 9 (1), pp. 43-62.

Antonopoulou R., Adam S., Kim K., Masterson T. and Papadimitriou D. B. (2014), Responding to the unemployment challenge: A job guarantee proposal for Greece, Levy Economics Institute of Bard College, April, Annandale-on-Hudson, New York.

Bakas D. and Papapetrou E. (2014), Unemployment in Greece: Evidence from Greek regions using panel unit root tests, *The Quarterly Review of Economics and Finance,* vol. 54, pp. 551-62.

Balourdos D. and Chryssakis M. (1998), Programmes of continuing vocational training: Statistical indications, evaluation and perspectives (in Greek), in Maratou-Alipranti L. and Hatzigianni A. (eds), *Unemployment, employment, education-training in Greece and France*, Proceedings of the Franco-hellenic Colloquium, EKKE, Athens, pp. 133-50.

Becker G. S. (1962), Investment in human capital: A theoretical analysis, *Journal of Political Economy,* 70 (supplement), October, pp. 9-49.

Becker G. S. (1964), Human capital, New York: Columbia University Press.

Becker G.S. (1975), Human capital: A theoretical and empirical analysis with special reference to education (2nd ed.), New York: Columbia University Press.

Ben-Porath Y. (1967), The production of human capital and the life cycle of earnings, *Journal of Political Economy,* vol. 75, pp. 352-65.

Berman E., Bound J. and Griliches Z. (1994), Changes in the demand for skilled labor within US manufacturing industries: Evidence from the annual survey of manufacturing, *Quarterly Journal of Economics*, CK, pp. 367-98.

Bettio F. and Plantenga J. (2004), Comparing care regimes in Europe, *Feminist Economics,* vol. 10 (1), pp. 85-113.

Blaug M. (1975), The empirical status of human capital theory, *Journal of Economic Literature,* 14, pp. 827-55.

Bosworth D. (1993), Skill shortages in Britain, *Scottish Journal of Political Economy,* vol. 40, pp. 241-71.

Bosworth D., Dutton P. and Lewis J. (1992), 'Introduction,' in Bosworth D., Dutton P. and Lewis J. (eds), *Skill shortages: Causes and consequences*, Avebury, Aldershot.

Bouzas N. and Ketsetzopoulou M. (1998), Policy to fight the exclusion from the labour market (in Greek), in *Social inequalities and social exclusion*, Athens: Sakis Karagiorgas Foundation, pp. 184-94.

Castles F. and Ferrera M. (1996), Home ownershipand the welfare state: Is Southern Europe different?, *South European Society and Politics*, vol. 1 (2), pp. 163-84.

CEC (Commission of the European Communities-1996), Teaching and learning towards the learning society, White Paper on education and training, Luxembourg.

Chasapis D. (1994), Quality of the CVT in Greece (in Greek), Greek National Unit of Co-ordination for FORCE / EUROTECNET in the context of the FORCE study: Quality of the CVT in Europe. Co-ordinators: Gronwold P. and Verardi A., EC Task Force Human Resources, Brussels, under the auspices of the Consultative Committee for FORCE/EUROTECNET, Brussels - Athens.

Chasapis D. (1996), Report to the access in the CVT in Greece according to the decision of 30 June 1993 of the Council, National Institute of Labour, Athens (in Greek).

Cheng S., Wu T., Lee K. and Chang T. (2014), Flexible Fourier unit root test of unemployment for PIIGS countries, *Economic Modelling*, vol. 36, pp. 142-8.

Chevalier A. and Lindley J. (2006), Over-education and the skills of UK graduates, IZA Discussion Paper No 2442, IZA, Bonn.

Chevalier A. and Lindley J. (2007), Over-education and the skills of UK graduates, Centre for the Economics of Education, LSE, DP 79.

Chletsos M. (1998), The education as an active employment policy: Limits and preconditions of implementation. The case of Greece (in Greek), in Maratou-Alipranti L. and Hatzigianni A. (eds), *Unemployment, employment, education-training in Greece and France*, Proceedings of the Franco-hellenic Colloquium, EKKE, Athens, pp. 151-79.

Cockx B., van der Linden B. and Karaa A. (1998), Active labour market policies and job tenure, *Oxford Economic Papers*, vol. 50(4), pp. 685-708.

Dedoussopoulos A. (ed. - 1995), Economics of labour: The supply of labour, vol. A, Publications O Politis, Athens (in Greek).

Dedoussopoulos A. (1996), Guiding directions of CVT programmes, Panteion University, Athens (in Greek).

Dedoussopoulos A. and collaborators (1998), Active and passive policies to tackle unemployment: The role of OAED (1983-1993), Panteion University, Department of Urban and Regional Development, Athens, March (in Greek).

Dedoussopoulos A. and Karamessini M. (1998), Active labour market policies in Greece: Conditions for effectiveness, 20th Conference of the International Working Party on Labour Market Segmentation (IWPLMS), Arco (Trento), 9-14 July.

Dedoussopoulos A., Aranitou V., Koutentakis F. and Maropoulou M. (2013), Assessing the impact of the memoranda on Greek labour market and labour relations, Project financed by the European Commission, ILO, Geneva, November, Working Paper No. 53.

Dedoussopoulos A., Kafkalas G., Getimis P. and Kazantzopoulos G. (1995), Comparative study (Central Macedonia, South Wales and Lower Saxony) on regional systems for the anticipation of skill needs and the design, implementation and evaluation of training programmes, vol. 4, Synthesis Report – Executive Summary, prepared for DGXXII, URDP, October.

Diamandouros N. (1993), Politics and culture in Greece, 1974-91, in Clogg R. (ed.), Greece, 1981-89: The Populist Decade, London: Macmillan.

Diamandouros N. (1994), Cultural dualism and political change in post-authoritarian Greece, Madrid: Instituto Juan March, Working paper no. 50.

Dimoulas K. and Michalopoulou K. (2008), Active employment policies. The case of integrated interventions in the NUTS-3 areas of Arta, Thesprotia, Preveza, Larissa and Fthiotida, INE/GSEE-ADEDY, Athens.

Dolton P. and Marcenaro-Gutierrez O. (2009), Overeducation across Europe, in Dolton P., Asplund R. and Barth E. (eds.), *Education and inequality across Europe*, Ch. 4, Cheltenham, Northampton, Mass: Edward Elgar Publishing.

Economou D. (1997), The impact of the first Community Support Framework for Greece: The anatomy of failure, *European Urban and Regional Studies*, vol. 4 (1), pp. 71-84.

EKOM Business Consulting Services (1994), Region of Central Macedonia, Study of the local labour market, Spatial and sectoral analysis of the relation between vocational training and employment at a geographical unit lower than county, May (in Greek).

Esping-Andersen G. (1999), Social foundations of post-industrial economies, Oxford: Oxford University Press.

ESYE (National Statistical Service of Greece), National Accounts Directorate, Athens (various years - in Greek).

ESYE (www.statistics.gr).

European Industrial Relations Observatory (EIRO) (2007), Greece industrial relations country profiles, 9 February: http://eurofound.europa.eu/eiro/ country/greece4.html.

European Industrial Relations Observatory (EIRO) - Karakioulafi Ch. (IN.E./GSEE-ADEDY) (2006), Greece - Annual survey for 2005 (http://eurofound.europa.eu/ eiro/2006/01 /feature/gr0601102f.html).

Eurostat (1995), Education and Employment prospects.

Eurostat (1997), Unemployment in the EU, No 7.

Featherstone K. (2008), Varieties of Capitalism and the Greek case: Explaining the constraints on domestic reform?, Hellenic Observatory Papers on Greece and Southeast Europe, GreeSE Paper No 11, European Institute, LSE, February.

Ferrera M. (1996), The southern model of welfare in social Europe, *Journal of European Social Policy*, 6 (1), pp. 17-37.

Gallie D. and Paugam S. (2000), The social regulation of unemployment, in Gallie D. and Paugam S. (eds.), *Welfare regimes and the experience of unemployment in Europe*, Oxford: Oxford University Press.

Getimis P. and collaborators (1994a), The contribution of the Greek public administration to the mobilisation of the endogenous potential in the Region of Central Macedonia, Final report, volume A, Panteion University, Department of Urban and Regional Development, January (in Greek).

Getimis P. and collaborators (1994b), The contribution of the Greek public administration to the mobilisation of the endogenous potential in the Region of Central Macedonia, Final report, volume B, annexes, Panteion University, Department of Urban and Regional Development, January (in Greek).

Getimis P. and Gravaris S. (1994), Labour market and labour market policy in the Region of Central Macedonia. Modernisation, networks and institutional changes, Panteion University, Department of Urban and Regional Development and University of Hannover, Institute of Political Science, Athens (in Greek).

Giner S. (1982), Political economy, legitimation and the State in Southern Europe, *The British Journal of Sociology*, 33 (2), pp. 172-99.

Goetschy J. (1999), The European Employment Strategy: Genesis and development, *European Journal of Industrial Relations*, 5(2), pp. 117-37.

González M.-J., Jurado T. and Naldini M. (eds.) (2000), Introduction: Interpreting the transformation of gender inequalities in Southern Europe, in *Gender inequalities in Southern Europe: Women, work and welfare in the 1990s*, London: Frank Cass.

Gough I., Eardley T., Bradshaw J., Ditch J. and Whiteford P. (1997), Social assistance in OECD countries, *Journal of European Social Policy*, vol. 7(1), pp. 17-43.

Goumenakis G. and Michaelides P. G. (1995), The effectiveness of labour market oriented training courses for the long-term unemployed, in Vocational training in Greece, Part 2, TSER Programme, University of Crete, Department for Elementary Teacher Education, Laboratory for Science Teaching, Rethymno.

Green F., Machin S. and Wilkinson D. (1998), The meaning and determinants of skills shortages, *Oxford Bulletin of Economics and Statistics*, 60 (2), pp. 165-87.

Green F., McIntosh S. and Vignoles A. (1999), Over-education and skills – Clarifying the concepts, Discussion Paper No 435, CEP, LSE.

Gu W. and Wong A. (2010), Estimates of human capital in Canada: The lifetime income approach, Economic Analysis (EA) Research Paper Series, Catalogue no. 11F0027M, No. 062, Economic Analysis Division, Statistics Canada.

Guichard S. and Rusticelli E. (2010), Assessing the impact of the financial crisis on structural unemployment in OECD countries, OECD Economics Department Working Papers, No 767.

Hall P. and Soskice D. (eds) - (2001), Varieties of capitalism: The institutional foundations of comparative advantage, Oxford: Oxford University Press.

Hartog J. (1997), On returns to education: Wandering along the hills of ORU land, Keynote speech for the LVIIth Conference of the Applied Econometrics Association, Maastricht, May.

Haskel J. and Martin C. (1993a), Do skill shortages reduce productivity? Theory and evidence from the United Kingdom, *Economic Journal,* vol. 103, pp. 386-94.

Haskel J. and Martin C. (1993b), The causes of skill shortages in Britain, *Oxford Economic Papers*, vol. 45, pp. 573-88.

Heyes J. (2007), Training, social dialogue and collective bargaining in Western Europe, *Economic and Industrial Democracy*, 28, pp. 239-58.

Iliades N. (1995), Continuing vocational training in Greece, National Report (in the context of FORCE), National Institute of Labour, January (in Greek).

IN.E. (Institute of Labour)/GSEE (General Confederation of Workers of Greece) - ADEDY (Civil Servants' Supreme Administrative Council) (1999), The Greek economy and the employment, Annual Report, Reports no 1, Athens, August (in Greek).

IN.E./GSEE-ADEDY (2000), The Greek economy and the employment, Annual Report, Reports no 2, Athens, August (in Greek).

IN.E./GSEE-ADEDY (2007), The Greek economy and the employment, Annual Report, chapter 5, pp. 155-76, Athens, August (in Greek).

IN.E./GSEE-ADEDY (2008), The Greek economy and the employment, Annual Report, chapter 6, pp. 149-60, Athens, August (in Greek).

International Monetary Fund (2009), World Economic Outlook Database, IMF, April.

Iversen T. and Soskice D. (2001), An asset theory of social policy preferences, *American Political Science Review,* 95(4), pp. 875-93.

Jones R. and Chiripanhura B. (2010), Measuring the U.K.'s human capital stock, *Economic and Labour Market Review,* 4 (11), pp. 36-63.

Jones R. and Goss D. (1991), The role of training strategy in reducing skills shortages: Some evidence from a survey of small firms, *Personnel Review*, vol. 20, pp. 24-30.

Jurado Guerrero T. and Naldini M. (1997), Is the South so different? Italian and Spanish families in comparative perspective, in Rhodes M. (ed.), *Southern European welfare states: Between crisis and reform*, London: Frank Cass.

Kafkalas G., Tombrou K. and Foutakis D. (1995), Comparative study on regional systems for the anticipation of skill needs and the design, implementation and evaluation of training programmes, vol. 3, Central Macedonia Final Regional Report, prepared for DGXXII, Aristotelian University of Thessaloniki-URDP, June.

Kanellopoulos C. N. (1996), Recent developments in Greek education, *International Journal of Educational Development*, vol. 16 (1), pp. 65-77.

Kanellopoulos K., Mavromaras K. and Mitrakos T. (2003), Education and the labour market, Athens: KEPE (in Greek).

Karamessini M. (2007), The Southern European social model: Changes and continuities in recent decades, International Institute for Labour Studies, Discussion Paper Series, ILO, Geneva.

Karamessini M. (2008), The absorption of university graduates in the labour market, Athens: Network of the Career Offices of Universities and Dionicos (in Greek).

Karamessini M. (2010), Transition strategies and labour market integration of Greek University graduates, Hellenic Observatory papers on Greece and Southeast Europe, GreeSE paper No 32, The Hellenic Observatory, European Institute, LSE, February.

Kassimati K. et al. (1984), The OAED Apprenticeship Centres: Findings, problems, proposals, EKKE, Athens (in Greek).

Katrougalos G. and Lazaridou G. (2003), Southern European welfare states: Problems, challenges and prospects, Basingstoke: Palgrave Macmillan.

Katsikas C. (2005), Studies-Vocation and labour market, Athens: Atrapos Publishing (in Greek).

KEPE-REMACO Business Consultants S.A. (1998), Initial approach to the interim evaluation of CSF-2, ch. 2 (Athens: Ministry of National Economy, unpublished study).

KODE (1991), Study of the OAED apprenticeship system, University of Piraeus, Piraeus (in Greek).

KOE (1994), Study evaluating the OAED intensive vocational training system, Athens, KOE, Economic University of Athens (mimeo) - (in Greek).

Le T., Gibson J. and Oxley L. (2003), Cost and income-based measures of human capital, *Journal of Economic Surveys*, 17 (3), pp. 271-307.

Leibfried S. (1992), Towards a European welfare state? On integrating poverty regimes in the European Community, in Ferge Z. and Kolberg J. E. (eds.), *Social policy in a changing Europe*, Boulder: Westview Press.

Li H., Liang Y., Fraumeni B., Liu Z. and Wang X. (2010), Human capital in China, Paper prepared for the 31st General Conference of the International Association for Research in Income and Wealth, St. Gallen, Switzerland, August 22-28, 2010.

Liagouras G., Protogerou A. and Kalogirou Y. (2003), Exploring mismatches between higher education and the labour market in Greece, *European Journal of Education,* 38 (4), pp. 413-26.

Linardos-Rylmon P. (1995), Skills, labour market and training (in Greek), in Unemployment, economic policy and employment policies, Notebooks of IN.E., issue no. 4, IN.E./GSEE, Athens, Oct.-Dec., pp. 33-42.

Linardos-Rylmon P. (1998), Vocational training and labour market: Indispensable changes into the function of the continuing training system in Greece (in Greek), in Maratou-Alipranti L. and Hatzigianni A. (eds), *Unemployment, employment, education-training in Greece and France*, Proceedings of the Franco-Hellenic Colloquium, *EKKE,* Athens, pp. 233-6.

Liu G. and Greaker M. (2009), Measuring the stock of human capital for Norway: A lifetime labour income approach, Documents 2009/12, Statistics Norway.

Livanos I. (2007), The incidence of long-term unemployment: Evidence from Greece, *Applied Economics Letters*, 14 (6), pp. 405-8.

Livanos I. (2009a), Modelling the incidence of unemployment: The case of Greece, *Applied Economics Letters*, 16 (16), pp. 1607-11.

Livanos I. (2009b), The relationship between higher education and labour market in Greece: The weakest link?, MPRA Paper No 16239, Munich.

Livanos I. and Pouliakas K. (2009), Wage returns to University disciplines in Greece: Are Greek higher education degrees Trojan horses?, MPRA Paper No 18821, Munich.

Machin S. (1996), Wage inequality in the UK, *Oxford Review of Economic Policy*, XII, pp. 47-64.

Machin S. and van Reenen J. (1998), Technology and changes in skill structure: Evidence from seven OECD countries, *The Quarterly Journal of Economics,* November, pp. 1215-44.

Meghir C., Ioannides Y. and Pissarides C. (1989), Female participation and male unemployment duration in Greece, *European Economic Review,* vol. 33 (2-3), pp. 395-406.

Mincer J. (1974), Schooling, experience and earnings, New York: Columbia University Press.

Mingione E. (2002), Labour market segmentation and informal work, in Gibson H. (ed.), *Economic transformation, democratization and integration into the European Union: Southern Europe in comparative perspective*, Basingstoke, Hampshire: Palgrave.

Mitrakos T. M., Tsakloglou P. and Cholezas I. (2010), Determinants of youth unemployment in Greece with an emphasis on tertiary education graduates, Bank of Greece, *Economic Bulletin,* No. 33, May, pp. 21-62.

Molina O. and Rhodes M. (2005), Varieties of capitalism and mixed market economies, APSA-EPS Newsletter, 38.

Morgan G., Whitley R. and Moen E. (eds) - (2005), Changing capitalisms? Internationalization, institutional change, and systems of economic organization, Oxford: Oxford University Press.

Mouzelis N. (1993), The State in late development, Greek Political Science Review, 1, pp. 53-89.

Murray A. and Steedman H. (1998), Growing skills in Europe: The changing skills profiles of France, Germany, the Netherlands, Portugal, Sweden and the UK, TSER, Discussion Paper No 399, CEP, LSE.

OECD (1990), Employment Outlook, Paris: OECD.

OECD (1993), Active labour market policies: Assessing macro-economic and micro-economic effects, Employment Outlook, ch. 2, Paris: OECD, pp. 39-80.

OECD (2001), Regulatory reform in Greece, OECD Reviews of Regulatory Reforms, Paris: OECD Publishing.

OECD (2009), Economic Survey Greece, Paris: OECD Publishing.

OECD (2010), Employment Outlook, Paris: OECD Publishing.

OECD (2011), OECD Economic Surveys: Greece 2011, Paris: OECD Publishing.

Oliver J. and Turton J. (1982), Is there a shortage of skilled labour?, *British Journal of Industrial Relations,* vol. 20, pp. 195-200.

Pagoulatos G. (2003), Greece's new political economy: State, finance and growth from postwar to EMU, edited by Oxford, St. Antony's Series. London and New York: Palgrave Macmillan.

Panteion University-PLA.NE.T. A.E. (1993), Study for the establishment and function of a regional experimental Institute for Labour in the Region of Central Macedonia, On-going report, Phase A, September (in Greek).

Papadimitriou D. B., Nikiforos M. and Zezza G. (2013), The Greek economic crisis and the experience of austerity: A strategic analysis, Strategic Analysis Annandale-on-Hudson, N.Y.: Levy Economics Institute of Bard College, July.

Papadopoulos T. (2006), Support for the unemployed in a familistic welfare regime, in Mossialos E. and Petmesidou M. (eds), *Social Policy Developments in Greece*, Aldershot: Ashgate, pp. 219-38.

Papakonstantinou G. (1998), Education-training as factors of investment in human capital (in Greek), in Maratou-Alipranti L. and Hatzigianni A. (eds), *Unemployment, employment, education-training in Greece and France*, Proceedings of the Franco-Hellenic Colloquium, EKKE, Athens, pp. 125-32.

Patrinos H. (1997), Over-education in Greece, *International Review of Education*, vol. 43 (2/3), pp. 203-23.

Petmesidou M. (1996), Social protection in Southern Europe: Trends and prospects, *Journal of Area Studies,* vol. 9, pp. 95-125.

Petrinioti X. (1999), The unemployment (in Greek), in Petrinioti X. and Koukoules G.F. (eds), Labour Yearbook 1998, Athens: Panteion University Publications, pp. 55-75.

Prais S. J. (1995), Productivity, education and training: An international perspective, National Institute for Economic and Social Research, Cambridge University Press.

Prokou E. (2011), The aims of employability and social inclusion: Active citizenship in lifelong learning policies in Greece, *The Greek Review of Social Research*, special issue 136 C, pp. 203-23.

Rees A. (1973), The economics of work and pay, New York: Harper and Row.

Rhodes M. (1997), Southern European welfare states: Identity, problems and prospects for reform, in Rhodes M. (ed.), *Southern European welfare states. Between crisis and reform*, London: Frank Cass.

Rodokanakis S. (2009), Comparing the probability of unemployment in Southern Greece vis-à-vis the entire country, Bulletin of Geography – Socio-economic Series, No 12, pp. 17-43.

Rodokanakis S. (2010a), The dynamics of regional labour markets and training programmes: Greek evidence, *European Spatial Research and Policy*, vol. 17 (1), pp. 93-115.

Rodokanakis S. (2010b), Comparing the probability of unemployment in Northern Greece vis-à-vis the entire country, *Journal of Economic Asymmetries,* vol. 7 (1), pp. 137-74.

Rodokanakis S. (2011), Measuring the unemployment risk in Greece as a whole from the LFS micro-data: Comparison among the three CSFs, Proceedings (CD-Rom) following a selection of papers presented at the 17th European Colloquium on Quantitative and Theoretical Geography (ECQTG2011), Athens, 2-5 Sep., pp. 492-99.

Rodokanakis S. and Tryfonidis D. (2009), Unemployment hazard in the Aegean islands: Econometric analysis of the LFS micro-data, in Brox J. A. and Baltas N. (eds), *The global economics of a changing environment: Studies in the structure, performance and reform of economics, organizations and business throughout the globe*, chapter 14, Waterloo, Canada: North Waterloo Academic Press, June, pp. 211-24.

Rodokanakis S. and Vlachos V. (2012), Measuring the unemployment risk in Northern Greece from the LFS micro-data during the period 1994-2006, *Review of Economic Analysis*, vol. 4 (2), pp. 224-46.

Rodokanakis S. and Vlachos V. (2013a), Unemployment in the Greek regions of Attica and Central Macedonia: Comparative econometric analysis between the 2nd and the 3rd CSFs, *International Journal of Economics and Business Research*, vol. 6 (2), pp. 140-57.

Rodokanakis S. and Vlachos V. (2013b), Evaluating the employment probability: Men and women in comparative perspective in Attica and Central Macedonia, *Journal of Economic and Social Studies*, vol. 3 (1), pp. 119-51.

Rubery J., Bosch G. and Lehndorff S. (2008), Surviving the EU? The future for national employment models in Europe, *Industrial Relations Journal,* vol. 39 (6), pp. 488-509.

Saraceno C. (2000), Gendered policies: Family obligations and social policies in Europe, in Boje T. and Leira A. (eds.), *Gender, welfare state and the market: Towards a new division of labour*, London and New York: Routledge.

Seferiades S. (2003), The European Employment Strategy against a Greek benchmark: A critique, *European Journal of Industrial Relations*, 9 (2), pp. 189-203.

Seferiades S. (2006), Employment policy in the European Employment Strategy era: What prospects?, in Petmesidou M. and Mossialos E. (eds.), *Social policy developments in Greece*, Ashgate, chapter 9, pp. 194-218.

Spanou C. (1996), On the regulatory capacity of the Hellenic state: A tentative approach based on a case study, *International Review of Administrative Sciences*, vol. 62 (1), March, pp. 219-37.

Stevens M. (1994), An investment model for the supply of training by employers, *Economic Journal,* vol. 104, pp. 556-70.

Streeck W. (2012), Skills and politics: General and specific, in Busemeyer M. R. and Trampusch C. (eds), *The political economy of collective skill formation*, Oxford: Oxford University Press, pp. 317-52.

Thomaidou F., Kikilias E., Mitrakos T., Politis T., Tsakloglou P. and Holezas I. (2009), Study of the employment of higher education graduates in Greece, Athens: Cultural and Development Initiative (in Greek).

T.Q.M. Hellas Ltd (1994), Study on the needs in continuing training structures and retraining of main sectors and branches of economic activity in the Region of Central Macedonia, June (in Greek).

Training Agency (1990), 'Labour Market and Skill Trends, 1991/1992,' Employment Department, UK.

Trifiletti T. R. (1999), Southern European welfare regimes and the worsening position of women, *Journal of European Social Policy,* vol. 9 (1), pp. 49-64.

Tsakloglou P. and Cholezas I. (2005), Education and inequality in Greece, IZA Discussion Paper, No. 1582, IZA, Bonn.

Tsoukalas C. (1993), Greek national identity in an integrated Europe and a changing world order, in Psomiades H. and Thomadakis S. (eds.), *Greece, the new Europe and the changing international order*, New York: Pella, pp. 57-78.

Tsoukalis L. (1997), Beyond the Greek paradox, in Graham T. A. and Nicolaidou K. (eds), The Greek paradox: Promise vs. performance.

University of Macedonia (1994), Assessment of the OAED apprenticeship system (by Tsekouras I., Stavrou S. and Papatheodossiou Th.), Department of Economic and Political Sciences, Thessaloniki, November (in Greek).

University of Patra (1994), OAED study on the workers in the automotive repair sector, University of Patra/OAED (in Greek).

University of Piraeus (1990), Study on the apprenticeship system of OAED, Centre of Economic and Administrative Research, OAED/ University of Piraeus (in Greek).

University of Piraeus Research Centre (1994), Evaluation of the Intra-firm Training Programme for the improvement of the competitiveness of the Greek private companies, Athens: OAED (in Greek).

URDP (1992), Action plan for interfund synergy in the framework of MOPs and IMPs in Greece, Athens, Study for the CEC/DGXVI (in Greek).

van Smoorenburg M.S.M. and van der Velden R.K.W. (2000), The training of school leavers: Complementarity or substitution*?, Economics of Education Review,* 19, pp. 207-17.

Vasconcelos Ferreira L. and Figueiredo A. (2005), Welfare regimes in the EU 15 and in the enlarged Europe: An exploratory analysis, FEP Working Papers No 176, Universidade do Porto.

World Bank (2010), Doing Business 2010: Making a difference for entrepreneurs, The International Bank For Reconstruction and Development/the World Bank, Washington, DC.

Zartaloudis S. (2014), The impact of European Employment Strategy in Greece and Portugal: Europeanization in a world of neglect, Palgrave: Macmillan, London.

In: Unemployment
Editor: Tabitha Fletcher

ISBN: 978-1-63485-181-7

Chapter 10

UNEMPLOYMENT RATE, SMOKING AND DRINKING IN CHINA: ARE THEY RELATED?

*Qing Wang**
School of Business, Dalian University of Technology,
Panjin, Liaoning, China

ABSTRACT

Background: The exact nature of the relationship between unemployment rate and health behaviors remains unclear due to the mixed results observed in the literature review. There is no study focused on the impact of macroeconomic environments on smoking and drinking in China. The paper aims to estimate the effects of area unemployment rate on smoking and drinking in China.

Methods: Using nationally representative data from the 1991 and 2011 China Health and Nutrition Survey (CHNS), Random Effects Logit model and Random Effects model were applied. 51,706 observations were available for statistical analysis.

Results: One percent increase in the unemployment rate resulted in an increase in the likelihood of smoking about 1.45 percent, cigarette consumption daily by 0.22 percent, the likelihood of drinking about 0.87 percent, the likelihood of drinking frequently about 0.78 percent, the likelihood of heavy drinker about 0.5 percent. Compared to employed respondents, the effects of area-level unemployment rate on health behaviors were stronger for those who were unemployment.

Conclusion: Findings showed that the unemployment rate was positively and significantly associated with smoking and drinking behaviors in China. Health behaviors intervention strategies may not only focus on the individual characteristics, but also the physical environment in which unemployment rate tend to rise.

Keywords: unemployment rate, current smoker, number of cigarettes smoked daily, current drinker, drink frequently, heavy drinker, China

---

* Email: wangqing1984@126.com.

INTRODUCTION

As leading risk factors for global disease burden, smoking and alcohol consumption are of particular interest [1]. About 20 percent of the world's adult population smoke cigarettes [2]. Tobacco caused 100 million deaths over the course of the 20th century [3]. China is the largest producer and consumer of cigarettes [4]. In 2013, China consumed more than 30 percent of the world's cigarettes and smoking accounts for 1.36 million deaths annually there [5].

Worldwide 38.3% of the population aged 15 years or older had drunk alcohol in the past 12 months in 2012. Among them, about 16.0 percent of drinkers engaged in heavy episodic drinking. About 3.3 million deaths, or 5.9 percent of all global deaths, were attributable to alcohol consumption. The most prevalent tendency worldwide is an increase in recorded alcohol consumption, which is mainly driven by an increase consumption in China and India [6]. Estimates from China Health and Nutrition Survey (CHNS) 1991-2011 indicated that the prevalence of drinking adults was over 34 percent.

The unemployment rate reflects the macro-economic environment where an individual resides, that may influence her or his behavior [7]. There is controversy over whether area unemployment rate inhibits or promotes consumption of these substances [8]. Some studies reported that the area-level unemployment rate was positively associated with smoking [7, 9-10], whereas some studies found increased unemployment rate followed by decreased cigarette consumption in the U.S and Sweden [11-14]. Charles and DeCicca found an increase in smoking among those who are least likely to be employed; however, smoking declined for those in the highest employment decile in U.S. [15]. The spillover effects of high unemployment rates are less well understood [16].

The association between unemployment and alcohol consumption was more complex. Some studies suggested that unemployment rate is a risk factor for alcohol abuse and increased alcohol consumption [17-20], some were null or decreased alcohol consumption [21-23], and 3 showed mixed findings [24-26]. The three studies with mixed findings highlight interesting complexity in how unemployment rate affects drinking behavior. First, it appeared that while rising unemployment rate to be associated with high measures for drinking frequency but low measures for drinking quantity [24]. Second, unemployment was positively associated with alcohol consumption overall, but negatively associated with drinking participation [25]. Third, the relationship between unemployment rate and drinking may be change cross periods [26]. One possible explanation is that the relationship between drinking and unemployment rate depends on the type of user and whether use is examined in developing or developed countries. For example, in developed countries, heavy drinkers consume less in a downturn, while light drinkers consume more. This positive relationship found for heavy drinking does not hold for developed countries where disposable income is low [27].

This study, examining the impacts of unemployment rate on smoking and drinking in China, contributes to the literature in two aspects. First, this study contributed to a better understanding of the relationship in an under-studied Chinese population.None of study has focused on the impacts of macroeconomic environments [28]. The relationship between health behaviors and unemployment rate may depend on whether use is examined in developing or developed countries. For example, in developed countries, drinkers might consume more in a downturn. This positive relationship found for drinking does not hold for developing countries where disposable income is low. The Chinese macroeconomic policies and environments are drastically different from those of the U. S. and European countries where similar comparisons and implications may not appropriately be made between China and those countries. In addition, we attempt to examine the effects of the area-based unemployment rate on smoking and drinking of individuals who are either employed or unemployed. Contextual effects of unemployment may exhibit different signs on alternative social groups. Previous studies have calculated an "average" effect of unemployment on smoking and drinking behaviors, research is lacking on the effects of unemployment on such behaviors of workforce and non-workforce populations, respectively [17].

CONCEPTUAL FRAMEWORK

Economic factors such as unemployment can lead individuals to change their behaviors without much attention to the potential effects on their personal health [29]. The canonical economic model of health-related decisions derived by Grossman was applied to examine the association between the unemployment rate and health behaviors [30]. Individuals would consider and make trade-off between current benefits obtained from risky and unhealthy behaviors and future cost of such behaviors including potentially undesirable consequences related to their health and well-being. The decision to smoke or drink can be seen as divestment in the stock of health capital in return for a short-run increase in welfare [31].

Mounting evidence has shown substantial costs being associated with smoking and drinking in the long-run. Smokers have higher risks of developing debilitating and often serious illnesses such as cancer, cardiovascular and circulatory diseases, and chronic respiratory diseases. The chemicals in tobacco damage the lungs, blood vessels, and other tissues and keep them inflamed; disrupting the way body heals itself [32]. Alcohol consumption has been identified as a component cause for more than 200 health conditions covered by ICD-10 disease and injury codes [6]. Most notably, new evidence points to a causal link between alcohol and infectious diseases such as tuberculosis and pneumonia [33, 34]. Also, it is important to note that alcohol consumption can contribute to more than one type of disease or injury in the drinker [6]. In short, smoking and drinking decreases the individual's health capital and productivity in the long-run.

However, smokers and drinkers may experience short-term benefits from smoking and drinking, such as relieves in anxiety or appetite suppression [35, 36], both of which may help people to ease stresses resulting from possible budget constraints given an environment where the unemployment rate is increasing. For Chinese people, job insecurity due to increased unemployment usually results in stress, anxiety, and psychological hardship [37], one outlet for coping with this stress is to take up or increase smoking and drinking [38-40].

Unemployment often provokes a shift from a preference towards the future to a preference leaning towards the present time [41]. Many studies have found that unemployment leads to an erosion of biographical plans, an abandonment of the future and a loss of hope [42-44]. A short-term perspective not only increases the likelihood of seeking short-term rewards that may result in unhealthy behavior such as smoking and drinking, but also leads to underestimating the long-term consequences of the unhealthy behavior (e.g., health risks associated with these behaviors).

On the other hand, budget constraints due to increased unemployment may also have opposite effects on smoking or drinking [45]. Because unemployment leaves individuals with less discretionary income, individuals may simply decide to abstain or reduce tobacco or alcohol consumption in order to save money [46]. For example, in China between 1990 and 2005, urban poor families used 7.7% of their reported expenditures on smoking and the rate among rural family was 11.2% [47]. Given that smoking or drinking represents a significant share of an individual's disposable income, higher rates of unemployment may force individuals to reduce or quit risky behaviors such as smoking and drinking.

In addition, the unemployment rate may influence smoking and drinking not only on those who have lost their jobs but also on those who remain employed [7]. High unemployment induces a negative externality on the employed. If workers attach their future prospects to their local unemployment rate, anxiety that one might be the next on the list of fired persons will grow with rising unemployment rates.

METHODS

Data

Data was obtained from CHNS, 1991-2011, which is publicly available (http://www.cpc.unc.edu/projects/china/data/datasets/longitudinal). CHNS was a longitudinal survey covering Guangxi Zhuang and eight other provinces with substantial variations in terms of geography, economic development, public resources, and health indicators in the years 1991, 1993, 1997, 2000, 2004, 2006, 2009, and 2011. The nine provinces accounted for approximately 45% of China's population in 2011. The survey collected data on detailed information on measures of health behaviors, demographic and social economic status, such as smoking, drinking, education and household income.

A multistage, random cluster process was included to draw the sample surveyed in each province. Counties in the nine provinces were stratified by income level (low, middle, and high). Four counties were randomly selected from each province by a weighted-sampling scheme (1 in low, 2 in middle, and 1 in high-income levels). In addition, the provincial capital and the lowest-income city were also included. Villages and townships within the counties and urban and suburban neighborhoods within the cities were selected randomly. There were about 4400 households in the survey, covering about 19,000 individuals in the most recent wave. A detailed description of the design of the CHNS is accessible at http://www.cpc.unc.edu/projects/china.

CIGARETTE SMOKING VARIABLE

In the CHNS questionnaire, respondents were asked if they were active smokers at the time of the survey. The respondents who answered "yes" were further asked on the number of cigarettes smoked per day. Two variables were constructed to measure smoking behavior.

The first was smoking status, which was classified into smoker or non-smoker. The second was log of "number of cigarettes consumed daily." Such a continuous measure of smoking could capture the intensity of smoking dependence among respondents, which may not be obtained in the present widely used binary indicator of being a current smoker.

ALCOHOLIC BEHAVIOR

Respondents were asked if they drank beer or any other alcoholic beverage during the previous 12 months. Those who had drunk in the past 12 months were asked further questions about: frequency of drinking (almost every day, 3-4, 1–2 times per week; 1-2 a month; no more than once a month); types of beverage (beer, grape wine, liquor) and amount of alcohol drunk each week (reported by number of bottles (640ml) for beer, and number of liang (50g) for wines and liquor) [48].

Three variables were constructed to measure drinking behavior. The first one was drink status. Respondents were classified into two main drinking categories: current drinker was defined as those who had drunk alcohol in the past 12 months or non-drinker. The second one was drink frequency. Respondents were classified into frequently drinker were defined as those who drank alcohol in the past 12 months almost every day. The third one was heavy drinker. Level of alcohol consumption was calculated as grams of pure alcohol per week, based on the beverage type, amount drunk and frequency (days per week), assuming the following alcohol content by volume (v/v) typically seen in China: beer 4%, grape wine 12%, liquor 45%. Heavy drinking episodes were classified as the consumption of >60 g of alcohol on one occasion for men, and >40 g for women [49].

CITY-LEVEL UNEMPLOYMENT RATE

The key independent variable was city-level urban investigated unemployment rate. City-level urban unemployment rate refers to as the percentage of residents in the city between 16 and 65 years of age who were unemployed. The results from China Health and Nutrition Survey (CHNS) produced the number for the unemployment rate. In China, the registered unemployment rate is reported. As National Bureau of Statistics of People's Republic of China website presents, the registered unemployment rate refers to the rate between the registered unemployed persons and total labor force. Unemployed individuals, who have not registered as either employed or unemployed, are not regarded as unemployed persons. Therefore, individuals, who were not currently working or were actively looking for work but did not go to the government employment service agencies for registration, were excluded in the calculation of registered unemployment rate. The registered unemployment rate is lower than the investigated unemployment rate, which is used widely in developed countries. In order to compare with other country, city-level investigated unemployment rate calculated from CHNS results were used.

Individual Socio-Economic Status and Demographic Variables

Several control variables were included when we ran the health-related economic decision model, derived by Grossman [29]. Demographic variables included old people (age >65), gender (reference group: female) and marital status (married was the reference). Education, job status, and income are the most commonly used measures of social economic status [50-51]. Educational attainment was defined at three levels: primary school or below, junior high school, senior high school or above. Two dummy variables were created, with primary school or below serving as the reference group. Job status was either unemployed or employed. It is noted that the employed category included those who were employed or retired. Household income divided by the number of household members was ranked and divided into three groups (i.e., affluent, middle and poor) with the poor group being the reference. Another dummy variable, 'Living in Urban Area,' indicated whether or not an individual lived in an urban area.

Analytical Techniques

The study estimated the following empirical specification:

$$S_{ijt} = \beta_0 + X_{ijt}\beta_1 + U_{jt}\beta_2 + v_j + u_t + \varepsilon_{ijt}$$

S_{ijt} represents smoking status for individual i living in province j in year t.

X_{ijt} represents a vector of observed individual characteristics, such as age, marital status, education, income, etc.

U_{jt} is the average unemployment rate of city.

v_j, u_t represents state and wave specific fixed effect, and ε_{ijt} is the error term.

Since smoking status, drinking behavior were measured by ordered outcomes, Random Effects Logit model was applied to analyze the relationship between area-level unemployment rate and behaviors, controlling for the individual socio-economic status and demographic variables. When it refers to the association between number of cigarettes consumed daily and unemployment rate, Random Effects Model was estimated. We took into account the potential clustering factor at the level of city by using Huber–White corrected standard errors. All analyses were performed using the STATA version 12.0.

RESULTS

The average city-level unemployment rate was 12%. Variations in the unemployment rate existed across waves and regions, with the lowest being 6.9% in 1991 and the highest being 16.7% in 2011; and with the lowest being 7.7% in Guizou, the highest being 16% in Hunan.

Table 1 shows descriptive statistics for the variables. The sample size was 51,706. The average age of current smokers was 46.5 years. 29% of the respondents identified themselves as smokers; they smoked cigarettes 4.47 daily. Compared to individuals who were unemployed, employed individuals were more likely to smoke and smoke more cigarette daily (smoking prevalence: employed individuals 34% V.S. unemployed individuals 20.3%; number of cigarettes consumed daily: employed individuals 5.39 V.S. unemployed individuals 2.8).

Table 1. Individual socioeconomic and life style characteristics

Sample	All individuals		Employed individuals		Unemployed individuals	
Variable	Mean	Std. Error	Mean	Std. Error	Mean	Std. Error
Demographics						
Age	45.01	16.41	40.79	12.9	54.73	18.46
Male	0.47	0.50	0.52	0.50	0.38	0.49
Unmarried	0.02	0.14	0.02	0.13	0.03	0.19
Educational						
Primary school and below	0.45	0.50	0.42	0.49	0.53	0.50
Middle school	0.31	0.46	0.33	0.47	0.26	0.44
High school and above	0.24	0.42	0.25	0.43	0.21	0.41
Economic status						
Individual income	7454.40	10785.56	8160.1	10348.72	7343.12	
Job status	0.75	0.43	1	0	0	0
Urban	0.31	0.46	0.26	0.44	0.44	0.50
Life style						
Current smoker	0.29	0.45	0.34	0.47	0.20	0.40
Number of cigarettes consumed daily	4.47	8.54	5.39	9.23	2.8	6.83
Current drinker	0.34	0.49	0.40	0.50	0.26	0.44
Drink almost every day	0.10	0.29	0.11	0.31	0.08	0.28
Heavy drinker	0.13	0.33	0.17	0.37	0.08	0.27

Table 2. Marginal effects of unemployment rate on smoking and drinking behaviors

Sample	All individuals		Employed individuals		Unemployed individuals	
	Marginal effects	Std. Error	Marginal effects	Std. Error	Marginal effects	Std. Error
Current smoker	1.45***	0.37	1.43***	0.43	2.14***	0.72
Number of cigarettes consumed daily	0.22***	0.06	0.18**	0.07	0.33***	0.10
Current drinker	0.87***	0.24	0.38	0.27	3.05***	0.51
Drink almost every day	0.78**	0.36	0.49	0.4	3.15***	0.75
Heavy drinker	0.5*	0.22	0.22	0.24	1.38***	0.5

* $p < 0.1$, ** $p < 0.05$, *** $p < 0.01$.

Huber–White corrected standard errors.

The average age of current drinker was 45.7 years. Overall, 34% of respondents surveyed reported having drunk some alcohol in the past year. Among them, 10% drank almost every day, 13% were considered as heavy drinker. The prevalence of drinking was higher among employed person than those without job (drinker: unemployed individuals 26% V.S. employed individuals 40%; drink almost every day: unemployed individuals 8% V.S. employed individuals 11%; heavy drinker: unemployed individuals 8% V.S. employed individuals 17%).

Table 2 shows marginal effects of unemployment rate on smoking and drinking behaviors after controlling for socio-economic status and other demographic characteristics. The positive association supported the hypothesis that the unemployment rate had positive impacts on smoking. One percent increase in the unemployment rate resulted in the increase in the likelihood of smoking about 1.45 percent, number of cigarette smoked daily by 0.22 percent. Area unemployment rate had stronger effects on smoking behavior for unemployed person than employed person (smoking status 2.14% V.S. 1.43%; number of cigarette smoked daily 0.33% V.S. 0.18%).

The results were consistent on the drinking effects of unemployment rate. Area unemployment rate was significant associated with drinking status, frequency and the likelihood being heavy drinker. One percent increase in the unemployment rate resulted in the increase in the likelihood of drinking about 0.87 percent, the likelihood of drinking frequently about 0.78 percent, the likelihood of heavy drinker about 0.5 percent. Also, compared to employed person, unemployed respondents

were more likely to be influenced by area unemployment rate. One percent increase in area unemployment rate increased the likelihood of drinker by 3.05 percent, the likelihood of drinking frequently about 3.15 percent, the likelihood of heavy drinker about 1.38 percent; however, unemployment rate had no significant effect for employed individuals.

CONCLUSION AND DISCUSSION

This is the first study to quantify relationship between area unemployment rate and individual smoking and drinking based on a large representative sample of China. We observed a strong positive association of unemployment rate and smoking/drinking. In China, the increased unemployment rate provoked a shift from a preference towards the future to a preference leaning towards the present time, which resulted in increased smoking and drinking. Changes in smoking and drinking resulting from financial burdens were less substantial. The growth of consumer incomes in China has been much faster than the increase in consumer expenditures on cigarettes and alcohol in recent years. For example, From 1990 to 2005, the former, on average, was about 2.8 times as much as the latter. The ability to pay for cigarettes has doubled as well [47].

According to most studies, smoking and drinking patterns appear to be procyclical in developed countries [7,9-10,17-20]. A decrease in smoking and drinking was followed when the unemployment rate increases. In contrast, a countercyclical trend was observed in China, which was consistent with those findings among individuals with lower social-economic status (e.g. construction workers, African Americans), old people or women in developed countries [11-14, 21-23]. Combing our findings with existing literature, the positive association may be explained by the social supports that individuals enjoy [52]. Since the social safety net is not yet well developed, fluctuations in the unemployment rate tend to easily affect individual physical living conditions and increase the psychological stress. It was possible that, without the protection from a sophisticated social welfare safety net, the high unemployment rate created anxiety for individuals, and as a result, trig the increase in their cigarette and alcohol consumption. According to the economics theory, this is the case that individuals change their time preference toward the present versus the future and use smoking and drinking as a form of self-medication [40]. Effects of unemployment rate on smoking were stronger for those who were unemployed than employed person, which was consistent with the explanation that the psychological stress rather than instant budget constrain played a bigger role in smoking and drinking decision with the background of unemployment rate change and macroeconomic fluctuation.

Our findings in combination with other research shed light on the implementation of public regulation of smoking and alcohol control. Combing our findings with existing literature, therefore, highlights the need for multi-level approaches aimed at smoking and alcohol control. The fact that the unemployment rate was associated with smoking and drinking behaviors suggests that policy interventions for smoking and alcohol control should not only focus on the individual characteristics but also take the macro-economic environment into consideration. The findings of positive impact of the unemployment rate on smoking and drinking from our study indicate potentially effective policy strategies consisting of improving the social welfare safety net and increasing cigarette and alcohol tax. The government, especially during the economic recession period, should increase recourse allocation in health to strengthen the social welfare safety net to help ease economic hardship and mental stress, focusing on unemployed individuals. To achieve this, one option is to increase tax to compensate the social welfare safety net and meantime adjust cigarette and alcohol demand. Other policies may include offering more smoking and drinking reduction and cessation services during economic recessions and strengthen anti-smoking or anti-drinking education and campaign especially during the economic booming period.

Our findings also have global public health implications. The vast majority of the world's smokers live in low- and middle-income countries, which results in nearly 80 percent of deaths occurred in middle- and low-`income countries [2]. At present, global health is affected by economic fluctuation. Compared to developed countries, the social welfare safety net in developing countries is weaker [53]. Smoking behaviors in developing countries are more easily to be affected by economic downturn. The gap between the numbers of smokers in developing countries versus developed countries is expected to be widened [2]. As a result, special attention should be paid to smoking and alcohol control in developing countries, especially during the economic recession.

REFERENCES

[1] Lim, S.S., Vos, T., Flaxman, A. D., Danaei, G., Shibuya, K., Adair-Rohani, H., Ezzati, M. 2013. A comparative risk assessment of burden of disease and injury attributable to 67 risk factors and risk factor clusters in 21 regions, 1990-2010: a systematic analysis for the Global Burden of Disease Study 2010. *Lancet* 380 (9859), 2224-2260.

[2] Erikson, M., Judith, M., and Hana, R. 2012. *The tobacco atlas*. Atlanta: American Cancer Society.

[3] World Health Organization. WHO report on the global. The MPOWER package. *Geneva Switzerland Who* 34(3):581-581.

[4] Chinese Center for Disease Control and Prevention (2011) *Global Adult Tobacco Survey (GATS) China 2010. Country Report.* Beijing: China Sanxia Press.

[5] National Health and Family Planning Commission of the People Republic of China. 2014. Promote the increase in tobacco tax to reduce the risk of second-hand smoke, http://www.sc.xinhuanet.com/content/2014-12/11/c_1113602410.htm, access by 11 December 2014.

[6] World Health Organization. 2015. Global status report on alcohol and health 2014. http://who.int/substance_abuse/publications/global_alcohol_report/en/.access by 2015.

[7] Kendzor, D., Reitzel L. R., Mazas, et al. 2012. Individual- and area-level unemployment influence smoking cessation among African Americans participating in a randomized clinical trial. *Social Science Medicine* 74(9):1394-401.

[8] Henkel, D. 2011. Unemployment and substance use: a review of the literature (1990-2010). *Current Drug Abuse Review* 4 (1): 4.

[9] Okechukwu, C., Bacic, J., et al. 2012. Smoking among construction workers: the nonlinear influence of the economy, cigarette prices, and antismoking sentiment. *Social Science and Medicine* 75 (8): 1379–1386.

[10] Latif, E. 2014. The impact of recession on drinking and smoking behaviors in Canada. *Ecoonomic Model.* 42: 43–56.

[11] Novo, M., Hammarström, A. and Janlert U. 2000. Smoking habits-a question of trend or unemployment? a comparison of young men and women between boom and recession. *Public Health* 114: 460-463.

[12] Novo, M., Hammarström, A. and Janlert U. 2000. Do high levels of unemployment influence the health of those who are not unemployed? A gendered comparison of young men and women during boom and recession. *Social Science and Medicine* 53: 293–30.

[13] Ruhm CJ. 2005. Healthy living in hard times? *Journal of Health Econ.* 24 (2): 341–363.

[14] Goel, R. K. 2014. Economic stress and cigarette smoking: evidence from the United States. *Economic Modelling*, 40(C), 284–289.

[15] Charles, K.K., DeCicca, P. 2008. Local labor market fluctuations and health: is there a connection and for whom? *Jounal of Health Economic* 27 (6): 1532–1550.

[16] Schwarz, P. 2012. Neighborhood effects of high unemployment rates: Welfare implications among different social groups. *The Journal of Socio-Economics* 41. 180–188.

[17] Dee, T.S., 2001. Alcohol abuse and economic conditions: evidence from repeated cross-sections of individual-level data. *Health Economics.* 10, 257–270.

[18] Ruhm, C.J., 1995. Economic conditions and alcohol problems. *Journal of. Health Economics*. 14, 583–603.

[19] Freeman, D. G. 1999. A note on economic conditions and alcohol problems. *Journal of Health Economics*, 18, 661–670.

[20] Dávalos, M. E., Fang, H., French, M. T. 2011. Easing the pain of an economic downturn: macroeconomic conditions and excessive alcohol consumption. *Health Economics*. 22(11), 1318-1335.

[21] Ruhm, C.J., 2000. Are recessions good for your health? *Quarterly Journal of. Economics*. 115, 617–650.

[22] Stuckler, D., Basu, S., Suhrcke, M., et al. 2009. The public health effect of economic crises and alternative policy responses in Europe: An empirical analysis. *The Lancet*, doi:10.1016/S0140-6736(09)61124-7. Published online July 8, 2009.

[23] Khang, Y.-H., Lynch, J. W. 2005. Letter: Regarding 'changes in mortality after the recent economic crisis of South Korea.' *Annals of Epidemiology*, 15(7), 535–537.

[24] Celia C. Lo, Tyrone C. Cheng. 2013. Heavy drinking during periods of high unemployment: 15-Year trend study of the role of race/ethnicity. *Drug and Alcohol Dependence* 133, 383– 390.

[25] Ruhm, C. J., Black, W. E. 2002. Does drinking really decrease in bad times? Journal of Health Economics, 21, 659–678.

[26] Johansson, E., Bockerman, P., Prattala, R, Uutela, A. 2006. Alcohol-related mortality, drinking behavior, and business cycles: Are slumps really dry seasons?. *The European Journal of Health Economics,* 7(3), 215–220.

[27] Rosalie Liccardo Pacula. Substance use and recessions: What can be learned from economic analyses of alcohol?. *International Journal of Drug Policy* 22 (2011) 326–334.

[28] Zhang DM., Hu Z, Orton S, et al. Socio-economic and psychosocial determinants of smoking and passive smoking in older adults. *Biomedicine Environmental Science* 2013; 26(6): 453-67.

[29] Schunck R, Rogge BG. Unemployment and its association with health relevant actions: Investigating the role of time perspective with German census data. *International J Pubic Health* 2010; 55 (4): 271–8.

[30] Grossman, M. 1972. On the concept of human capital and demand for health. *Journal of Political Economy* 80(2): 223-55.

[31] Cawley, J. and Ruhm, C. 2011 The economics of risky health behavior. In: Pedro Pita Barros, Tom McGuire, and Mark Pauly(eds.) H*andbook of health economics,* New York: Elsevier.

[32] Hisham, M., Fakhreddine, B., Kanj, A., et al., 2014. The growing epidemic of water pipe smoking: Health effects and future needs. *Respiratory Medicine* 108(9): 1241-1253.

[33] Crisp, A., Sedgwick, P., Halek, C., et al. Why may teenage girls persist in smoking?[J]. Journal of Adolescence, 1999, 22(5):657–672.1999. Why may teenage girls persist in smoking?. *Journal of adolescence health* 22: 657-72.

[34] Yadav, D., Hawes, R. H., et al. 2009. Alcohol consumption, cigarette smoking, and the risk of recurrent acute and chronic pancreatitis.. *Archives of Internal Medicine*, 169(11), 474.

[35] Rehm, J. 2011. The risks associated with alcohol use and alcoholism.. *Alcohol Research & Health the Journal of the National Institute on Alcohol Abuse & Alcoholism*, 34(2), 135-143.

[36] Aubin HJ, Farley A, et al. 2012. Weight gain in smokers after quitting cigarettes: meta-analysis. BMJ. 345: e4439.

[37] Catalano, R., Goldman-Mellor, S., et al. 2011. The health effects of economic decline. *Annual review of public health* 32: 431-50.

[38] Hill, T. D. and Angel, R. J. 2005. Neighborhood disorder, psychological distress, and heavy drinking. *Social Science and Medicine* 61: 965–975.

[39] Kassel, J. D., Stroud, L. R. and Paronis, C. A. 2003. Smoking, stress, and negative affect: Correlation, causation, and context across stages of smoking. *Psychological Bulletin* 129 (2): 270–304.

[40] Pierce, R. S., Frone, M. R., Russell, M. and Cooper, M. L. 1994. Relationship of financial strain and psychosocial resources to alcohol use and abuse: the mediating role of negative affect and drinking motives. *Journal of Health Social Behavior* 35 (4): 291–308.

[41] Montgomery, S.M., Cook, D.G., et al. 1998. Unemployment, cigarette smoking, alcohol consumption and body weight in young British men. *European Journal of Public Health* 8 (1): 21–27.

[42] Fryer, D. and Stambe, R. 2015. Unemployment and Mental Health. *International Encyclopedia of the Social & Behavioral Sciences* 2: 733-737.

[43] Drydakis, N. 2015. The effect of unemployment on self-reported health and mental health in Greece from 2008 to 2013: A longitudinal study before and during the financial crisis. *Social Science and Medicine* 128: 43-51.

[44] Karsten, I.P. and Moser, K. 2009. Unemployment impairs mental health: Meta-analyses. *Journal of Vocation Behavior* 74(3): 264-282.

[45] Janlert, U. and Hammarström, A. 2009. Which theory is best? Explanatory models of the relationship between unemployment and health. *BMC Public Health* 9.

[46] Falba, T., Teng, H. M., Sindelar, J. L., et al. 2005. The effect of involuntary job loss on smoking intensity and relapse. *Addiction* 100 (9): 1330–1339.

[47] Hu, T. W., Mao, Z., Shi, J. and Chen W. 2008. *Tobacco Taxation and Its Potential Impact in China.* Paris: International Union Against Tuberculosis and Lung Disease.

[48] Millwood, I. Y., Liming, L., et al. 2013. Alcohol consumption in 0.5 million people from 10 diverse regions of china: prevalence, patterns and socio-demographic and health-related correlates. *International Journal of Epidemiology, 42*(3), 816-827.

[49] Yang L., Zhou M., Sherliker P., et al. 2012. et al. 2012. Alcohol drinking and overall and cause-specific mortality in China: nationally representative prospective study of 220 000 men with 15 years of follow-up. *International Journal of Epidemiology* 41(4),1–13.

[50] Schaap, M. M. and Kunst, A. E. 2009. Monitoring of socio-economic inequalities in smoking: learning from the experiences of recent scientific studies. *Public Health* 123: 103-109.

[51] Shavers, V. L. 2007. Measurement of socioeconomic status in health disparities research. *Journal of the National Medicine Association* 99: 1013-1023.

[52] Suhrcke, M. and Stuckler, D. 2012. Will the recession be bad for our health? It depends. *Social Science and Medicine* 74(5): 647-653.

[53] Wang, W.P. 2006. The social security level: international comparison and enlightenment. *Social Science of Beijing* 3: 27-32.

INDEX

C

D

E

F

G

H

I

N

O

P

Q

R

S

T

U